WITHDRAWN
PRINT

Dogs 101: A Guide to American Kennel Club Breed Groups, Vol. 2 - The Hound Group

Jacob Cleveland

Contents

Articles

References

Breed Groups (dog)

A **Breed Group** is a categorization of related breeds of animal by an overseeing organization, used to organize the showing of animals. In dogs, kennel clubs define the *Breed Groups* and decide which dog breeds are to be included in each *Breed Group*. The Fédération Cynologique Internationale *Breed Groups* are used to organize dogs for international competition. *Breed Groups* often have the names of, and are loosely based on, ancestral dog types of modern dog breeds.

Recognized Breed Groups

International

The Fédération Cynologique Internationale makes sure that dogs in its 84 member countries can compete together, by establishing common nomenclature and making sure that pedigrees are mutually recognized in all the member countries. So internationally, dog breeds are organized in ten groups, each with subsections according to breed type and origin.

- **Group 1 - Sheepdogs and Cattle Dogs (except Swiss Cattle Dogs)**
- **Group 2 Pinscher and Schnauzer - Molossoid Breeds - Swiss Mountain and Cattle Dogs**
  - Section 1: Pinscher and Schnauzer type
  - Section 2: Molossoid breeds
  - Section 3: Swiss Mountain and Cattle Dogs
- **Group 3 Terriers**
  - Section 1: Large and medium-sized Terriers
  - Section 2: Small-sized Terriers
  - Section 3: Bull type Terriers
  - Section 4: Toy Terriers
- **Group 4 Dachshunds**
- **Group 5 Spitz and Primitive types**
  - Section 1: Nordic Sledge Dogs
  - Section 2: Nordic Hunting Dogs
  - Section 3: Nordic Watchdogs and Herders
  - Section 4: European Spitz
  - Section 5: Asian Spitz and related breeds
  - Section 6: Primitive type
  - Section 7: Primitive type - Hunting Dogs
  - Section 8: Primitive type Hunting Dogs with a ridge on the back

- **Group 6 Scenthounds and Related Breeds**

  - Section 1: Scenthounds
  - Section 2: Leash (scent) Hounds
  - Section 3: Related breeds (Dalmatian and Rhodesian Ridgeback)

- **Group 7 Pointing Dogs**

  - Section 1: Continental Pointing Dogs
  - Section 2: British and Irish Pointers and Setters

- **Group 8 Retrievers - Flushing Dogs - Water Dogs**

  - Section 1: Retrievers
  - Section 2: Flushing Dogs
  - Section 3: Water Dogs

- **Group 9 Companion and Toy Dogs**

  - Section 1: Bichons and related breeds
  - Section 2: Poodle
  - Section 3: Small Belgian Dogs
  - Section 4: Hairless Dogs
  - Section 5: Tibetan breeds
  - Section 6: Chihuahueñ o
  - Section 7: English Toy Spaniels
  - Section 8: Japan Chin and Pekingese
  - Section 9: Continental Toy Spaniel
  - Section 10: Kromfohrländer
  - Section 11: Small Molossian type Dogs

- **Group 10 Sighthounds**

  - Section 1: Long-haired or fringed Sighthounds
  - Section 2: Rough-haired Sighthounds
  - Section 3: Short-haired Sighthounds

The Kennel Club

The Kennel Club (UK) is the original and oldest kennel club; it is not a member of the Fédération Cynologique Internationale. For The Kennel Club, dogs are placed in the following groups:

- Hound Group
- Gundog Group
- Terrier Group
- Utility Group
- Working Group

- Pastoral Group
- Toy Group

Working is here meant to indicate dogs that are not hunting dogs that work directly for people, such as police dogs, search and rescue dogs, and others. It does not imply that other types of dogs do not work. Dogs that work with livestock are in the Pastoral Group.

Australia and New Zealand

The Australian National Kennel Council and the New Zealand Kennel Club recognize similar groups to The Kennel Club.

Australian National Kennel Council recognized Breed Groups:

- Group 1 (Toys)
- Group 2 (Terriers)
- Group 3 (Gundogs)
- Group 4 (Hounds)
- Group 5 (Working Dogs)
- Group 6 (Utility)
- Group 7 (Non Sporting)

New Zealand Kennel Club recognized Breed Groups:

- Toy Group
- Terrier Group
- Gundogs
- Hound Group
- Working Group
- Utility Group
- Non Sporting Group

North America

The Canadian Kennel Club and the two major kennel clubs in the United States have similar groups, although they may not include the same dogs in the same groupings. Canadian Kennel Club recognized Breed Groups:

- Group 1, Sporting Dogs
- Group 2, Hounds
- Group 3, Working Dogs
- Group 4, Terriers
- Group 5, Toys
- Group 6, Non-Sporting
- Group 7, Herding

American Kennel Club recognized Breed Groups:

- Sporting Group
- Hound Group
- Working Group
- Terrier Group
- Toy Group
- Non-Sporting Group
- Herding Group

United Kennel Club (US) recognized Breed Groups:

- Companion Dog Group
- Guardian Dog Group
- Gun Dog Group
- Herding Dog Group
- Northern Breed Group
- Scenthound Group
- Sighthound & Pariah Group
- Terrier Group

Other

The major national kennel club for each country will organize breeds in breed groups. The naming and organization of *Breed Groups* may vary from country to country. In addition, some rare new breeds or newly documented traditional breeds may be awaiting approval by a given kennel club, and may not yet be assigned to a particular *Breed Group*.

In addition to the major registries, there are a nearly infinite number of sporting clubs, breed clubs, minor kennel clubs, and internet-based breed registries and dog registration businesses in which breeds may be organized into whatever Breed Group the club, minor registry, or dog business may devise.

See also

- Dog type
- Dog breed
- Conformation show
- General Specials

External links

- http://www.dogsonline.com
- http://www.dogsindepth.com/index.html Dog Breed Groups from dogsindepth.com the online dog encyclopedia
- http://www.u-c-i.de/

American Kennel Club

The **American Kennel Club** (or **AKC**) is a registry of purebred dog pedigrees in the United States. Beyond maintaining its pedigree registry, this kennel club also promotes and sanctions events for purebred dogs, including the Westminster Kennel Club Dog Show, an annual event which predates the official forming of the AKC, the National Dog Show, and the AKC/Eukanuba National Championship. Unlike most other country's kennels clubs, the AKC is not part of the Fédération Cynologique Internationale (World Canine Organization).

Dog registration

The AKC is not the only registry of purebred dogs, but it is the only non-profit registry and the one with which most Americans are familiar. Founded in 1884, the AKC is the largest purebred dog registry in the world. Along with its nearly 5,000 licensed and member clubs and affiliated organizations, the AKC advocates for the purebred dog as a family companion, advances canine health and well-being, works to protect the rights of all dog owners and promotes responsible dog ownership. An example of dogs registered elsewhere in the U.S. is the National Greyhound Association which registers racing greyhounds (which are legally not considered "pets").

For a purebred dog to be registered with the AKC, the dog's parents must be registered with the AKC as the same breed, and the litter in which the dog is born must be registered with the AKC. If the dog's parents are not registered with the AKC or the litter is not registered, special registry research by the AKC is necessary for the AKC to determine if the dog is eligible for AKC registration. Once a determination of eligibility is met, either by litter application or registry research, the dog can be registered as purebred by the AKC.To register a mixed breed dog with AKC as a Canine Partner, you may go to the AKC website and enroll the dog via an online form. Once registered, your mixed breed dog will be eligible to compete in the AKC Agility, Obedience and AKC Rally® Events. 2010 Most Popular Dogs in the U.S.

1. Labrador Retriever

2. German Shepherd Dog

3. Yorkshire Terrier

4. Golden Retriever

5. Beagle

6. Boxer

7. Bulldog

8. Dachshund

9. Poodle

10. Shih Tzu

Registration indicates only that the dog's parents were registered as one recognized breed; it does not necessarily indicate that the dog comes from healthy or show-quality blood lines. Nor is registration necessarily a reflection on the quality of the breeder or how the puppy was raised. Registration is necessary only for breeders (so they can sell registered puppies) or for purebred conformation show or purebred dog sports participation. Registration can be obtained by mail or online at their website.

AKC and health

Even though the AKC supports some canine health research and has run advertising campaigns implying that the AKC is committed to healthy dogs, the AKC's role in furthering dog health is controversial. Temple Grandin maintains that the AKC's standards only regulate physical appearance, not emotional or behavioral health. The AKC has no health standards for breeding. The only breeding restriction is age (a dog can be no younger than 8 months.) Furthermore, the AKC prohibits clubs from imposing stricter regulations, that is, an AKC breed club cannot require a higher breeding age, hip dysplasia ratings, genetic tests for inheritable diseases, or any other restrictions. Parent clubs do have the power to define the looks of the breed, or breed standard. Parent club may also restrict participation in non-regular events or classes such as Futurities or Maturities to only those dogs meeting their defined criteria. This enables those non-regular events to require health testing, DNA sampling, instinct/ability testing and other outlined requirements as established by the hosting club of the non-regular event.

As a result, attention to health among breeders is purely voluntary. By contrast, many dog clubs outside the US do require health tests of breeding dogs. The German Shepherd Club of Germany [1], for example, requires hip and elbow X-rays in addition to other tests before a dog can be bred. Such breeding restrictions are not allowed in AKC member clubs. As a result, some US breeders have established parallel registries or health databases outside of the AKC; for example, the Berner Garde [2] established such a database in 1995 after genetic diseases reduced the average lifespan of a Bernese Mountain Dog to 7 years. The Swiss Bernese Mountain Dog club introduced mandatory hip X-rays in 1971.

For these, and other reasons, a small number of breed clubs have not yet joined the AKC so they can maintain stringent health standards, but, in general, the breeders' desire to show their dogs at AKC shows such as the Westminster Dog Show has won out over these concerns.

Contrary to most western nations organized under the International Kennel Federation (of which the AKC is not a member), the AKC has not removed docked tails and cropped ears from the requirements of many AKC breed standards, even though this practice is opposed in the U.S. by the American Veterinary Medical Association, and banned by law in many other countries.

The Club has also been criticized for courting large scale commercial breeders.

Purebred Alternative Listing Program / Indefinite Listing Privilege Program

The Purebred Alternative Listing Program (PAL), formerly the Indefinite Listing Privilege Program (ILP), is an AKC program that provides purebred dogs who may not have been eligible for registration a chance to register "alternatively" (formerly "indefinitely"). There are various reasons why a purebred dog might not be eligible for registration; for example, the dog may be the product of an unregisterable litter, or have unregisterable parents. Many dogs enrolled in the PAL and ILP programs were adopted from animal shelters or rescue groups, in which case the status of the dog's parents is unknown. Dogs enrolled in PAL/ILP may participate in AKC companion and performance activities, but not conformation. Enrollees of the program receive various benefits, including a subscription to *Family Dog* Magazine, a certificate for their dog's place in the PAL, and information about AKC Pet Healthcare and microchipping. Dogs that were registered under the ILP program keep their original numbers.

AKC National Championship

The AKC/Eukanuba National Championship is an annual event held in both Tampa, FL, and Long Beach, CA. The show is by invitation only. The dogs invited to the show have either finished their championship from the bred-by-exhibitor class or ranked in the Top 25 of their breed. The show can often be seen on major television stations.

Open foundation stock

The Foundation Stock Service (FSS) is an AKC program for breeds not yet accepted by the AKC for full recognition, and not yet in the AKC's Miscellaneous class. The AKC FSS requires that at least the parents of the registered animal are known. The AKC will not grant championship points to dogs in these breeds until the stud book is closed and the breed is granted full recognition.

Activities

The AKC sanctions events in which dogs and handlers can compete. These are divided into three areas:

- Conformation shows
  - Junior Showmanship
- Companion events, in which all registered and PAL/ILP dogs can compete. These include:
  - Obedience trials
  - Tracking trials
  - Dog agility
  - Rally obedience
- Performance events, which are limited to certain entrants; PAL/ILP dogs of the correct breed are usually eligible:
  - Coonhound events (coonhounds; no PAL/ILP dogs)
  - Field trials (hounds)
  - Earthdog trials (small terriers and Dachshunds)
  - Sheepdog trials (herding tests) (herding breeds, Rottweilers, and Samoyeds)
  - Hunt tests (most dogs in the Sporting Groups and Standard Poodles)
  - Lure coursing (sighthounds only)
  - Working Dog Sport (obedience, tracking, protection) German Shepherds, Doberman Pinschers, Rottweilers, Bouvier des Flandres

AKC policy toward working dog sport events that include protection phases, such as Schutzhund, has changed according to prevailing public sentiment in the United States. In 1990, as well-publicized dog attacks were driving public fear against many breeds, the AKC issued a ban on protection sports for all of its member clubs. After the terrorist attacks of 9/11/2001, Americans began to take a more positive attitude toward well-trained protection dogs, and in July 2003 the AKC decided to allow member clubs to hold a limited number of protection events with prior written permission. In 2006 the AKC released rules for its own Working Dog Sport events, very similar to Schutzhund.

In 2007, the American Kennel Club accepted an invitation from the Mexican Kennel Club to participate in the Fédération Cynologique Internationale World Dog Show in Mexico City.

Recognized breeds

As of July 2009, the AKC fully recognizes 163 breeds with 12 additional breeds granted partial status in the Miscellaneous class. Another 62 rare breeds can be registered in its Foundation Stock Service.

The AKC divides dog breeds into seven *groups*, one *class*, and the Foundation Stock Service, consisting of the following (as of July 2009):

- Sporting Group: 28 breeds developed as bird dogs. Includes Pointers, Retrievers, Setters, and Spaniels.

- Hound Group: 25 breeds developed to hunt using sight (sighthounds) or scent (scent hounds). Includes Greyhounds and Beagles.

- Working Group: 26 large breeds developed for a variety of jobs, including guarding property, guarding livestock, or pulling carts. Includes Siberian Huskies and Bernese Mountain Dogs.

- Terrier Group: 27 feisty breeds some of which were developed to hunt vermin and to dig them from their burrows or lairs. Size ranges from the tiny Cairn Terrier to the large Airedale Terrier.

- Toy Group: 21 small companion breeds Includes Toy Poodles and Pekineses.

- Non-Sporting Group: 17 breeds that do not fit into any of the preceding categories, usually larger than Toy dogs. Includes Bichon Frises and Miniature Poodles.

- Herding Group: 22 breeds developed to herd livestock. Includes Rough Collies and Belgian Shepherds.

- Best in Show:over 150 breeds All Breeds

- Miscellaneous Class: 11 breeds that have advanced from FSS but that are not yet fully recognized. After a period of time that ensures that good breeding practices are in effect and that the gene pool for the breed is ample, the breed is moved to one of the seven preceding groups.

- Foundation Stock Service (FSS) Program: 62 breeds. This is a breed registry in which breeders of rare breeds can record the birth and parentage of a breed that they are trying to establish in the United States; these dogs provide the *foundation stock* from which eventually a fully recognized breed might result. These breeds cannot participate in AKC events until at least 150 individual dogs are registered; thereafter, competition in various events is then provisional.

The AKC Board of Directors appointed a committee in October, 2007, to evaluate the current alignment of breeds within the seven variety groups. Reasons for the action included the growing number of breeds in certain groups, and the make-up of breeds within certain groups. The number of groups and group make-up has been modified in the past, providing precedent for this action. The Group Realignment Committee completed their report in July, 2008.

The committee recommended that the seven variety groups be replaced with ten variety groups. If this proposal is approved, the Hound Group would be divided into "Scent Hounds" and "Sight Hounds"; the Sporting Group would be divided into "Sporting Group – Pointers and Setters" and "Sporting Group –

Retrievers and Spaniels"; a new group called the "Northern Group" would be created; and the Non-Sporting Group would be renamed the "Companion Group". The Northern Group would be populated by Northern/Spitz breeds, consisting of the Norwegian Elkhound, Akita, Alaskan Malamute, Siberian Husky, Samoyed, American Eskimo, Chinese Shar-Pei, Chow Chow, Finnish Spitz, Keeshond, Schipperke, Shiba Inu and Swedish Vallhund. In addition, the Italian Greyhound is proposed to be moved to the Sight Hound Group, and the Dalmatian is proposed to be moved to the Working Group.

See also: American Kennel Club Groups

Other AKC programs

The AKC also offers the Canine Good Citizen program. This program tests dogs of any breed (including mixed breed) or type, registered or not, for basic behavior and temperament suitable for appearing in public and living at home.

The AKC also supports Canine Health with the Canine Health Foundation http://www.akcchf.org/

Another AKC affiliate is AKC Companion Animal Recovery (AKC CAR), the nation's largest not-for-profit pet identification and 24/7 recovery service provider. AKC CAR is a leading distributor of pet microchips in the U.S. and a participant in AAHA's free Pet Microchip Lookup tool.

AKC and legislation

The AKC tracks all dog related legislation in the United States, lobbies lawmakers and issues legislative alerts on the internet asking for citizens to contact public officials. They are particularly active in combating breed-specific legislation such as bans on certain breeds considered dangerous. They also combat most legislation to protect animals such as breed-limit restrictions and anti-puppy mill legislation. While they argue that their motive is to protect legitimate breeders and the industry, many argue their incentive is purely financial.

See also

- List of dog breeds
- United Kennel Club
- DOGNY
- American Dog Club
- World Wide Kennel Club
- List of Kennel Clubs by Country

External links

- Official website [3]
- AKC CAR's Official website [4]
- 2007 Registration Data [5]
- The Politics of Dogs: Criticism of Policies of AKC [6] The Atlantic, 1990
- Digging into the AKC: Taking cash for tainted dogs [7] The Philadelphia Inquirer, 1995
- Doogle.Info Worldwide online dog database and pedigree [8]

Hound Group

Hound Group is the name of a breed group of dogs, used by kennel clubs to classify a defined collection of dog breeds, and does not necessarily include all hound-type dogs. Most major English-language kennel clubs include a *Hound Group* (including The Kennel Club (UK), the American Kennel Club, the Canadian Kennel Club, the Australian National Kennel Council, and the New Zealand Kennel Club) although different kennel clubs may not include the same breeds in their *Hound Group*. The international kennel club association, the Fédération Cynologique Internationale, does not have a *Hound Group*, and includes most hound-type dogs in *Group 6, Scenthounds and related Breeds*, and *Group 10, Sighthounds*.

Hounds

Most hound type dogs share the common ancestral trait of being used for hunting. Some use acute scenting powers to follow a trail. Others demonstrate a gift of stamina as they relentlessly run down quarry. Beyond this, however, generalizations about hounds are hard to come by, since the type encompasses quite a diverse lot. There are Pharaoh Hounds, Norwegian Elkhounds, Afghans and Beagles, among others. Some hounds share the distinct ability to produce a unique sound known as baying.

Hound Group breeds

Major registries

Abbreviations used in this section are:

- AKC: American Kennel Club
- ANKC: Australian National Kennel Council
- CKC: Canadian Kennel Club
- KC: The Kennel Club (UK)
- NZKC: New Zealand Kennel Club
- UKC: United Kennel Club

Dogs listed in the *Hound Group* of various kennel clubs. Differences between kennel clubs are noted in parentheses.

Afghan Hound	American Foxhound (recognised only by the AKC and CKC)	Australian Dingo (recognised only by the ANKC)
Azawakh (recognised only by the KC)	Basenji	Basset Bleu de Gascogne (recognised only by the KC)
Basset Fauve de Bretagne (recognised only by the ANKC, KC and NZKC)	Basset Hound	Bavarian Mountain Hound (recognised only by the KC)
Beagle	Black and Tan Coonhound (recognised only by the AKC and CKC)	Bloodhound
Bluetick Coonhound (recognised only by the AKC, ANKC, and NZKC)	Borzoi	Cirneco dell'Etna (recognised only by the KC)
Dachshund	Drever (recognised only by the CKC)	English Foxhound
Finnish Spitz (AKC Non-sporting Group)	Grand Basset Griffon Vendéen (recognised only by the KC)	Grand Bleu de Gascogne (recognised only by the KC)
Greyhound	Hamiltonstövare (not recognised by the AKC and CKC)	Harrier (not recognised by the KC)
Ibizan Hound	Irish Wolfhound	Norrbottenspets (recognised only by the CKC)
Norwegian Elkhound	Norwegian Lundehund (recognised only by the KC and the CKC)	Otterhound
Petit Basset Griffon Vendéen	Pharaoh Hound	Plott Hound (recognised only by the AKC)
Portuguese Podengo (small) (recognised only by the KC)	Redbone Coonhound (recognized by the AKC)	Rhodesian Ridgeback
Saluki	Scottish Deerhound	Segugio Italiano (recognised only by the KC)

Sloughi (recognised by the KC, NZKC and
ANKC; not recognised by the AKC or CKC)

Whippet

Other organizations

"Hound Group" may also be a term used by minor kennel clubs, breed clubs, sporting clubs, and internet-based dog businesses. Each may or may not define the term separately. In addition, there are many new or rare breeds that are not yet recognized by any major registry that may eventually be listed in the "Hound Group" of a major kennel club.

See also

- Breed Groups (dog)
- Hound
- Hunting dog
- Sighthound
- Scent hound

External links

- Profile of AKC Hound Group Dogs [1]
- The Hound Club of South Australia Inc [2]
- Hound Dog Breeds from dogsindepth.com the online dog encyclopedia [3]

Afghan Hound

Afghan Hound

A gold coated Afghan Hound	
Other names	Sage Baluchi, Tazhi Spai, De Kochyano Spai, Tazi, Ogar Afgan
Country of origin	Afghanistan

Traits

Weight	Male	20-27 kg (45-60 lb)
Height	Male	61–73 cm (24–29 in)
Coat	Long and fine	
Color	Any	
Litter size	6-8 puppies	
Life span	11-13 years	

Classification and standards

FCI	Group 10 Section 1 #228	standard [1]
AKC	Hound	standard [2]
ANKC	Group 4 - (Hounds)	standard [3]
CKC	Group 2 - (Hounds)	standard [4]
KC (UK)	Hound	standard [5]
NZKC	Hounds	standard [6]
UKC	Sighthounds and Pariah Dogs	standard [7]

Dog (*Canis lupus familiaris*)

The **Afghan Hound** is one of the oldest, if not the first, sighthound dog breed. Distinguished by its thick, fine, silky coat and its tail with a ring curl at the end, the breed acquired its unique features in the cold mountains of Afghanistan, where it was originally used to hunt hares and gazelles by coursing them. Its local name is **Sag-e Tāzī** (Persian: گس زات‌ی) or **Tāžī Spai** (Pashto: زات‌ ي‌پس‌ی). Other alternate names for this breed are *Kuchi Hound*, *Tāzī*, *Balkh Hound*, *Baluchi Hound*, *Barutzy Hound*, *Shalgar Hound*, *Kabul Hound*, *Galanday Hound*, or sometimes incorrectly *African Hound*.

Description

Appearance

The Afghan Hound is tall, standing 24 to 29 inches (61 to 74 cm) in height and weighing 45 to 60 pounds (20 to 27 kg). The coat may be any colour, but white markings, particularly on the head, are discouraged; many individuals have a black facial mask. Some specimens have facial hair that looks like a Manchu moustache that are called "mandarins." Some Afghan Hounds are almost white, but particolour hounds (white with islands of red or black) are not acceptable and may indicate impure breeding. The long, fine-textured coat requires considerable care and grooming. The long topknot and the shorter-haired saddle on the back in the mature dog are distinctive features of the Afghan Hound coat. The high hipbones and unique small ring on the end of the tail are also characteristics of the breed.

Temperament

The temperament of the typical Afghan Hound can be aloof and dignified, but happy and clownish when playing. This breed, as is the case with many sighthounds, has a high prey drive and may not get along with small animals. The Afghan Hounds' reasoning skills have made it a successful competitor in dog agility trials as well as an intuitive therapy dog and companion. Genomic studies have pointed to the Afghan Hound as one of the oldest of dog breeds.

The breed has a reputation among some dog trainers of having a relatively slow "obedience intelligence" as defined by author Stanley Coren. However, these tests are reliant on quickly obeying commands and completing obedience tasks, things for which Afghans are not naturally inclined. It is an independent dog, with strong pack allegiance and prey drive, which has helped it survive as a breed for several thousand years. Coren says of breeds such as the Afghan, "They did the work all by themselves. They didn't have to cooperate with the human being [to get food]." As such, Afghans are likely to refuse or ignore commands from humans or trainers with which they have not developed a close working relationship, but even owners should not be surprised if their Afghan hounds sometimes choose to ignore commands.

Although seldom used today for hunting in Europe and America where they are popular, Afghan hounds are frequent participants in lure coursing events and are also popular in the sport of conformation showing.

Health

Mortality

Afghan Hounds in UK surveys had a median lifespan of about 12 years and 18 years if the dog is taken care of, which is similar to other breeds of their size. In a 2004 UK Kennel Club survey, the most common causes of death were cancer (31%), old age (20%), cardiac (10.5%), and urologic (5%).

Morbidity and health concerns

Major health issues are allergies, and cancer. Sensitivity to anesthesia is an issue the Afghan hound shares with the rest of the sighthound group, as sighthounds have relatively low levels of body fat. Afghan hounds are also among the dog breeds most likely to develop chylothorax, a rare condition which causes the thoracic ducts to leak, allowing large quantities of chyle fluid to enter the dog's chest cavity. This condition commonly results in a lung torsion (in which the dog's lung twists within the chest cavity, requiring emergency surgery), due to the breed's typically deep, "barrel"-shaped chest. If not corrected through surgery, chylothorax can ultimately cause fibrosing pleuritis, or a hardening of the organs, due to scar tissue forming around the organs to protect them from the chyle fluid. Chylothorax is not necessarily, but often, fatal.

The Afghan Hound needs to be taken on a long daily walk or jog. While out on the walk the dog must be made to heel beside or behind the person holding the lead, as in a dog's mind the leader leads the way, and that leader needs to be the human. Dogs who do not get to go on daily walks are more likely to display behavior problems. Teach them to enter and exit door and gateways after the humans. They will also enjoy running free in an open fenced, safe area.

History

Sighthounds are among the oldest recognisable types of dogs, and genetic testing has placed the Afghan Hound breed among those with the least genetic divergence from the wolf on some markers; this is taken to mean that such dogs are descended from the oldest dog types, not that the breeds tested had in antiquity their exact modern form. Today's modern purebred breed of Afghan Hound descends from dogs brought in the 1920s to Great Britain, and are a blending of types and varieties of long haired sighthounds from across Afghanistan and the surrounding areas. Some had been kept as hunting dogs, others as guardians.

Although demonstrably ancient, verifiable written or visual records that tie today's Afghan Hound breed to specific Afghan owners or places is absent, even though there is much speculation about possible connections with the ancient world among fanciers and in non-scientific breed books and breed websites. Connections with other types and breeds from the same area may provide clues to the history. A name for a desert coursing Afghan hound, Tazi (sag-e-tazi), suggests a shared ancestry with the very similar Tasy breed from the Caspian Sea area of Russia and Turkmenistan.) Other types or breeds of similar appearance are the Taigan from the mountainous Tian Shan region on the Chinese border of Afghanistan, and the Barakzay, or Kurram Valley Hound, from India/Pakistan. There are at least thirteen types known in Afghanistan, and some are being developed (through breeding and recordkeeping) into modern purebred breeds. As the lives of the peoples with whom these dogs developed change in the modern world, often these landrace types of dogs lose their use and disappear; there may have been many more types of longhaired sighthound in the past.

Once out of Persia, India and Afghanistan, the history of the Afghan Hound breed becomes an important part of the history of the very earliest dog shows and The Kennel Club (UK). Various sighthounds were brought to England in the 1800s by army officers returning from India (which at the time included Pakistan), Afghanistan, and Persia, and were exhibited at dog shows, which were then just becoming popular, under various names, such as Barukzy hounds. They were also called "Persian Greyhounds" by the English, in reference to their own indigenous sighthound.

One dog in particular, *Zardin*, was brought in 1907 from India by Captain Bariff(http://www. afghanhoundtimes.com/zardinb.htm), and became the early ideal of breed type for what was still called the Persian Greyhound. Zardin was the basis of the writing of the first breed standard in 1912, but breeding of the dogs was stopped by World War I.

Out of the longhaired sighthound types known in Afghanistan, two main strains make up the modern Afghan Hound breed. The first were a group of hounds brought to Scotland from Baluchistan by Major and Mrs. G. Bell-Murray and Miss Jean C. Manson in 1920, and are called the *Bell-Murray strain*. These dogs were of the lowland or steppe type, also called kalagh, and are less heavily coated. The second strain was a group of dogs from a kennel in Kabul owned by Mrs. Mary Amps, which she shipped to England in 1925. She and her husband came to Kabul after the Afghan war in 1919, and the foundation sire of her kennel (named Ghazni) in Kabul was a dog that closely resembled Zardin. Her *Ghazni strain* were the more heavily coated mountain type. Most of the Afghans in the United States were developed from the Ghazni strain from England. The first Afghans in Australia were imported from the United States in 1934, also of the Ghazni strain.) The French breed club was formed in 1939 (FALAPA). The mountain and steppe strains became mixed into the modern Afghan Hound breed, and a new standard was written in 1948, which is still used today.

The spectacular beauty of Afghan Hound dogs caused them to become highly desirable showdogs and pets, and they are recognised by all of the major kennel clubs in the English-speaking world. One of the Amps Ghazni, *Sirdar*, won BIS at Crufts in 1928 and 1930. An Afghan hound was featured on the cover of Life Magazine, November 26, 1945. "Afghan Hounds were the most popular in Australia in the 1970s…and won most of the major shows". An Afghan Hound won BIS (Best in Show) at the 1996 World Dog Show in Budapest. Afghan hounds were BIS at the Westminster Kennel Club Dog Show in 1957 and again in 1983. That win also marked the most recent win at Westminster for an breeder-owner-handler, Chris Terrell.

The Afghan Hound breed is no longer used for hunting, although it can be seen in the sport of lure coursing.

In popular culture

Because of its distinctive appearance, the Afghan hound has been represented in animated feature films, including Universal Pictures' Balto (Sylvie), Disney's Lady and the Tramp II (Ruby), an Afghan hound also appeared on 101 Dalmatians and the television series What-a-Mess (Prince Amir of Kinjan). Afghan hounds have also been featured in television advertisements and in fashion magazines. The Afghan hound is represented in books as well, including being featured in a series of mystery novels by Nina Wright (Abra), and a talking Afghan Hound in David Rothman's The Solomon Scandals (2008, Twilight Times Books). In the novel *Between the Acts*, Virginia Woolf uses an Afghan hound (named Sohrab) to represent aspects of one of the book's human characters.

On August 3, 2005, Korean scientist Hwang Woo-Suk announced that his team of researchers had become the first team to successfully clone a dog, an Afghan Hound named Snuppy. In 2006 Hwang Woo-Suk was dismissed from his university position for fabricating data in his research. Snuppy, nonetheless, was a genuine clone, and thus the first cloned dog in history.

External links

- Afghan Hound [8] at the Open Directory Project - An active listing of Afghan Hound links.

American Foxhound

American Foxhound

American Foxhound	
Nicknames	Foxhound
Country of origin	United States

Traits		
Weight	Male	65-75 pounds (29-34kg)
Height	Male	22-25 inches (53-64cm)
Coat	Short, hard	
Color	red, tri, black n tan, blue	
Litter size	1-12 puppies	
Life span	10-12 years	

Classification and standards		
FCI	Group 6 Section 1 #303	standard [1]
AKC	Hounds	standard [2]
CKC	Group 2 - Hounds	standard [3]
UKC	Scenthounds	standard [4]
Dog (*Canis lupus familiaris*)		

The **American Foxhound** is a breed of dog that is cousin to the English Foxhound. They are scent hounds, bred to hunt foxes by scent.

Description

Appearance

While standards call for the American Foxhound to be about 21-25 inches (530-640 mm) tall to the withers, and weigh anywhere between 65-75 pounds (29-34 kg), many of them are larger in structure (especially the show strains), with males standing 26-29 inches (660-740 mm) and females 25-28 inches (640-710 mm) and smaller in weight, typically between 40-65 pounds (20-29 kg). Some breeders have theorized that this is due to the considerably improved diet the dogs receive. For years it was traditional to feed Foxhounds on a diet of "dog bread", a variation on cornbread. The legs of a Foxhound are very long and straight-boned. The foxhound's chest is rather narrow. It has a long muzzle, and a large, domed skull. The dog is a Virginia Common pet.The ears are wide and low-set. The eyes are hazel or brown, and are large and wide-set. The coat is short and harsh. Overall, they are very similar to the Beagle, only standing higher and being larger. Their coats come in four colors: red, tri, black and tan, and blue.

Temperament

The American Foxhound is sweet, kind, loyal, and very loving at a home. As with all hounds they need careful training, constant socialization, and owners who are willing to give them ample exercise: a bored foxhound will find ways to keep themselves entertained and can be very destructive, some examples of destruction include everything from scratching at doors to tearing apart objects including toilet paper, being very rambunctious and, being rather long, they have the ability to take things from counter-tops. If routine walks are not an option, access to a secure yard is a good alternative; however the best option would be constant access via a dog door and a secure yard.

Intelligent creatures as they are, many foxhounds quickly learn to open gates or scale small fences to go wandering. While on the hunt the foxhound is a warrior, once a scent is picked up he or she will follow it neglecting any commands. Because their hunting instinct is strong they should never be trusted off-lead. Foxhounds are rarely street savvy and will follow a scent trail into the street where they could get hit by a car.

Foxhounds are easy to live with and thrive as members of a family; however, they are not ideal apartment dogs and shouldn't be left alone indoors for extended periods of time. They do however, get along very well with children, especially small children; although one must always keep an eye when children and animals are interacting as it is not beyond any animal to bite or claw when they feel they are threatened.

Foxhounds do not make good watchdogs; while more skittish hounds may howl when they see a newcomer, more often than not they will greet the newcomer affectionately hoping for treats or scratches behind the ears. This is due to centuries of breeding; any hound that growled or bared its teeth at its master would not be bred, or in some cases would be killed.

Most scent hounds are bred to give "voice". Foxhounds are not nuisance barkers but they do have loud, deep voices that carry a great distance. Although most people love the sound, many urban or suburban neighbors do not appreciate the deep barks or melodious howling of a foxhound. They have a special bark: a normal bark followed by a hight pitch howl.

They cannot be expected to act like retrievers because, though affectionate, they are independent by nature. Although a few foxhounds have been trained in obedience, most will not follow commands unless it suits them. Training a foxhound can be a trying experience, training a retired foxhound that grew up in a Fox Hunt can be even worse, as they can be stubborn.

Health

This breed is not generally a breed that carries genetic disorders. Overfeeding these dogs can easily cause them to gain weight. A minor health risk in American Foxhounds is thrombocytopathy, or platelet disease. While dysplasia was largely unknown in Foxhounds, it is beginning to crop up occasionally, along with some eye issues. It is not typical or customary for Foxhound breeders to screen for any hereditary disorders at this time.

The breed's lifespan is generally 10-12 years.

The American Foxhound is an energetic breed. According to some veterinarians and trainers, it needs plenty of exercise, for example, a fairly long walk followed by a game of fetch.

History

In 1650, Robert Brooke sailed to Crown Colony in America with his pack of hunting dogs, which were the root of several strains of American Hounds. These dogs remained in the Brooke family for nearly 300 years.

George Washington received French Foxhounds, Grand Bleu de Gascogne, (which look much like an American Bluetick hound) as a gift from the Marquis de Lafayette. Many of the dogs Washington kept were descended from Brooke's, and when crossed with the French hounds, helped to create the present day American Foxhound.

Though there has long been a rumor that the new breed was originally used for hunting Indigenous peoples of the Americas, this is not true. The breed was developed by landed gentry purely for the sport of hunting foxes. With the importation (or migration) of the red fox, Irish Foxhounds were added to the lines, to increase speed and stamina in the dog, qualities still prevalent in today's dogs.

Today there are a bunch of different strains of American Foxhound, including Walker, Goodman, Trigg, July and Penn-Marydel. Though the different strains look quite different, they are all recognized as members of the same breed. Most show hounds are Walkers, many of the pack hounds (used with hunting foxes on horseback) are Penn-Marydel and hunters use a variety of strains to suit their hunting style and quarry.

Australian Dingo

The **Australian Dingo** is an ancient, free roaming, primitive canine unique to the continent of Australia. Its original ancestors are thought to have arrived with humans from southeast Asia thousands of years ago, when dogs were still relatively undomesticated and closer to their wild Asian Gray Wolf parent species, *Canis lupus*. Since that time, living largely apart from people and other dogs, together with the demands of Australian ecology, has caused them to develop features and instincts that distinguish them from all other canines. Australian Dingoes have maintained ancient characteristics that unite them, along with other primitive dogs, into a taxon named after them, *Canis lupus dingo*, and has separated them from the domestic dog, *Canis lupus familiaris*.

Dingoes play an important role in the various ecosystems of Australia; they are apex predators and the largest terrestrial predators on the continent.

Due to its habit of attacking livestock and the vulnerability of sheep, dingoes and other wild dogs are seen as a pest by the sheep industry and the resulting control methods normally run counter to dingo conservation efforts.

Today, it is estimated that the majority of the modern "dingoes" are also descended from other domestic dogs. The number of these so-called dingo-hybrids had increased significantly over the last decades and the dingo was therefore classified as vulnerable.

Nomenclature

Canis lupus dingo has several names in both scientific and non-scientific literature, of which the word *dingo* is the most common term. Furthermore, on the Australian continent, the term *wild dog* is now used very often in both areas. In most cases this term includes dingoes, dingo-hybrids, and all other feral dogs.

Scientific name

Since its first official nomenclature in 1792 (*Canis antarcticus*) the scientific name of the dingo has changed several times.

While *Canis familiaris dingo*, which treats the dingo as a subspecies of domestic dog (and the domestic dog as a species separate from wolves), has been the most frequently used term over the last 50 years, according current taxonomy, the accepted name is *Canis lupus dingo*, which treats the dingo as a subspecies of gray wolf separate from *Canis lupus familiaris*. It should be noted that the current edition of Mammal Species of the World classifies both these subspecies as domestic dogs. Furthermore, the terms *Canis dingo* , which classes the dingo as a separate species from both dogs and wolves, and *Canis lupus familiaris dingo*, which classifies the dingo as a variety of the familiar dog,.

Colloquial name

The most common name in the colloquial language is the term "dingo". This term originated in the early times of European colonization in New South Wales and most likely derived from the word "tingo", a term used by the aboriginal people of Port Jackson to describe their camp dogs.

The dingo has many names in the different Indigenous Australian languages. Those names include the terms *Joogong*, *Mirigung*, *Noggum*, *Boolomo*, *Papa-Inura*, *Wantibirri*, *Maliki*, *Kal*, *Dwer-da*, *Kurpany*, *Aringka*, *Palangamwari*, *Repeti* and *Warrigal*. At the same time there are different names for the dogs depending on where they live. The Yarralin for instance call the dogs that live with them *Walaku* and the ones living in the wilderness *Ngurakin*.

Depending on the area where they live, the dingoes in Australia are occasionally called alpine dingoes, desert dingoes, northern dingoes, Cape York dingoes, or tropical dingoes. In recent times people have begun to call them "Australian native dogs" or reasoning that they are a subspecies of *Canis lupus*, an "Australian wolf".

Description

The dingo shares many characteristics with south-east Asian domestic dogs and Indian pariah dogs.

Dingoes have a relatively broad head, a pointed muzzle, and erect ears. Eye colour varies from yellow over orange to brown. Compared to other similarly-sized domestic dogs, dingoes have longer muzzles, larger carnassials, longer canine teeth, and a flatter skull with larger nuchal lines.

The average dingo is 52–60 cm tall at the shoulders and measures 117 to 124 cm from nose to tail tip. The average weight is 13 to 20 kg, however there was a report of a wild dingo weighing 27 kg. Males are typically larger and heavier than females of the same age. Dingoes from the North and the North-West of Australia are larger than Central and South-Australian populations. Australian dingoes are invariably heavier than Asian ones.

The legs are about half the length of the body and the head put together. The hind feet make up a third of the hind legs and have no dewclaws. Dingoes can have sabre-form tails (typically carried erect with a curve towards the back) or tails which are carried directly on the back.

Fur

The fur of adult dingoes is short, bushy on the tail, and varies in thickness and length depending on the climate. The fur colour is mostly sandy to reddish brown, but can include tan patterns and be occasionally black, light brown, or white. Completely black dingoes probably were prevalent in Australia in the past, but have been sighted only rarely in recent times and are now more common in Asia than in Australia.

Most dingoes are at least bicoloured, with small white markings on the chest, muzzle, tag, legs, and paws being the most common feature. In the case of reddish individuals, there can be small, distinctive, and dark stripes on the shoulders. All other colour and colour-patterns on adult dingoes are regarded as evidence for interbreeding with other domestic dogs.

Communication

Like all domestic dogs, dingoes tend towards a phonetic communication, the difference being that they howl and whimper more and bark less than domestic dogs. During research, eight sound classes with 19 sound types could be concretized.

Barking

It is often wrongly asserted that dingoes do not bark. Compared to most other domestic dogs, the bark of a dingo is short and monosyllabic. During observations, the barking of Australian dingoes revealed itself to have a relatively small variability, and the sub-groups of barking characteristic of domestic dogs could not be found. Furthermore, only 5% of the observed vocalisations were made up of barking. Australian dingoes bark only in swooshing noises or in a mixture atonal/tonal. Also, barking is almost exclusively used for giving warnings. Warn-barking in a homotypical sequence and a kind of "warn-howling" in a heterotypical sequence has also been observed. The bark-howling starts with several barks and then fades into a rising and ebbing howl and is probably, similarly to coughing, used to warn the puppies and members of the pack. Additionally, dingoes emit a sort of "wailing" sound, which they mostly use when approaching a water hole, probably to warn already present dingoes.

According to the present state of knowledge, it is not possible to get Australian dingoes to bark more frequently by having them in contact with other domestic dogs. However Alfred Brehm reported a dingo that completely learned the more "typical" form of barking and knew how to use it, while its brother did not. Whether dingoes bark or bark-howl less frequently in general is not certain.

Howling

Dingoes have three basic forms of howling (moans, bark-howl, and snuffs) with at least 10 variations. Usually there are three kinds of howls distinguished: long and persistent, rising and ebbing, and short and abrupt.

Observations have shown that every kind of howling has several variations, though their meanings are unknown. The frequency of howling varies depending on season and time of day, and is also influenced by breeding, migration, lactation, social stability, and dispersal behaviour. Also, howling can be more frequent in times of food shortage, because the dogs become more widely distributed within their home range. Additionally howling seems to have a group-function and is sometimes an expression of joy (for example, greeting-howls). Overall howling was observed less frequently than among grey wolves. It can happen that one dog starts to howl and several or all other dogs howl back and bark from time to time. In the wilderness, dingoes howl over long distances to attract other members of the pack, to find other dogs, and to keep intruders at bay. Dingoes howl in chorus with significant pitches and with increasing number of pack-members the variability of pitches also increases. Therefore it is suspected that dingoes can measure the size of a pack without visual contact.

Other forms of communication

During observations, growling made up 65% of the observed vocalizations. It was always used in an agonistic context, as well as for dominance and as a defensive sound. Similar to many other domestic dogs, a reactive usage of defensive growling could only be observed rarely or not at all. Growling very often occurs in combination with other sounds, and was observed almost exclusively in swooshing noises (similar to barking).

During observations in Germany, there was a sound found among Australian dingoes which the observers called "Schrappen". It was only observed in an agonistic context, mostly as a defense against obtrusive cubs or for defending resources. It was described as a bite intention, where the receiver is never touched or hurt. Only a silent, but significant, clashing of the teeth could be heard.

Aside from vocal communication, dingoes communicate like all domestic dogs via scent marking specific objects (for example, Spinifex) or places (waters, trails, hunting grounds, and so forth) using chemical signals from their urine, feces, and scent glands. Males scent-mark more frequently than females, especially during the mating season. They also scent-rub whereby a dog rolls on its neck, shoulders, or back on something that is usually associated with food or the scent markings of other dogs.

Unlike wolves, dingoes can react to social cues and gestures from humans.

Behavior

Dingoes are very often nocturnal in warmer regions, but more active during the day in cooler areas. Their main time of activity is around dusk and dawn. The periods of activity are short (often less than one hour) with short times of resting. They have two kinds of movement: a searching movement, apparently associated with hunting, and an exploratory movement, probably for contact and communication with other dogs.

In general, dingoes are shy towards humans. However, there are reports of dingoes that were not impressed by the presence of humans, for instance around camps in national parks, near streets or suburbs. According to studies in Queensland, the wild dogs there move freely at night through urban areas and cross streets and seem to get along quite well.

Dietary habits

170 species (from insects to buffalo) have been identified as being part of the dingo diet. In general, livestock seems to make up only a small proportion of its diet. In continent-wide examinations, 80% of the diet of wild dogs consisted of 10 species: Red Kangaroo, Swamp Wallaby, cattle, Dusky Rat, Magpie Goose, Common Brushtail Possum, Long-haired Rat, Agile Wallaby, European rabbit and the Common Wombat. This narrow range of major prey indicates that wild dogs are rather specialized, but in the tropical rain forests of North-Eastern Australia dingoes are supposed to be opportunistic hunters of a wide range of mammals. In certain areas, they tend to specialize on the most common prey, with a preference for medium to large sized mammals. The consumption of domestic cats has also been proven. Non mammalian prey is irregularly eaten and makes up only 10% of the dingo's diet. Big reptiles are only rarely captured, at least in Eastern Australia, although they are widespread. It is possible that especially big Monitor Lizards are too defensive and well armed or simply able to flee fast enough into dens or climb trees.

Dietary composition varies from region to region. In the gulf region of Queensland, feral pigs and Agile Wallabies are the dingo's main prey. In the rain forests of the North the main prey consists of Magpie-Geese, rodents and Agile Wallabies. In the southern regions of the Northern-Territory, the dogs mainly eat European rabbits, rodents, lizards, and Red Kangaroo; in arid central Australia rabbits, rodents, lizards, Red Kangaroo, and cattle carcass; and in the dry North-West Eastern Wallaroos and Red Kangaroo. In the deserts of the South-West they primarily eat rabbits and in the eastern and south-eastern highlands wallabies, opossums, and wombats. To what extent the availability of rabbits influences the composition of the diet could not be clarified. However because Rabbit Hemorrhagic Disease killed a large part of the Australian rabbit population at the end of the 20th century, it is suspected that the primary prey of the dogs has changed in the affected areas. Also, on Fraser Island, fish were proven to be a part of the dingo diet. However the main prey species were Bandicoots and several rodents. They also ate a lot of echidnas, crabs, small skinks, fruits, and other plants, as well as insects (mostly beetles). During these observations only 10% of the examined feces-samples contained human garbage (in earlier studies 50% were reported).

When scavenging for food, wild dogs(we presume the author is referring to all dogs free to roam, not just dingoes)) primarily eat cattle and kangaroo carcasses. Dingoes in coastal regions regularly patrol the coast for dead fish, seals, penguins, and other washed up birds.

Dingoes in general drink one liter of water a day in the summer and about half a liter a day in winter. During the winter in arid regions, dingoes could potentially live from the liquid in the bodies of their prey, as long as the number of prey is sufficient. Similarly, weaned cubs in central Australia are able to draw their necessary amount of liquid from their food. There, regurgitation of water by the bitches for the cubs was observed. During lactation, females have no higher need of water than usual, since they consume the urine and feces of the cubs and therefore recycle the water and keep the den clean.

Hunting behavior

Dingoes often kill by biting the throat and adjust their hunting strategies to suit circumstances. For bigger prey, due to their strength and potential danger, two or more individuals are needed. Such group formations are unnecessary when hunting rabbits or other small prey.

Kangaroo hunts are probably more successful in open areas than in places with high densities of vegetation, and juvenile dingoes are killed more often than adults. Dingoes typically hunt large kangaroos by having lead dingoes chase the quarry toward their waiting pack mates, which are skilled at cutting corners in chases. In one area of Central Australia, dingoes hunted kangaroos by chasing them toward a wire fence which would hinder their escape. Birds can be captured when they do not fly or fail to take off fast enough. Dingoes also steal the prey of eagles and the coordinated attack of three dingoes for killing a large monitor lizard was observed. On Fraser Island, dingoes supposedly hunted and killed horses in coordinated attacks. Additionally, active fishing has been proven on the island. There are also reports which state that some dingoes virtually live entirely on human food through stealing, scavenging, or begging. In fact dingoes are well-known for such a behavior in some parts of Australia. It is suspected that this might cause the loss of hunting strategies or a change in the social structures.

During studies at the Fortescue River in the mid 1970s, it was observed how most of the studied dingoes learned to hunt and kill sheep very quickly, even when they never had prior contact with sheep. Although the dingoes killed many sheep at that time, they still killed and ate kangaroos. During the early 1990s, wild dogs were observed to have an extraordinarily high success rate when killing sheep and did not have to hunt in a coordinated manner to achieve this. Often a dog only chases and outruns a single sheep, just to turn away suddenly and chase another. Therefore, only a small proportion of the hurt or killed sheep and goats are also eaten which seems to be the rule and not the exception. The dog probably falls into some kind of "killing spree", due to the rather panicked and uncontrolled flight behavior of the sheep, who run in front of the dingoes time and again and therefore cause one attack after another. Dingoes often attack sheep from behind during the sheep's flight, which causes injuries on the sheep's hind legs. Rams are normally attacked from the side — probably to avoid the horns — or sometimes on the testicles. Inexperienced dingoes or those who kill "for fun", sometimes cause significant damage on the sheep's hind legs, which often causes death.

Nearly all dingo attacks on cattle and Water Buffalo are directed against calves.Hunting success depends on the health and condition of the adult cattle and on their ability to defend their calves. The defense behavior of the mother can be sufficient to fend off an attack. Therefore the basic tactics of attacks are: distracting the mother, rousing the herd/group and waiting (sometimes for hours), and testing of the herd to find the weakest members. While locating a cattle herd, it could be observed how the dingoes made several feint attacks, at which they concentrated on the calves at first and, later on, attacked the mothers to distract them. Thereupon, the dingoes retreated and waited at a distance from the herd, until the rest of the cows had gathered their calves and moved on. During another occasion of an attack, "sub-groups" of a dingo-pack were observed to take turns in attacking and resting, until the mother was too tired to effectively defend her calf. It was also observed how dingoes hunting a water buffalo with an estimated weight of 200 kg took turns in biting the buffalo's legs during the chase.

Social behavior

Although dingoes are usually seen alone (especially in areas where they are persecuted), most belong to a social group whose members meet from time to time and are permanently together during the mating season in order to breed and raise cubs. Dingoes are generally highly social animals and form, where possible, stable packs with clearly defined territories, which only rarely overlap with the territories of neighboring packs. Intruders are mostly killed. These packs as a rule consist of 3–12 individuals (mostly the alpha-pair, as well as the current litter and the previous year's litter), who occupy a territory throughout the whole year. However, there are regional variants which show the flexible social structure of the dingo. Apparently, specialization on bigger prey boosts social behavior and the formation of bigger groups. During times of drought, packs in Australia fragment and the mortality rate of all the members, regardless of social status, is very high.

Packs have different (but not completely separate) hierarchies for males and females, and the ranking order is mostly established through ritualized aggression, especially among males. Overawing and agonistic behavior occurs only in a reduced state among Australian dingoes. Serious fights could only be observed rarely and under extreme circumstances. Dogs of higher rank show this behavior from time to time, to confirm their status, while those of lower rank are more prone to show conflict-preventive behavior.

Bigger packs are often splintered into sub-groups of flexible size. Additionally, lone individuals can occur in already occupied areas and can have loose contact with the groups, including participation in foraging for food. Desert areas have smaller groups of dingoes with a more loose territorial behavior and sharing of the water sites. On Fraser Island, dingoes had pack sizes of two to nine dogs with overlapping territories. However, they had a very high rate of infanticide, probably due to the high density of the island's dingo-population when compared to the size of the island and prey population. Territory size and individual areas change over time depending on the availability of prey, but are not connected to pack size. Wild dogs only rarely move outside of their territories. The areas of individuals can overlap. When territories of neighboring packs overlap, the packs tend to avoid contact. How big the territory and home range of dogs are depends for the most part on the availability of prey. Home ranges are generally stable, but can change over time due to outside circumstances or changes in social organization. Individuals who start to detach themselves from the pack have bigger home ranges at first before they finally disperse.

Territories around human dominated areas tend to be smaller and contain a relatively higher number of dingoes due to the better availability of food. According to studies in Queensland, the local wild dogs in urban areas have smaller territories of occasionally only two to three square-kilometers in diameter.

There, the existence of a territory of a single dingo could be proven, which only consisted of a small patch of bush near the fringe of a primary school in the heart of a small town.

Most dingoes stay near their area of birth and do not travel more than 20 km per day, but some, especially young males, disperse. The size of the individual home range increases with age. The biggest recorded home ranges (90–300 km^2) came from the deserts of Southwest-Australia. In the center of the Northern Territory home ranges of up to 270 km^2 were observed. Home ranges in other parts of the continent can be 45–113 km^2 in the Northwest, 25–67 km^2 in Central Australia, on average 3 km^2 in the tropic North and 10–27 km^2 in the forests of the Eastern mountains.

Reproduction

Dingoes breed once annually, depending on the estrus-cycle of the females who, according to most sources, only come in heat once per year. Dingo bitches can come in heat twice per year, but can only be pregnant once a year, with the second time only seeming to be pregnant (at most).

Males are virile throughout the year in most regions, but have a lower sperm production during the summer in most cases. During studies on dingoes from the Eastern Highlands and Central Australia in captivity, no breeding cycle could be observed. All were potent throughout the year. The breeding was only regulated by the heat of the females. There was a rise in testosterone in the males during the breeding season, however this was attributed to the heat of the females and copulation. In contrast to the captive dingoes, captured dingo males from Central Australia did show evidence of a male breeding cycle. Those dingoes showed no interest in females in heat (this time other domestic dogs) outside of the mating season (January to July) and did not breed with them.

The mating season usually occurs in Australia between March and May (according to other sources between April and June). In Southeast Asia, mating occurs between August and September. During this time dingoes may actively defend their territory using vocalizations, dominance behaviour, growling, and barking.

Most females in the wild start breeding at the age of two years, and within packs the alpha-female tends to go into heat before the subordinates and will actively suppress the mating attempts of the other females. Males become sexually mature between the age of 1–3 years. The precise start of breeding varies depending on age, social status, geographic range, and seasonal conditions. Among dingoes in captivity, the pre-estrus was observed to last 10–12 days. However, it is suspected that the pre-estrus may last as long as 60 days in the wild.

In general, the only dingoes in a pack that successfully breed are the alpha-pair and the other pack-members help with raising the cubs. Subordinates are actively prevented from breeding by the alpha-pair and some subordinate females have a false pregnancy. Low ranking or solitary dingoes can successfully breed if the pack structure breaks up.

The gestation period lasts for 61–69 days and the size of the litter can range from one to ten cubs (usually five cubs), with the number of the males tending to be higher than that of the females. Cubs of subordinate females usually get killed by the alpha-bitch, which causes the population increase to be low even in good times. It is possible that this behaviour developed as an adaptation to the fluctuating environmental conditions in Australia. Cubs are usually born between May and August (the winter period) but in tropical regions, breeding can occur at any time of the year.

At the age of three weeks, the cubs leave the den for the first time and will leave it completely upon reaching the age of eight weeks. In Australia, dens are mostly underground. There are reports of dens in abandoned rabbit burrows, rock-formations, under boulders in dry creeks, under large spinifex, in hollow logs, in augmented burrows of monitor lizards, and wombat burrows. The cubs usually stray around the den within a radius of 3 km and are accompanied by older dogs during longer travels. The transition to consuming solid food is normally accompanied by all members of the pack during the age of nine to twelve weeks. Apart from their own experiences, cubs also learn through observation. Young dingoes usually become independent at the age of three to six months or they voluntarily disperse at the age of twelve months when the next mating season starts.

Migration

Dingoes usually remain in one area and do not undergo seasonal migrations. However, during times of famine, even in normally "safe" areas, dingoes travel into pastoral areas, where intensive human-induced control measures are undertaken. It was already noted in Western Australia in the 1970s that young dogs can travel for long distances when necessary. About 10% of the dogs who were captured back then - all younger than twelve months - were later recaptured far away from their first position. Among these, 10% of the travelled distance for males was 21.7 km and for females 11 km. Therefore, travelling dingoes had lower chances of survival in foreign territories and it was assumed to be unlikely that they would survive long migrations through occupied territories. The rarity of long migration routes seemed to confirm this assumption. During investigations in the Nullarbor Plain, even longer migration routes were recorded. The longest recorded migration route of a radio collared dingo was about 250 km.

Mortality and health

Dingoes are susceptible to the same diseases as domestic dogs. Up to now, 38 species of parasites and pathogens have been detected in Australian dingoes. The bulk of these diseases have a low influence on the survival of adult wild dogs. The exceptions include canine distemper, hookworms, and heart worms in North-Australia and southeastern Queensland. Cubs can also be killed by lungworms, whipworms, hepatitis, coccidiosis, lice, and ticks. Sarcoptic mange is a widespread parasitic disease among the dingoes of Australia, but seldom debilitating. Free roaming dogs are the primary host of Echinococcosis-tapeworms and have an infection rate of 70 to 90%.

Statistics on the average age of dingoes living in the wild range between five to ten years. In captivity, dingoes have a lifespan of 13 to 15 years, and in exceptional cases even up to 24 years have been recorded. The main mortality factors for dingoes are killings by humans, crocodiles, and dogs (including other dingoes). Additional causes for dingo mortality are starvation and/or dehydration during times of drought or after strong bush fires, infanticide, snake bites, killing of cubs by Wedge-tailed Eagles, as well as injuries caused by cattle and buffalo.

Present day distribution

It is only possible to give a crude description of the dingo's distribution area and the accordant population density. It is difficult to give an exact assessment of the distribution of dingoes and other domestic dogs, since the exact extent of interbreeding between the two is not known. Therefore the following information on the distribution of the dingo applies to dogs which were classified as dingoes based on fur-color, body-form, and breeding-cycle, therefore the maps on their distribution might be conflicting.

Distribution in the past

Based on fossil, molecular, and anthropogenic evidence, it is assumed that dingoes once might have had a widespread distribution. These ancient dingoes would have associated to nomadic hunter-gatherer-societies and later with the rising agricultural centers. It is further assumed that they would have been tamed there and were then transported to various places in the world. Dingo-findings from Thailand and Vietnam are regarded as the oldest findings, which have been estimated to be respectively as old as 5,000–5,500 years. The age of findings from the highlands of Indonesia vary between a maximum of 5,000 to (in most cases) 2,500 to 3,000 years.

Originally, it was suspected that the dingo was introduced to Austraia in the Pleistocene by Aborigines, which led to confusion concerning the dingo's nomenclature. Today, the most common theory is that the dingo arrived in Australia about 4,000 years ago, because the oldest known fossils of dingoes were estimated to be about 3,500 years old and were found in various places in Australia, which indicates a rapid colonization. Findings are absent from Tasmania, which was separated from the main Australian landmass around 12,000 years ago due to a rise in sea level. Therefore, archeological data indicates an arrival between 3,500 to a maximum of 12,000 years ago. To reach Australia from Asia, there would have been at least 50 km of open sea to be crossed, even at the lowest sea level. Since there is no known case of a big land animal who made such a journey by itself, it is most likely that the ancestors of modern dingoes were brought to Australia on boats by Asian seafarers. A dance of the Aborigines on the coastal regions of the Kimberley, during which they depict dogs running excitedly up and down a boat and finally jumping into the water, is seen as further evidence for the introduction of dingoes by seafarers. It is possible that these dogs were used as food or eventually guard dogs. Potentially, the dingo came to Australia and the islands of Southeast Asia and the Pacific in the course of expansion of the Austronesian culture.

There are two main theories concerning the geographical origin and travel routes of the modern dingo's ancestors and their arrival in Australia:

- An East-Asian origin and a travel route over the Southeast-Asian islands due to their close proximity to Australia, and the relatively easy accessibility over the islands of the Southeast-Asian archipelago. This theory is supported by examination of the mtDNA of Australian dingoes.
- An introduction of sheepdogs from the Indus valley in Asia, over Timor by Indian seafarers, based on similarities in skeletal anatomy of Indian pariah dogs and Iranian wolves. Moreover, this theory implies that the oldest known fossils are 4,000 years old and were found on Timor, where the dogs coexisted for a while with pigs and sheep. This theory would be supported by the assumption that the simultaneous appearance of certain stone tools was caused by Indian influence. However this is disputed by other authorities.

Whether there were several introductions of dingoes to Australia or just one is not known yet.

The first official report of a "wild dog" in Australia comes from the year 1699 from Captain William Dampier. At the time, dingoes were probably widespread over the main part of the continent and lived in the wild as well as alongside the Aboriginals. They were mostly tolerated by the European settlers and sometimes kept as pets. The number of dingoes was probably low in those times and increased since then in some parts of Australia. Their number probably increased strongly around the 1880s due to the establishment of the pastoral economy and artesian water places and probably had its peak in the 1930s and 1950s. Afterwards the numbers have remained high, but the percentage of dingo-hybrids has significantly increased since then.

Present-day distribution

Today dingoes live in all kinds of habitats, including the snow-covered mountain forests of Eastern Australia, dry hot deserts of Central Australia, and Northern Australia's tropical forest wetlands. The absence of dingoes in many parts of the Australian grasslands is probably caused by human persecution. Based on skull characteristics, size, fur colour, and breeding cycles there could be distinct regional populations between Australia and Asia, but not in Australia.

Today the whole population of wild dogs on the Australian continent consists, besides dingoes, of a wide panoply of feral domestic dogs (mostly mixed-breeds and dingo-hybrids) with an enormous variety of colours. Due to the increased availability of water, native and introduced prey, as well as livestock and human provided food, the number of wild dogs is regarded as increasing. There are reports from some parts of Australia stating that wild dogs now hunt in packs there, although they had hunted on a solitary basis before. The density of the wild dog population varies between 0.003 and 0.3% per square kilometre, depending on habitat and availability of prey.

"Pure" dingoes are regarded as widespread in Northern, Northwest, and Central Australia; rare in Southern and Northeast Australia; and possibly extinct in the South-Eastern and South-Western areas. The establishment of agriculture caused a significant decrease in dingo numbers and they were practically expelled from the territories occupied by the sheep industry. This primarily affects big parts of Southern Queensland, New South Wales, Victoria, and South Australia. This situation was maintained by the construction of the Dingo Fence. Although dingoes were eradicated from most areas south of the Dingo Fence, they still exist in an area of about 58,000 km^2 in the dry Northern areas north of the Dingo Fence and therefore on about 60% of the whole area. In Victoria, wild dog populations are currently concentrated on the densely forested areas of the Eastern Highlands, from the border to New South Wales southern to Healesville and Gembrook. They also exist in the large desert in the Northwest of the state. Wild dog populations in New South Wales primarily exist along the Great Dividing Range and the Hinterlands on the coast, as well as in the Sturt National Park in the Northwest of the state. In the rest of the continent dingoes are regarded as widespread, with the exception of the arid eastern half of Western Australia. In the bordering areas of South Australia and the Northern Territory they are regarded as naturally scarce. Wild dogs are widespread in the Northern Territory, with the exception of the Tanami and Simpson Desert, where they are rare due to the lack of watering holes. However, local concentrations exist there near artificial water sources. According to DNA-examinations from the year 2004, the dingoes of Fraser Island are "pure". However, skull measurements from the mid 1990s had a different result.

Outside of Australia, dingoes were proven to exist in Thailand, based on comparisons between the skulls of Thai dogs and those of fossil and present-day dingoes. The population there probably has the biggest proportion of "pure" dingoes. They are widespread in Northern and Central Thailand and rare in the southern regions. They may also exist in Burma, China, India, Indonesia, Laos, Malaysia, Papua New Guinea, on the Philippines, and in Vietnam, but if they exist there, their distribution is unknown. Dingoes are regarded as widespread in Sulawesi, but their distribution in the rest of Indonesia is unknown. They are regarded as rare on the Philippines and are probably extinct on many islands. In Korea, Japan, and Oceania there exist a few local dog breeds with dingo-like features, but dingoes are considered extinct there.

Ecological impact of the dingo after its arrival in Mainland Australia

See also: Extinction of the thylacine in mainland Australia

It is suspected that the dingo caused the extinction of the thylacine, the Tasmanian Devil, and the Tasmanian Native-hen from mainland Australia, since there is a correlation in space and time between the arrival of the dingo and the extinctions of these species. However, dingoes do not seem to have had the same ecological impact the Red Fox had in later times. This might be connected to the dingo's way of hunting and the size of their favored prey, as well as the low number of dingoes in the time before European colonization.

The assumption that dingoes and thylacines may have been competitors for the same prey stems from the external similarities of the two species: the thylacine had a stronger and more efficient bite, but was probably dependent on relatively small prey, while the dingo's stronger skull and neck would have allowed it to bring down bigger prey. The dingo was probably a superior hunter, as it hunted cooperatively in packs and could better defend resources, while the thylacine was probably more solitary. Also, wild dingo populations might have had demographic support from conspecifics living with humans and may have introduced new diseases which affected the thylacine more severely. The extinction of the thylacine on the continent around 2000 years ago has also been linked with changes in climate and land use of the Aborigines. It is plausible to name the dingo as the cause of the extinction, but there are significantly morphological differences between the two, which suggested that the ecological overlapping of both species might be exaggerated: the dingo has the dentition of a generalist, while the thylacine had the dentition of a specialist carnivore, without any signs of consumption of carrion or bones. It is also argued that the thylacine was a flexible predator that should have withstood the competition by the dingo and was instead wiped out due to human persecution.

This theory also has problems with explaining how the Tasmanian Devil and the dingo coexisted on the same continent until about 430 years ago, when the dingo supposedly caused the Tasmanian Devil's demise. The group dynamics of dingoes should have successfully kept devils away from carrion, and since dingoes are able to break bones, there would have been little left for the devils to scavenge upon. Additionally, devils are successful hunters of small to medium sized prey, so there should have been an overlapping of the species in this area too. Furthermore, the arguments that the dingo caused the extinction of the thylacine, the devil, and the hen are in direct conflict with each other. If the dingo was so similar to the thylacine and the devil in its ecological role, and that it suppressed both, it is strange that the hen coexisted with both for such a long time. Although this is possible, critics regard the evidence for this as weak.

Impact

Reliable information about the exact ecological, cultural, and economical impact of wild dogs does not exist yet. Furthermore, the impact of wild dogs depends on several factors and a distinction between dingoes and other domestic dogs is not necessarily made.

The appearance of a wild dog is probably insignificant for its ecological impact. Here it is important what a dog does, and therefore what its place in the ecosystem is. In contrast to this the appearance of a wild dog is sometimes very important when it comes to their cultural and economical impact. Here it is often desired that the wild dog's appearance complies to what is demanded, that it is a "pure" dingo or at least looks like one. In case of their economic impact their appearance only seem to be important when "pure" dingoes are used as a tourist attraction. Where wild dogs are regarded as pests their appearance is only of minor importance, if it is of any importance at all.

The impact wild dogs have in urban areas and whether they are a danger to humans (direct attacks, diseases, and more) is unknown yet.

Ecological impact

Today the dingo is regarded as part of the native Australian fauna by environmentalists as well as biologists, especially since these dogs existed on the continent before the arrival of the Europeans and a mutual adaption of the dingoes and their surrounding ecosystems had occurred. However there is also the contrary view that dingoes are just another introduced predator respectively and that they are only native to Thailand.

Much of the present day place of wild dogs in the Australian ecosystem and especially in the urban areas remains unknown. Although the ecological role of dingoes in Northern and Central Australia is well understood, the same does not apply to the role of wild dogs in the East of the continent. In contrast to some claims it was undoubtedly disproven that dingoes are damaging to the Australian ecosystem in general. In most cases it is assumed that they have a positive impact.

Dingoes are regarded as apex predators and possibly perform an ecological key function. Therefore it is likely (with increasing evidence from scientific research) that they control the diversity of the ecosystem by limiting the number of prey and keeping the competition in check. Wild dogs hunt feral livestock like goats and pigs, as well as native prey and introduced animals. It is possible that the low number of feral goats in Northern Australia is caused by the presence of the dingoes, however whether they control the goats' numbers or not is still disputable. Studies from the year 1995 in the northern wet forests of Australia came to the conclusion that the dingoes there did not reduce the number of feral pigs but that their predation only has an impact on the pig population together with the presence of water buffalos (which hinder the pigs' access to food).

There were observations concerning the mutual impact of dingoes and fox and cat populations and evidence that dingoes limit the access of foxes and cats to certain resources. Therefore it is assumed, that a disappearance of the dingoes may cause an increase of Red Fox and feral cat numbers and therefore a higher pressure on native animals. During studies it was found out that the presence of dingoes is one of the factors that keep the fox numbers in an area low and therefore reduces the pressure on native animals which then do not have to disappear from the area. It could be proven that the countrywide numbers of Red Foxes are especially high where dingo numbers are low, however it was considered that there might be other factors responsible for this, depending on the area. There was evidence found for a competition between wild dogs and Red Foxes in the Great Blue Mountains of New South Wales, since there were many overlaps in spectrum of preferred prey. However, there was only evidence for a local competition not on a grand scale. It is also possible that dingoes can live side to side with Red Foxes and feral cats without reducing their numbers in areas with sufficient food resources (for example, high rabbit numbers) and hiding places. Nearly nothing is known about the relationship of wild dogs and feral cats, except that both mostly live in the same areas. Although wild dogs also eat cats, it is not known whether this has an impact on the cat populations. In many areas wild dogs live together with the most species of quolls, except for the Eastern Quoll who is probably extinct on the continent, and therefore wild dogs are not regarded as a threat for them.

Additionally, the disappearance of the dingoes might cause prevalence of kangaroo and rabbit numbers. In the areas outside of the Dingo Fence the number of dingoes and emus is lower than in the areas inside, however the number changed depending on the habitat. Since the environment is the same on both sides of the fence, it was assumed that the dingo is a strong factor for the regulation of these species. Therefore some people demand that dingo numbers should be allowed to increase or dingoes should reintroduced in areas with low dingo populations to lower the pressure on endangered populations of native species and to reintroduce them in certain areas.

Cultural impact

Opinions about the dingo are often based on its perceived "cunning" and that it is an intermediate to civilization and wilderness.

Some of the early European settlers compared dingoes to domestic dogs and perceived them as such, wile others compared them to wolves. Over the years, dingoes started to attack sheep and so their relationship to the Europeans changed very quickly: they were regarded as devious and cowardly since they did not fight bravely in the eyes of the Europeans and just vanished in the bush. Dingoes were seen as predators which killed wantonly, rather than out of hunger (similar claims are made today concerning dingo-hybrids). Additionally they were seen as promiscuous or as devils with a venomous bite or saliva, and thus, no reservations were required to kill one. Over the years, dingo trappers gained a kind of prestige for their work, primarily when they managed to kill dingoes which were especially hard to catch. Therefore, dingoes were associated with thieves, vagabonds, bushrangers, and parliamentary opponents. The oldest evidence of politicians calling their opponents "dingo" (therefore cowardly and treacherous) is from the 1960s and became very popular afterwards. Today the word "dingo" still stands for coward and cheat and the verb and adjective forms have the appropriate meanings.

Today, the image of the dingo ranges from romantic transfiguration of being completely harmless to the point of demonising them as a general danger for humans and nature. For some the dingo is a *beautiful, unique animal* and others do not regard it as a domestic dog but as a wolf. Dingoes are called an icon of Australia, which should be preserved (at least in its "pure" form), and its possible "extinction" is also compared to that of the thylacine. Where dingoes are regarded as pests regardless of their "rehabilitation", this attitude can degenerate into full hatred. In the process, it is sometimes said that dingoes are detrimental for the society and the environment (for example, that they are in general the cause for the extinction of native animals). Dingoes (no matter whether "pure" or not) are than treated as a scourge, that has to be eradicated. In such cases it is also deemed acceptable to kill all wild dogs if it would save one human life. Besides this, there is also among bureaucrats the opinion that wild dogs are cruel towards sheep and cattle and therefore every cruelty against them is justified.

Traditionally dogs have a privileged position in the aboriginal cultures of Australia (which the dingo may have adopted from the thylacine) and the dingo is a well known part of rock carvings and cave paintings. There are ceremonies (like a keen at the Cape York Peninsula in the form of howling) and dreamtime stories connected to the dingo, which were passed down through the generations. There are strong feelings that dingoes should not be killed and in some areas women are breast feeding young cubs. In most cases they are treated with extraordinary indulgence, although the reasons for this might not be any kindness, since dogs are sometimes treated quite brutally. Nonetheless there seems to be a big feeling of community although the reasons for this do not seem to always be clear. Similar to how Europeans acquired dingoes, the Aboriginal people of Australia acquired dogs from the immigrants very quickly. This process was so fast that Francis Barralier (the first European to explore the Outback) discovered in the year 1802 that five dogs of European origin were there before him. There is the theory that other domestic dogs will adopt the role of the "pure" dingo. In fact the majority of the myths about dingoes just call them dogs (whether that role was adopted or there was no difference for the storyteller is unknown) and other introduced animals like the water buffalo and the domestic cat have been adopted into the indigenous aboriginal culture in the forms of rituals, traditional paintings, and dreamtime stories.

The dingo is connected to holy places, totems, rituals, and dreamtime characters. There are stories that dogs can see the supernatural, are guard dogs, and warn against evil powers. There is evidence that dogs have been buried together with their owners to protect them against evil even after death. Most of the published myths hail from the Western Desert and show a remarkable complexity. In some stories dingoes are the central characters, in others only minor ones. One-time it is an ancestor from the dreamtime, who created humans and dingoes or gave them their current shape. Then there are stories about creation, socially acceptable behaviour, and explanations why some things are the way they are. There are myths about shapeshifters (human to dingo or vice versa), "dingo-people", and the creation of certain landscapes or elements of those landscapes, like waterholes or mountains. The dingo is also responsible for death. In other myths there are advice and warnings to those who do not want to follow the social rules. Stories can show the borders of one's territory or the dingo in it might stand for certain members of the community, for example, rebellious dingoes stand for "wild" members of the tribe. The dingo also has a wild and uncontrollable face in other stories and there are many stories about dingoes that kill and eat humans (for example, the Mamu, who catches and devours the spirit of every child who roams too far from the campfire). Other stories tell of a giant devil dingo, from which the real dingoes originate. The dog is thereby depicted as a homicidal, malicious creature that—apart from the lack of a subtle mind—is similar to a trickster, since it plays the role of a mischievous adversary for other mythological beings. Many of them fall victim to blood-thirsty dogs or escape them. Here individual beings have a significant meaning too or sometimes become part of the landscape. Even the actions of these dogs result for instance in the creations of stones and trees from flying around bones and meat or ochre from the spilled blood.

Economic impact

Wild dogs are responsible for a wide range of negative and undesired impacts on the livestock industry of Australia and are regarded as pests since the start of the European livestock industry. Thereby sheep are the most frequent prey, followed by cattle and goats. However research on the real extent of the damage and reason for this problem only started a very short time ago. There are many reasons for the death of livestock and when the body is found it is often too late to tell for sure what the cause of death was. Since the outcome of an attack on livestock depends to a high degree from the behaviour and experience of the predator and the prey there is no certain way (except for direct observation) to determine whether an attack was done by dingoes or some other sort of domestic dogs. Even the leftovers from the prey in the scat of wild dogs do not prove that they are pests, since wild dogs also eat carrion. Exact numbers or reliable estimates of the damage caused by wild dogs are therefore hard to get and seldom reliable. Even if livestock is not a big part of the dingo's diet, this says nothing about the extent of damage dingoes could cause to the livestock industry.

The significance of dingoes as a pest is mainly based on the predation of sheep and to a lower degree on cattle and is not only connected to the direct loss of livestock. Sheep of every age are susceptible to dingo attacks, in the case of cattle only the calves are susceptible. Harassment of sheep can cause a less optimal use of grassland and miscarriages.

The cattle industry can tolerate low to moderate and sometimes high grades of wild dogs (therefore dingoes are not so fast regarded as pests in these areas), in the case of sheep and goats a zero-tolerance attitude is common. The biggest threats are dogs that live inside or near the paddock areas. The extent of sheep loss is hard to determine due to the wide pasture lands in some parts of Australia. The numbers of cattle losses is much more variable and less well documented. Although the loss of cattle can rise up to 30%, the normal loss rate is about 0–10%. Thereby factors like availability of native prey, as well as the defending behaviour and health of the cattle play an important role for the number of losses. A study in Central Australia in the year 2003 confirmed, that dingoes only have a low impact on cattle numbers, when enough other prey like kangaroos and rabbits are available. In some parts of Australia it is assumed that the loss of calves can be minimized if horned cattle are used instead of hornless. The exact economical impact is not known in this case and it is regarded as unlikely that the rescue of some calves will compensate for the necessary costs of control measures. Calves usually suffer less lethal wounds than sheep due to their size and the protection by the adult cattle and have a higher chance of surviving an attack. Therefore it can happen that the evidence for a dog attack is only found after the cattle have been herded back in the enclosure and signs like bitten ears, tails, and other wounds are discovered. The opinions of cattle-owners about dingoes are more variable than the ones of sheep-owners and some cattle-owners believe that it is better that the weakened mother loses her calf in times of drought so she does not have to care for her calf too and therefore these owners hesitate more on killing dingoes. Laurie Corbett also stated this theory. Also the cattle industry may benefit from the predation of dingoes on rabbits, kangaroos, and rats. Furthermore the mortality rate of calves has many possible causes and it is hard to discriminate between them. The only reliable method to document the damage would be to document all pregnant cows and observe their development and that of their calves. The loss of calves in observed areas where dingoes were controlled was higher than in other ones. Loss of livestock is therefore not necessarily caused by the occurrence of dingoes and is independent from wild dogs.

Domestic dogs are the only terrestrial predators in Australia that are big enough to kill fully grown sheep and only a few sheep manage to recover from the severe injuries. In the case of lambs, death can have many causes apart from attacks by predators. Often the predators are blamed for the deaths, because they eat from the carcasses. Although attacks by Red Foxes appear, it happens more rarely than previously thought. The fact that the sheep and goat industry is much more susceptible for damage caused by wild dogs than the cattle industry is mostly due to two factors:

• The flight behaviour of the sheep and their quirk to flock together in the face of danger
• The hunting methods of wild dogs and the efficiency of their way of handling goat and sheep

Therefore the damage for the livestock industry is not in relation to the numbers of wild dogs in an area (except that there is no damage where no wild dogs occur). Even if there are only a few wild dogs in an area, the damage for the sheep industry can be very high, since surplus killing can occur. Sometimes extreme losses of livestock are reported (once supposedly 2000 sheep in one night) and are supposed to be increasing.

According to a report from the Government of Queensland, wild dogs cost the state yearly about 30 million dollars due to livestock-losses, spreading of diseases and control measures. Losses for the livestock-industry alone were estimated to be as high as 18 million dollars. According to a survey among cattle owners in 1995, performed by the Park and Wildlife Service, owners estimated their annual losses due to wild dogs (depending on the district) from 1.6% to 7.1%. Despite the variety of estimations, there is little doubt that predation by dingoes can cause enormous economical damage, especially in times of drought when natural prey is sparse and the dingo numbers are still relatively high. Furthermore wild dogs are involved in the spreading of Echinococcosis among cattle and sheep, as well as heartworms and parvoviruses among dogs under human care. An infection with Echinococcosis can leads to confiscation of 90% of the intestines, which further leads to a value decrease of the meat and high economical damage. Furthermore, bitten livestock can only be sold for a lower price.

Dogs are regarded as a delicacy in East-Asia and Oceania and are regularly killed for eating. In the northeast of Thailand about 200 dingoes are killed per week to be sold on the meat market. Before the start of the 20th century dingoes were also eaten by Indigenous Australians, but there are now reports about this practice in recent times. Among them dingoes were also used as hunting aids, living hot-water bottles, and camp-dogs. Their scalps were used as a kind of currency, teeth were traditionally used for decorative purposes, and their fur for traditional costumes. In some parts of Australia premiums are paid for dingo fur and scalps. Fur of dingoes mostly has only a low value and an export of this fur is forbidden in states where they are protected. There is also no widespread commercial catching and killing of dingoes for obtaining their fur. Sometimes "pure" dingoes have an importance for tourism, when they are used to attract more visitors. However this seems only to have been done on Fraser Island, where the dingoes are extensively used as a symbol to make the island more attractive. The experience of personally interacting with dingoes seems to be especially important for the tourists. Pictures of dingoes appear on the majority of brochures, many web sites, and post cards which advertise for the island. The usage of dingo-urine as a repellent against dingoes and wallabies was taken into consideration, but has not been economically implemented yet.

Legal status

The dingo was classified as vulnerable on the Red List of Threatened Species in the year 2004. This classification was done because the number of "pure" dingoes had decreased to about 30% due to interbreeding with other domestic dogs. The dingo is regarded as a regulated, native species (but not threatened) under the *Environment Protection and Biodiversity Conservation Act (1999)* in the Commonwealth of Nations and is therefore protected in the national parks of the Commonwealth, as well as in World Heritage Sites and other conservation areas. However, this law also allows that dingoes can be controlled in areas where they have a proven impact on the environment. The law forbids the export of dingoes or their body parts from Australia, except for cases where it is regulated by the law. The legal status of the dingo and other wild dogs varies across the Australian federal states and territories:

- Northern Territory: the dingo is regarded as protected, not threatened and native (due to its ecological impact) under the *Territory Parks and Wildlife Conservation Act (2000)*. Dingoes in the Northern Territory are regarded as having an important conservational value since interbreeding of dingoes and other domestic dogs is low in the area. However dingoes can be legally killed when they are a danger for the livestock industry.
- Western Australia: Dingoes and their hybrids are regarded as declared animals under the *Agriculture and Related Resources Protection Act (1976)*. Populations have to be controlled and can be kept as pets under certain conditions. Control measures are strictly confined to livestock areas and other domestic dogs are controlled in general. Dingoes are also regarded as unprotected native fauna under the *Western Australian Wildlife Conservation Act (1950)*. Although not protected, dingoes are normally not hunted without permission in conservation areas.
- South Australia: Dingoes and their hybrids are appointed pests in the sheep areas south of the Dingo Fence under the *Animal and Plant Control Board (Agricultural Protection and Other Purposes) Act (1986)*. There they have to be controlled and can only be kept in captivity of authorized zoos and wildlife parks. North of the Dingo Fence dingoes are regarded as legitimate wildlife and although they are not protected, they are given a certain protection in a puffer zone of 35 km northern of the Dingo Fence.

- Queensland: Dingoes and their hybrids are regarded as pests under the *Land Protection (Pest and Stock Route Management) Act 2002*. All landowners are legally committed to reduce the number of all wild dogs on their lands. The dingo is regarded as wildlife and native wildlife under the *Nature Conservation Act (1992)* and is a natural resource (therefore protected) in conservation areas. Outside of these areas dingoes are not regarded as native Australian and are not protected. Dingoes and their hybrids can only be kept in wildlife parks and zoos with ministerial agreement.
- New South Wales: *The Rural Lands Protection Act (1998)* allocates wild dogs the status of pests and demands from landowners, that they shall be decimated or eradicated. Although dingoes are not regarded as protected under the *National Parks and Wildlife Act (1974)*, they are granted full protection in national parks. The dingo is regarded as an native species under the *Threatened Species Conservation Act (1995)*, since these dogs had established populations before the European colonization. The *Wild Dog Destruction Act (1921)* includes dingoes in its definition of wild dogs. This law only affects the western part of the state, where landowners are committed to control wild dogs. The law forbids the ownership of dingoes in that region, except when you have a legal permission. In other parts of the federal state dingoes can be kept as pets due to the *Companion Animals Act (1998)*.
- Australian Capital Territory: Dingoes are regarded as protected under the *Nature Conservation Act (1980)*. On private land killing of wild dogs is allowed when you have permission from the state.
- Victoria: Wild dogs are regarded as established pests under the *Catchment and Land Protection Act (1994)* and landowners (except from the Commonwealth) have the legal duty to hinder the spreading of wild dogs on their lands and to eradicate them as much as possible. The term wild dogs includes here all dingoes, feral domestic dogs, dogs who became wild and crossbreeds (except for recognized breeds like the Australian Cattle Dog). The *Domestic (Feral and Nuisance) Animal Act (1994)* commits every dog owner to have their dogs under control on all times. The dingoes are granted a certain protection in areas that are managed by the *National Parks Act (1975)*. Since 1998 it is possible to own dingoes as pets. At the time there is the possibility that "pure" dingoes will become officially classified as a protected species, according to official statements, that would not stand in conflict with control measures against wild dogs.
- Tasmania: The import of dingoes to Tasmania is forbidden under the *National Parks and Wildlife Act (1970)*. The control of dogs that attack livestock is managed under the *Dog Control Act (1987)*.

Control measures

Dingo attacks on livestock lead to widescale efforts to repel them from areas with intensive agricultural usage, and all states and territories have enacted laws for the control of dingoes. In the early 20th century, fences were erected to keep dingoes away from areas frequented by sheep, and a tendency to routinely eradicate dingoes developed among some livestock owners. Established methods for the control of dingoes in sheep areas consisted in the employment of certain workers on every property.

The job of these people (who were nicknamed "doggers") was to reduce the number of dingoes using steel traps, baits, firearms and other methods. The responsibility for the control of wild dogs lay solely in the hands of the land owners. At the same time, the government was forced to decimate the number of dingoes that came from unoccupied areas or reserves that might have travelled to industrial areas. As a result, a number of measures for the control of dingoes developed over time. It was also considered that dingoes travel over long distances to reach areas with richer prey populations and the control was often concentrated along "paths" or "trails" and in areas that were far away from sheep areas. Every dingo was regarded as a potential danger and had to be hunted.

In the 1920s the Dingo Fence was erected on the basis of the *Wild dog act (1921)* and, until 1931, thousands of miles of dogfences had been erected in several areas of South Australia. In the year 1946, these efforts were directed to a single goal and the Dingofence was finally completed. The fence connected with other fences in New South Wales and Queensland. The main responsibilities in maintaining the dogfence still lies with the landowners, whose properties border on the fence and get financial support from the government.

A reward system (local, as well from the government) was active from 1846 to the end of the 20th century, but there is no evidence that − despite the billions of dollars used − it was ever an efficient control method. Therefore, its importance declined over time.

The eradication of dingoes due to livestock damage decreased along with the importance of the sheep industry and the usage of strychnine (which beforehand had been used for 100 years) in the 1970s. The number of doggers also decreased and the frequency of government approved aerial baiting increased. During this period, many farmers in Western Australia switched to the cattle industry, and findings in the area of biology lead to a significant change in control measures and techniques in association with reduced costs and increased efficiency. At the same time, the importance of 1080 increased and the first anxieties arose that the number of dingoes might have decreased so much that they may become locally extinct. Increasing pressure from environmentalists, against the random killing of dingoes as well as due to the impact on other animals, demanded that more information needed to be gathered to prove the necessity of control measures and to disprove the claim of unnecessary killings. Observations on the ecology of dingoes led to the practice to place baits near water holes, hiding places and prey sites.

Today, permanent population control is regarded as necessary to reduce the impact of all wild dogs and to ensure the survival of the "pure" dingo in the wild.

Owners of dingoes and other domestic dogs are sometimes asked to spay or neuter their pets and to keep them under observation in order to reduce the number of stray/feral dogs and prevent interbreeding with dingoes (for instance under the *Territory Parks and Wildlife Conservation Act (2000)*). The principle of caution is used at least in some control areas today, since dingoes are fully protected there, have cultural importance to the indigenous people and much data concerning the importance of dingoes and the impact of control measures on other species is missing. Historically, the attitudes and needs of indigenous people were not taken into account when dingoes were controlled. So called dingo conservation zones are regarded as a possible solution for this problem, and these zones would mainly be based on holy dingo sites and dreamtime-paths. Other factors that might be taken into account are the genetic status (degree of interbreeding) of dingoes in these areas, ownership and land usage, as well as a reduction of killing measures to areas outside of the zones. Land owners are increasingly committed to regularly record where individual dingoes and their tracks are most frequent and cause the most damage. Also, birth, damage and mortality rates of livestock should be recorded. However most control measures and the appropriate studies are there to minimize the loss of livestock and not to protect dingoes. In areas of cattle industries, there are few or no control measures, and efforts are mostly limited to occasional shootings and poisonings. Government controlled use of 1080 is performed only every third year, when field observations prove the claims of high livestock losses and dingo numbers.

Baits with 1080 are regarded as the fastest as safest method for dog control, since they are extremely susceptible: even small amounts of poison per dog are sufficient (0.3 mg per kg). The application of aerial baiting is regulated in the Commonwealth by the *Civil Aviation Regulations (1988)*. The assumption that the Tiger Quoll might be damaged by the poison led to the dwindling of areas where aerial baiting could be performed. In areas where aerial baiting is no longer possible, it is necessary to put down baits. Where steel traps and baits cannot or are not allowed to be used (for example, residential zones), cage traps are used.

Apart from the introduction of 1080 (extensively used for 40 years and nicknamed "doggone"), the methods and strategies for decimating wild dogs have changed little over time. Strychnine is still used in all parts of Australia. Trapping and removal is an essential part of the control measures in the highlands of South-eastern New South Wales and Northern Victoria. It does occur that dingoes are hunted and shot by people on horseback or that a premium is sold for shot dingoes. One method, that does not have any proven effect, is to hang dead dogs along the borders of the property in the belief that this would repel wild dogs. To protect livestock, livestock guardian dogs (for example, Maremmas), donkeys, alpacas, and llamas are used. Over the last years cyanide-ejectors and protection collars (filled with 1080 on certain spots) have been tested To keep wild dogs away from certain areas, efforts are taken to make these areas unattractive for them (for example, by getting rid of food waste) and therefore forcing them to move elsewhere. Control through deliberately spreading disease is normally not considered. Such attempts probably would not be successful, because typical dog diseases are already present in the population. Additionally, dogs under human care would also be susceptible. Other biological control methods are not regarded as achievable, since there would be a high risk of decimating dogs under human care.

The efficiency of control measures was questioned in the past and is still often questioned today. It is also questioned whether they stand in a good cost-benefit ratio. The premium system proved to be susceptible to deception and to be useless on a large scale and can therefore only be used for getting rid of "problem-dogs". Animal traps are considered as inhumane and inefficient on a large scale, for example, due to the limited efficacy of baits. Based on studies, it is assumed that only young dogs which would have died anyway can be captured. Furthermore, wild dogs are capable of learning and sometimes are able to detect and avoid traps quite efficiently. There is a known case in which a dingo bitch followed a dogger and triggered its traps one after another by carefully pushing her paw through the sand that covered the trap. Poisonous baits can be very effective when they are of good meat quality; however, they do not last long and are proven to be taken by Red Foxes, quolls, ants, and birds. Aerial baiting can nearly eliminate whole dingo populations. Livestock guardian dogs can effectively minimize livestock losses, but are less effective on wide open areas with widely distributed livestock. Furthermore they can be a danger to the livestock or be killed by control measures themselves when they are not sufficiently supervised by their owners. Fences are reliable in keeping wild dogs from entering certain areas, but they are expensive to built and need permanent maintenance. Further more they only cause the problem to be relocated.

According to studies, control measures can eliminate 66 to 84% of a wild living dog population, but the population can reach their old numbers very quickly over the course of a year and depending on the season, for instance by immigration of young dogs from other areas. If at all, only a cohesive coordinated control in all areas could be efficient in the long run. Control measures mostly result in smaller packs respectively in a disruption of the pack structure. Also the measures seem to be rather detrimental to the livestock industry because the empty territories are taken over by young dogs and the predation then increases. Nonetheless it is regarded as unlikely that the control measures could completely eradicate the dingo in Central Australia, and the elimination of all wild dogs is not considered as a realistic option.

Conservation

Dingoes are only officially protected in Australia and conservation areas for "pure" dingoes exist only there. All other wild dogs are considered pests. However, in reality all wild dogs are granted full protection in conservation zones, because a separate management is not possible. In Australia dingoes are only regarded as "legally protected" in national parks, natural reserves, in the Arnhem Land Aborigine Reserve and natural parks in the Northern Territory, national parks and reserves in New South Wales, national parks in Victoria and in the whole area of the Australian Capital Territory. Although dingoes are protected there, as well as in areas belonging to the World Heritage and Aboriginal-reserves, they are regarded as "declared" pests in the bulk of their remaining distribution area and landowners are committed to control the local populations.

The dingoes of Fraser Island are considered to be of significant conservational value, since they are often seen as the "most pure" population and to be most similar to the original dingoes, due to their geographical and genetically isolation. Supposedly the dingoes there are not "threatened" by interbreeding with other domestic dogs.

Groups that have devoted themselves to the conservation of the "pure" dingo by using breeding programs are for instance the *Australian Native Dog Conservation Society* and the *Australian Dingo Conservation Association*. The efforts of the dingo-conservation-groups are considered to be ineffective at the moment since most of their dogs are either untested or known to be hybrids.

The focus of attention in association with the conservation of dingoes is the stop of interbreeding between dingoes and other domestic dogs. Protection from interbreeding is extremely difficult, costly and conservation efforts are hampered by the facts that it is not known how many "pure" dingoes still exist in Australia and that conservation efforts are in conflict with control measures. Steps to conserve the "pure" dingo can only be effective when the identification of dingoes and other domestic dogs is absolutely reliable (especially in the case of living specimen). Conservation of "pure" and survivable dingo populations is regarded as promising in remote areas, where the contact with humans and especially other domestic dogs is rare. In parks, reserves and other areas not used by agriculture these populations shall only be controlled when they pose a threat to the survival of other native species. The introduction of "dog-free" buffer zones around areas with "pure" dingoes is regarded as a realistic method to stop interbreeding. At the moment this is enforced in the way that all wild dogs can be killed outside of the conservation areas. However studies from the year 2007 indicate that even an intensive control of core areas is probably not able to stop the process of interbreeding.

At the present there is no information on what kind of opinion the broad public has towards the conservation of dingoes. Additionally there is no unity on the definition of "pure" dingoes and how far they should be controlled.

As a pet and working dog

There is divided opinion on the topic of keeping dingoes as pets and working dogs. For some people, the dingo is by no means suitable for this while for others it is no different than other domestic dogs, and that to say otherwise would be far fetched. In this vein, dingoes would have the right to be recognized as a dog breed and that domestication would be the only reliable way to ensure the survival of the "pure" dingo.

Dingoes can be very tame when they come in frequent contact with humans. Furthermore there were and are dingoes that live with humans (due to practical, as well as emotional reasons). It is known that many indigenous Australians and early European settlers already lived alongside dingoes. Alfred Brehm reported of dingoes that were completely tame and, in some cases, behaved exactly like other domestic dogs (one was used for shepherding heavy livestock), as well as of specimens that remained wild and shy. He also reported of dingoes that were aggressive and completely uncontrollable, but was of the opinion that these reports *should not get more attention than they deserve*, since the behaviour depends on how the dingo was raised since early puppyhood. He also believed that these dogs could become very decent pets.

According to Eberhard Trumler dingoes are very smart and affectionate. These characteristics were the reason why he never recommended anyone to own dingoes if they could not provide the dog an enclosure (not a kennel) that was big enough and escape-proof and a partner of the opposite sex. During heat, dingoes are harder to manage than other domestic dogs, which combined with their attachment to their owners leads to problems, since they want to follow their owners all the time and never miss the opportunity to feed. They are supposed to find every weak spot of an enclosure or residence, escape for a while and stray through towns and villages. Their intellectual ability is supposedly connected to an enormous ability to learn and a lightning perception, but stops at the slightest hint of pressure. They would be suitable as shepherd dogs, as they see a purpose in it (keeping together a familiar group would be in their nature) and even today, some dingoes are used as shepherd dogs. Similar to other domestic dogs they can be housebroken.

In 1976, the *Australian Native Dog Training Society of N.S.W. Ltd* was founded, which was originally illegal because ownership of dingoes was forbidden. The dingo was officially recognized as Australia's national dog breed in mid-1994 by the Australian National Kennel Council, and a breed standard was published years later. However this does not legalize ownership in states where it is forbidden to own, breed or sell dingoes.

Today dingoes are bred by certain clubs and private individuals in Australia and the USA.

Whether or not dingoes are allowed to be kept as pets differs from country to country, as well as between the states of Australia. For example: in South Australia dingoes can only be kept in specially authorized zoos, circuses and research institutions. Ownership, planned domestication or commercial usage of dingoes is considered unacceptable, since this would lead to the reintroduction of dingoes in sheep areas.

The dingo is not regarded as a dog breed by the Fédération Cynologique Internationale. However the American Rare Breed Association (ARBA) regards the dingo as a breed belonging to the Spitz and Primitive Group. In addition the dingo is also listed in Group 4 (Hound) of the Australian National Kennel Council (ANKC).

Goals

Breeding programs are considered to be the best option to ensure the long-term existence of the dingo in its "pure" form (the reclassification of the dingo as a pet in New South Wales of the year 1998 was originally done to save the dingo from extinction), sometimes with the goal to later return them to the wild.

Apart from that, the breeding of dingoes is also there to produce dingoes that can be sold or used as working dogs. The first efforts to use dingoes at customs were done in 1976 in Victoria. However, some people speculated that these dogs were cross-breeds of dingoes and shepherd dogs.

Criticism

The ownership of dingoes as pets and their resulting breeding are criticised from many directions.

One point of criticism is that the activities and the resulting consequences of the dingo-conservation-groups, "dingo farms" and legislation for legal ownership of dingoes for people in public is supposed to be an additional threat to the survival of the "pure" dingoes. This fear exists because the majority of these breeding activities effectively expedite the interbreeding of dingoes and other domestic dogs, when the identification of a "pure" dingo is not absolutely correct respectively when hybrids are sold as "pure" dingoes.

Even supporters of breeding programs are sometimes only vaguely optimistic about the success of this step to preserve the "pure" dingo. Success in the form of a population viable for future re-wilding is only to be accomplished with difficulty from the start. According to David Jenkins, the breeding and reintroduction of "pure" dingoes is no easy option and at the time there were no studies that seriously dealt with this topic, especially in areas where dingo populations are already present. An additional threat is that breeders may unconsciously select for tamer dingoes by breeding individuals who are easier to manage. Therefore it may happen that, over the years, the tame populations become less suitable for living in the wild than their ancestors. Also, a loss of genetic diversity (thus resulting in a higher susceptibility to diseases) might occur due to a small founding population and negative changes could occur simply because the dogs were captive-bred. Furthermore, some features that are necessary for survival in the wild might "fade" under the conditions of domestication (for example, hunting techniques) because they are no longer practised.

Another point of criticism is that adult dingoes are not suitable as pets in the same way as other domestic dogs in the eyes of many people. Dingoes are hereby regarded as more independent minded than other domestic dogs, and domestication is supposedly difficult. Furthermore, it is stated that dingoes, as they age, succumb to their aggressive instincts and attacks on people become more likely and that dingoes often run away. Furthermore, most people could not give a dingo what it needs and dingoes would not react positively to domestication and training. Supposedly, only few dingoes and dingo-hybrids would reach an old age, since the owners would not know how to handle them. When a dingo is not socialized, it would be hard to control and develop behavioural problems from aspects of domestic life which are more easily tolerated by other dog breeds. To make dingoes more suitable as lapdogs, breeders would need to cross them with other domestic dogs.

Origin and genetic status

Since dingoes were the only big placental mammals in Australia, apart from humans, and looked similar to dogs under human care but lived in the wild, their origin was a subject of much speculation and debate since the 18th century and especially in the first half of the 20th century. Later archaeological and morphological studies indicated a relatively late introduction and a close relationship to other domestic dogs. The exact descent, place of origin and time of their arrival in Australia were not identified, nor whether they were domesticated or half-domesticated at the time of their arrival and therefore are feral or completely wild dogs respectively.

A widely distributed theory says that dingoes have evolved or were bred from the Canis lupus pallipes or Canis lupus arabs around 6.000–10.000 years ago (this was also assumed for all domestic dogs). This theory was based on the morphological similarities of dingo skulls and the skulls of these wolves. However genetic analyses indicated a much earlier domestication.

Analyses of amino sequences of the hemoglobin of a "pure" dingo in the 70s supported the theory that dingoes are more closely related to other domestic dogs than to grey wolves or coyotes. Additionally it was assumed that dingoes and other Asian domestic dogs are members of a group of domestic dogs that went feral very early. At the same time, DNA-studies on Australian dingoes and other domestic dogs were performed to differentiate between both populations in a reliable way and determine the extent of the interbreeding. At the first two examinations, during which at first 14 loci and later 5 of these loci were examined, no genetic difference could be found. Later on the analyses were expanded to 16 loci. This time dingoes from Central Australia, the Eastern Highlands, dingo-hybrids and domestic dogs of other origin were examined. The researchers were surprised that they could not find any differences no matter what kind of examination they used. It was reasoned that dingoes and other domestic dogs have a very similar gene pool. However, since also only few differences in the enzymes of different species of the genus canis could be found, it was assumed that a lack of differences might not indicate a close taxonomical relationship. It was also reasoned that the degree of interbreeding in the wild is only hard to determine.

During analyses in the end of the 1990s researchers also analysed 14 loci and detected a significantly lower genetic variability among Australian dingoes than among other domestic dogs and a small founding population was considered. There was one loci found that might have been suitable for differentiation, but not in the case of interbreeding of a dingo-hybrid with other "pure" dingoes. Additionally it was suspected that findings of other suitable loci might be used to determine whether there are clearly separate sub-populations of the "pure" dingoes.

To determine the origin and time of arrival of Australian dingoes, mtDNA-sequences of 211 dingoes and 19 archaeological samples from pre-European Polynesia have been compared in 2004 with DNA-samples of 676 other domestic dogs and 38 grey wolves. The domestic dog samples came from China, Africa, Southwest-Asia, India, Siberia, the arctic America, Europe, Mongolia, Korea, Japan, Vietnam, Cambodia, Thailand, Indonesia, the Philippines, Malaysia, New Zealand, Hawaii and the highlands of New Guinea. The dingo-samples came from zoos, wildlife parks, dingo-conservation-groups, dingo-lovers and 192 wild living specimen from 27 areas scattered over the Australian continent, mainly from the Pilbara-region, New South Wales and the Northeast of Victoria. The wild specimen had been selected based on similarities of external appearance, to exclude the influence of dingo-hybrids and other domestic dogs as far as possible.

Compared to wolves and other domestic dogs the variation of mtDNA-sequences was very limited too. Among dingoes only 20 mtDNA-sequences differing in 2 point mutations at most could be found. In comparison: 114 mtDNA-sequences with a maximal difference of 16 point mutations between the DNA-types could be found among other domestic dogs. Two of the dingo mtDNA-types were similar to that of other domestic dogs (A9, A29), while the other 18 types were unique to dingoes. In a phylogenetic tree of wolves and domestic dogs, dingoes fell right into the main clade (A), which contained 70% of all domestic dog types. Within this clade the dingo-types formed a group around the type A29, which was surrounded by twelve less frequent dingo-types, as well as a set of other domestic dog types. This mtDNA-type was found in 53% of the dingoes and was also found among some domestic dogs from East-Asia, New-Guinea and the American Arctic. Based on these findings it was reasoned that all dingo-mtDNA-types originated in A29. A9 was only found in one individual and it was regarded as possible that this type is the result of a parallel mutation. Based on a mutation-rate of mtDNA and that A29 is the only founder–type it was regarded as most likely that dingoes arrived in Australia about 4,600 to 5,400 years ago, which was consistent with archaeological findings. However, it was also considered that dingoes might have arrived within 4,600 to 10,800 years ago, in case that the mtDNA-mutation rate was slower than assumed. Furthermore it was reasoned that these findings strongly indicate a descent of dingoes from East-Asian domestic dogs and not from Indian domestic dogs or wolves. In addition these findings indicated two possibilities of descent:

• All Australian dingoes are descended from a few domestic dogs, theoretically one pregnant female
• All Australian dingoes are descended from a group of domestic dogs, who radically lost their genetic diversity through one or several severe genetic bottlenecks on their way from the Asian continent over Southeast-Asia

Nonetheless, the existence of other mtDNA-types on the islands surrounding Australia indicate there have been other types apart from A29 and only one single founding event. These results also indicated that there hasn't been any significant introduction of other domestic dog on the Australian continent prior to the arrival of the Europeans. Also, a shared origin and some sort of genetic exchange between Australian dingoes and the New Guinea singing dogs was regarded as possible. The current state of the Australian dingoes was ascribed to the long wild existence of these dogs and assumed that they are an isolated example of early domestic dogs.

Despite accordant claims, these findings did not show that only dingo females mate with non-dingo males and not vice versa. The findings would not allow such a conclusion, since the mating of a dingo female with a non-dingo male could not be detected via analyses of mtDNA. Furthermore the researchers made sure from the start that dingo-hybrids were excluded as far as possible.

Interbreeding with other domestic dogs

European domestic dogs first arrived in Australia during the European colonization. These dogs reverted to the wild (both unintentionally and intentionally), produced feral populations and interbred with the dingoes. Hybrids of dingoes and other domestic dogs exist today in all populations of Australia, with their population being regarded as increasing to the point that completely "pure" populations may no longer exist. The degree of interbreeding is locally so high by now, for instance in urban and rural areas, that there are big populations consisting purely of hybrids. Estimates from the 90s already assumed a proportion of dingo-hybrids of about 78% in the wild. It is not clear how big the current population of Hybrids is today.

Dingo-like domestic dogs and dingo-hybrids can be generally distinguished from "pure" dingoes by their fur-colour, since there is a wider range of colours and patterns among them than among dingoes. Furthermore, the more dog-typical kind of barking exists among the hybrids. Furthermore, differences in the breeding-cycle, certain skull-characteristics and genetic analyses can be used for differentiation. Despite all the characteristics that can be used for distinguishing between dingoes and other domestic dogs, there are two problems that should not be underestimated. At first there is no real clarity from what point a dog is regarded as a "pure" dingo, second no distinguishing feature is one-hundred per cent reliable and it is not sure which characteristics permanently remain under the conditions of natural selection.

In the scientific area, there are two main opinions regarding this process of interbreeding. The first, and likely most common position, states that the "pure" dingo should be preserved via strong controls of the wild dog populations, and only "pure" respectively nearly "pure" dingoes should be protected. The second position is relatively new and is of the opinion that people must accept that the dingo has changed and that it is not possible to bring the "pure" dingo back. Conservation of these dogs should therefore be based on where and how they live, as well as their cultural and ecological role, instead of concentrating on precise definitions or concerns about "genetic purity". Both positions are controversially discussed.

It is verifiable that there is a wider range of fur-colours, skull-shapes and body size in the modern day wild dog population than in the time before the arrival of the Europeans. Over the course of the last 40 years there has been an increase of the average wild dog body size of about 20%. Currently it is unknown whether, in the case of the disappearance of "pure" dingoes, the then existing hybrids will alter the predation pressure on other animals. It is also unclear what kind of role these hybrids would play in the Australian ecosystems. However, it is regarded as likely that the dynamics of the various ecosystems will not be disturbed by this process.

Attacks on humans

As wild dogs are large predators, they can be potentially dangerous to humans. Fraser Island is a special centre of attention regarding such, since interaction between dingoes and humans there is very high due to tourism, therefore the majority of reported incidents originate there.

The likelihood of wild dogs being a danger to humans depends to a large degree on how humans behave toward them. The more frequently these dogs are fed or scavenge human leftovers, the more likely it is that they lose all caution and sometimes react aggressively towards humans when they no longer receive or find food.

Even when habituation to humans seems to be the cause for attacks, it is not clear what the ultimate cause for attacks and overall threat towards humans is. It is possible that some attacks result from the "play" of young cubs, especially with children. Attacks can also be caused by false reactions of humans to aggressive and dominance behaviour of dingoes. It is assumed that dingoes might have started to regard "human" food sources (garbage cans, leftovers, handouts, and so forth) as part of their territory and that attacks on humans can therefore occur because the dingoes see humans as competition and want to protect their food sources. That some dingoes might regard humans as prey was also deemed possible because humans, especially children, could be theoretically overpowered.

Two reports of dingo attacks on humans

- On 17 August 1980 a nine-week-old girl named Azaria Chamberlain was captured by a dingo near Uluru (Ayers Rock) and killed. Her mother was suspected and convicted of murder. Four years later she was released from prison when the jacket of the baby was found in a dingo den and the mother was therefore found innocent. This incident caused much outcry for and against the dingoes.
- On 30 April 2001 nine-year-old Clinton Cage was attacked and killed by two dingoes near Waddy Point on Fraser Island. The incident and the following culling of 31 dingoes caused much outcry among the residents. There were many protests and the suggestion was made to erect fences.

The behavior of humans might undermine efforts to prepare against dingo-attacks; therefore the change of human behavior is in the centre of attention. Warning signs like "Beware of Dingoes" seem to have lost their effect on Fraser Island, despite their high numbers. Furthermore, some humans do not realize how adaptive and quick dingoes are. Therefore they do not stay attentive enough and for instance do not consider that dingoes even steal food like fruits and vegetables. In addition some tourists seemed to be confused by the high numbers of rules in some parks and have been prompted in some cases to actively feed the wild animals.

Problems in classification

There is no general agreement, scientifically or otherwise, on what the dingo is in a biological sense, since it has been called "wolf", "dingo", "dog" and "wild dog". Even within the scientific community is the dingo given several names. In addition, there is no consensus on whether it is a feral or native animal or what kinds of dogs should be classed as dingoes. Thus some people consider the New Guinea Singing Dog, the Basenji, the Carolina Dog and other dog-populations to be dingoes, something which has yet to be proven. Evidence indicates a discord concerning the status of these dogs also. Dingoes have been variously considered to be wild dogs, the progenitor of domestic dogs, the ancestor of modern dog breeds, a separate species, a link between wolf and domestic dog, a primitive canine-species or primitive domestic dog, a "dog-like" relative of wolves. or a subspecies of the domestic dog Others consider them to be native dogs of Asia, a relatively unchanged form of early domestic dog., part wolf and part dog or to have been selectively bred from wolves Then again, others do not consider them feral anymore but completely wild, since they have been living under natural selection for a very long time. According to present scientific consensus and knowledge, they are domestic dogs that arrived at their present distribution with humans, adapted to the respective conditions and are no more "primitive" or "primordial" than other domestic dogs.

The AU Dingo has never been subject to the artificial selection that produced modern dog breeds and that the AU Dingo is an undomesticated descendent of an extinct Asian wolf. However, compared to the European grey wolf, dingoes have an approximately 30% lower relative brain size, reduced facial expressions reduced impressive behaviour, curled tails which can be carried over the back and generally a permanent fertility in males; features that all known domestic dogs share and that are considered to be caused by domestication. It might happen that one and the same source names the dingo as a subspecies of the grey wolf but lists all other domestic dogs as a separate species. Likewise, the scientific name of the dingo might be stated to be *Canis lupus dingo*, but the dingo regarded as a separate species nonetheless. Alfred Brehm originally considered the dingo to be a separate species, but after examining several different specimens came to the conclusion that they could only be domestic dogs. In contrast, William Jardine considered the dingo to be an entirely separate species, while contemporary French naturalists regarded them as feral dogs. Even among modern day scientists dingoes and other domestic dogs are sometimes considered two separate species, despite proven small genetic, morphological and behavioural differences. The phenomenon of interbreeding between both is then attributed to the statement that all wolf-like species can interbreed and produce fertile offspring. However, breeding experiments in Germany could only prove an unrestricted fertility in the offspring of domestic dogs and grey wolves. Hybrids between domestic dogs and coyotes, respectively domestic dogs and Golden Jackals, had communication problems among each other, as well to the parent species. From the third hybrid-generation on, a decrease in fertility and an increase in genetic damage was observed among the coyote-hybrids and jackal-hybrids. Observations of this kind have never been made for hybrids of dingoes and other domestic dogs, only that dingoes and other domestic dogs can freely interbreed with each other.

The choice of classification can have a direct impact on the dingo. Dingoes officially cease to exist outside of national parks and become unprotected wild dogs. This term itself sometimes only includes dingoes and their hybrids respectively excludes dingoes. Another change of name is that dingoes are "only" feral outside of national parks, with this term having a more negative meaning than the term "wild".

On the other hand, dingoes have been "rehabilitated" in some way, by changing their status from pests to "Australia's native dog" or more subtly, from a subspecies of the domestic dog to that of the grey wolf. The undertone in the Australian press seemed to be that being a grey wolf or an Asian wolf means that the dingo is more "wild" and therefore more desirable than a companion animal (domestic dog). It is possible that the habit of calling the dingo only dog (not wild dog) in colloquial language indicates a kind of familiarity or debasing. In the last case it might be morally easier to kill a dingo when it causes problems because it would not have the "high status" of a wolf or dingo. Sometimes, it is considered to be bad that dingoes are domestic dogs, as well as being descended from them and not "directly" from the grey wolf. If the dingo regarded as native, than it is worthy of protection. But if it is considered to be "just" a variant of the domestic dog, it is regarded as a pest and should be eradicated.

English

- J.S. Bacon: *The Australian Dingo: The King of the Bush*. McCarron Bird, Melbourne 1955.
- R. Breckwoldt: *A Very Elegant Animal: the Dingo*. Angus and Robertson, Australia 1988.
- Lawrence K. Corbett: *The Dingo in Australia and Asia*. Cornell University Press, Ithaca 1995, ISBN 0-8014-8264-X.
- Deborah Bird Rose: *Dingo makes us Human, Life and Land in an Aboriginal Australian culture*. Cambridge University Press, New York, Oakleigh 1992, ISBN 0-521-39269-1.
- Chris R. Dickman: *A Symposium on the Dingo*. Royal Zoological Society of New South Wales, Sydney 1999, ISBN 0-9586085-2-0.
- Erich Kolig: *Aboriginal dogmatics: canines in theory, myth and dogma* [1]. In: *Bijdragen tot de Taal-, Land- en Volkenkunde 134*. Nr. 1, Leiden 1978, Seite 84–115.
- Kate Lawrance and Karen Higginbottom: *Behavioural Responses of Dingos to Tourist on Fraser Island* [2]. In: *Wildlife Tourism Research Report Series*. Nr. 27, 2002.
- Claudio Sillero-Zubiri, Michael Hoffmann, David W. Macdonald (editors): *Canids: Foxes, Wolves, Jackals and Dogs* [3]. IUCN – The World Conservation Union, 2004.
- E. Beckmann and Gillian Savage: *Evaluation of Dingo Education Strategy and Programs for Fraser Island and Literature review: Communicating to the public about potentially dangerous wildlife in natural settings* [4]. Environmetrics in conjunction with Beckmann and Associates, Commissioned by Queensland Parks and Wildlife Service, Juni 2003.

- Peter Fleming, Laurie Corbett, Robert Harden, Peter Thomson: *Managing the Impacts of Dingoes and Other Wild Dogs*. Bureau of Rural Sciences, Commonwealth of Australia, 2001.
- *Western Australian Wild Dog Management Strategy 2005* [5]. August 2005.
- Georgette Leah Burns, Peter Howard: *When wildlife tourism goes wrong: a case study of stakeholder and management issues regarding dingoes on Fraser Island*. Faculty of Environmental Sciences, Griffith University.

German

- Dorit Urd Feddersen-Petersen: *Hundepsychologie*. 4. Auflage. Franck-Kosmos-Verlag & Co. KG, Stuttgart 2004, ISBN 978-3-440-09780-9.
- Dorit Urd Feddersen-Petersen: *Ausdrucksverhalten beim Hund*. Franck-Kosmos-Verlag, Stuttgart 2008, ISBN 978-3-440-09863-9.
- Eberhard Trumler: *Meine wilden Freunde – Die Wildhundarten der Welt*. Piper, München 1981, ISBN 3-492-02483-1.
- Eberhard Trumler: *Mit dem Hund auf du – Zum Verständnis seines Wesens und Verhaltens*. 4. Auflage. Piper, München 1996.
- Eberhard Trumler: *Ein Hund wird geboren – Der Ratgeber für den Hundefreund*. Piper, München 1982, ISBN 3-492-02775-X.
- Erik Zimen: *Der Hund: Abstammung – Verhalten – Mensch und Hund*. 1. Auflage. Bertelsmann, München 1988.
- Hans Hoenig: *Vergleichend-anatomische Untersuchungen über den Hirnfurchungstypus der Caniden mit besonderer Berücksichtigung des Canis Dingo*. Trenkel, Berlin 1912.
- Helmut Hemmer: *Domestikation, Verarmung der Merkwelt*. Vieweg, Braunschweig 1983, ISBN 3-528-08504-5. (also available in english: *Domestication: the decline of environmental appreciation*, translated by Neil Beckhaus, Edition: 2, illustrated. Published by Cambridge University Press, 1990. ISBN 0-521-34178-7, 9780521341783

External links

- "Dingo found to be one of the world's oldest dog breeds." From *Times Online* March 18, 2010. [6]
- BBC story on dingo mitochondrial DNA study [7]
- Dingo Quick Facts [8]
- Primitive and Aboriginal Dog Society [9]
- A big collection of dingo pictures on Flickr [10]
- A documentation about Australian Dingos [11]

Azawakh

Azawakh

Typical Azawakh male	
Other names	Idi Hanshee Oska Rawondu Bareeru Wulo (formerly)Tuareg Sloughi
Country of origin	"Officially" Mali but also Burkina Faso, Niger, southern Algeria and throughout the western Sahel.

Traits

Classification and standards

FCI	Group 10 Section 3 #307	standard [1]
AKC	Hound (FSS)	standard [2]
	The AKC Foundation Stock Service [3] (FSS) is an optional recording service for purebred dogs that are not yet eligible for AKC registration.	
KC (UK)	Hound	[? standard]
UKC	Sighthounds and Pariah Dogs	standard [4]

Dog (*Canis lupus familiaris*)

The **Azawakh** is a sighthound dog breed from Africa.

Description

Appearance

His morphology is very close to that of the Middle Eastern and of the North African sighthounds, all swift, highbred coursing hounds, although at first glance obvious physical singularities present themselves. For example, a short, flat back atop long legs accentuates his lofty bearing, and his hips appear higher than the withers. His natural beauty is austere and architectural, sharply contrasting the arabesque loveliness of the Saluki, or the rather somber dignity of the Sloughi. Almond eyed, lean and graceful, his profile is at once sere but harmonious, his presence aristocratic and aloof. He moves with a distinctly feline plastique, collected, elastic, and articulate, his demeanor guarded and mysterious, his glance feral, untamed. In his land of ancestry he can be found in a variety of colors as well as varying degrees of refinement, though format is basically constant.

The standards call for a hound from 33 to 55 pounds (15 to 25 kg); its height is 24 to 29 inches (61 to 74 cm). The coat is very short and almost absent on the belly. Its bone structure shows clearly through the skin and musculature. Its muscles are "dry", meaning that they lie quite flat, unlike the Greyhound and Whippet. In this respect it is similar in type to the Saluki.

In Africa, Azawakh are found in a variety of colors such as red, blue fawn (that is, with a lilac cast), grizzle, and, rarely, blue and black. The Azawakh in its native land also comes with various white markings including Irish marked (white collar) and particolour (mostly white). Because of this wide color variation in the native population, the American standard used by the AKC and UKC allows any color combination found in Africa. In the United States, the FCI standard is modified to have no color restrictions at a minimum and there is a strong sentiment that the FCI standard should be heavily edited or replaced.

Colors permitted by the FCI breed standard are clear sand to dark fawn/brown, red and brindle (with or without a dark mask), with white bib, tail tip, and white on all feet (which can be tips of toes to high stockings). Currently, white stockings that go above the elbow joint are considered disqualifying features in France, as is a white collar or half collar (Irish marked).

The Azawakh's light, supple, lissome gait is a notable breed characteristic, as is an upright double suspension gallop.

Health

Azawakhs are an incredibly sound coursing hound. Serious coursing injuries are rare. The dogs heal very quickly from injury.

Azawakh have no known incidence of hip dysplasia. There is a small occurrence of adult-onset idiopathic epilepsy in the breed. Wobbler disease or cervical vertebral instability does rarely occur. Some breeders believe this is a largely developmental problem where puppies grow too quickly due to a high-protein western diet.

Like the Basenji, the Azawakh bitch often has a single annual estrus. Unassisted birth of healthy puppies is the norm. Litter sizes are usually from 4 to 6 puppies but litters as small as 1 and as large as 8 occur.

Azawakh need a fairly high level of exercise and should have regular runs off lead in large enclosed areas to run off steam. The dogs are very social and emotional. They need a master that provides firm but fair leadership. Azawakh thrive companionship of other Azawakh.

Temperament

Unlike other sighthounds, the primary function of the Azawakh in his native land is that of protector. He develops an intense bond with his owner, yet does not look to his master for instructions. Azawakh are a study in opposing tensions: attentive yet aloof, affectionate yet fierce, refined yet rugged. With those they accept, Azawakh are gentle and extremely affectionate. With strangers many are reserved and prefer not to be touched, but are not inherently aggressive. Although raised to protect livestock, they do not have innate aggression toward canine nor human unless they are threatened.

Azawakh have high energy and tremendous endurance. They are excellent training companions for runners and are nearly impervious to heat. They will happily run in weather over 100 degrees Fahrenheit that would kill a Greyhound. They often dig holes in the garden.

Many Azawakh detest rain and cold weather.

Azawakh are pack oriented and form complex social hierarchies. They have tremendous memories and are able to recognize each other after long periods of separation. They can often be found sleeping on top of each other for warmth and companionship.

Origin

Recent genetic, blood protein and archaeological studies as well as direct observation in the field offer a glimpse into the origin of the contemporary Azawakh breed. He comes out of the population of pariah dogs of sub-Saharan Africa—also called *bush dogs* or *senji*--and is also closely related to the Sloughi of the Maghreb. Despite morphological similarities, mitochondrial DNA evidence shows that he is only very distantly related to other sight hounds. Azawakh have a rare glucose isomerase allele (GPI^B) that occurs only in foxes, jackals, Italian wolves, Sloughi dogs and a handful of other quite unrelated rare dogs found mostly in Japan. The presence of the GPI^B suggests an ancient differentiation of the Azawakh from other dog populations near the base of the dog family tree divergence from wolves or perhaps a uniquely African cross-breeding with local African canids such as jackals. Petroglyph rock art dating from 8,000 to 10,000 years ago during the Green Sahara (also known as the Holocene and Neolithic Subpluvial) shows cursorial dogs in conjunction with hunters. Archaeologists have found dog bones buried in Holocene settlements in the Sahara. At the close of the Holocene Wet Phase in the 4th millennium Before Christ, the Sahara returned to desert and created a formidable physical barrier to travel. Together, this evidence suggests that the Azawakh population has a unique genetic heritage that has been largely isolated from other dog populations for millennia.

In the common era the Sahel dogs are almost totally isolated from northern dogs by the Sahara, but the ties to the pariah dogs to the south are extremely close. Azawakh are virtually indistinguishable from the Sahel pariah dog population from which they are drawn. In addition to a basic physical structure, the Azawakh share a number of unique traits with the pariah dogs:

- intense suspicion of the unknown
- strong guarding instinct
- pack hunting behavior
- complex social hierarchies
- unique vocalizations
- extra pre-molar teeth
- strong instinct to dig dens

Throughout the Sahel, very elegant puppies can be found among rustic siblings. The Sahel nomads do not have the same breed concepts as in the West and, unlike the Bedouin of the North, do not recognize a strict separation of *al hor* (noble) from *kelb* (mongrel) dogs. The nomads act as an extra level of selection on top of the intense natural selection pressure of the Sahel environment. The approach to selection is diametrically opposed to Western breeding. Instead of selecting which dogs to breed upon maturity, they decide which puppies should live. This approach has the advantage of maintaining a large reservoir of genetic variability and resilience.

The peoples of the Sahel control dam lines and cull puppies heavily at birth according to locally held aesthetic criteria that we do not fully understand. In the Sahel, color is not a selection criterion. The alpha male dog from the local population is usually the sire. Unless it is a wet year, only one puppy from a litter might be selected to live. Females are usually culled unless the family projects a need for more dogs in the future.

History

Bred by the Tuareg, Fula and various other nomads of the Sahara and sub-Saharan Sahel in the countries of Mali, Niger, Burkina Faso, and southern Algeria, the breed is used there as a guard dog and to hunt gazelle and hare at speeds up to 40 miles per hour. The austerity of the Sahel environment has ensured that only the most fit dogs survive and has accentuated the breed's ruggedness and independence. Unlike some other sighthounds, the Azawakh is more of a pack hunter and they bump down the quarry with hindquarters when it has been tired out. In role of a guard dog, if an Azawakh senses danger it will bark to alert the other members of the pack, and they will gather together as a pack under the lead of the alpha dog, then chase off or attack the predator. The Sloughi, by comparison, is more of an independent lone hunter and has a high hunting instinct.

They are relatively uncommon in Europe and North America but there is a growing band of devotees. Azawakhs have a range of temperaments from lap dog to quite fierce. Lifelong socialization and firm but gentle handling are critical. Well socialised and trained, they can be good with other dogs, cats, children, and strangers. Azawakh may be registered with the FCI in the USA via the Federación Canófila de Puerto Rico (FCPR). European FCI clubs and the AKC recognize the FCPR as an acceptable registry. The AKC recognizes Azawakh as a Foundation Stock Service breed and they are eligible to participate in AKC-sanctioned performance events. Azawakh may be registered with the UKC and ARBA. The breed is not yet registered by CKC. Azawakh are eligible for ASFA lure coursing and NOFCA open field coursing events.

References

- *Colour, Pattern and Marking Varieties of the Azawakh in the Regions of Origin* [1], 2005, Dr. Gabriel Meissen.
- *Dogs of Africa*, 2003, by Sian Hall, Alpine Blue Ribbon Books.
- *Dog's Best Friend*, 1999, by Ursula Birr, Gerald Krakauer and Daniela Osiander, Park Street Press.
- *The Functional Saluki* [2], 1993, Dan Belkin, Ph.D., Transcribed from a seminar given at the Saluki Club of America National Specialty.
- *The Genetics of the Dog*, 2001, Anatoly Ruvinsky and J. Sampson, CABI Publishing
- *Genetic evidence for an East Asian origin of domestic dogs* 2002, Savolainen P, Zhang YP, Luo J, Lundeberg J, and Leitner T, Science 298: 1610-3
- *The Genetic Impoverishment of the Azawakh Breed* [3], 2003, Elisabeth Naumann.
- *Sloughi*, 2004, by Dr. M.-D Crapon de Caprona, Kennel Club Books.

External links

- Association Burkinabe Idi du Sahel [4]
- Rare Breed Network: The Azawakh [5]
- American Azawakh Association [6]
- The Azawakh Club [7]
- Azawakh Community Pedigree Database [8]
- Azawakh Friends [9]
- Foundation Azawakhs and Other Imports from Africa [10]
- World Wide Azawakhs [11]
- Azawakh Breed Dog from dogsindepth.com the online dog encyclopedia [12]

Basenji

Basenji	
A red basenji with white markings	
Other names	African Bush Dog African Barkless Dog Ango Angari Congo Dog Zande Dog
Country of origin	Democratic Republic of the Congo

Traits

Classification and standards

FCI	Group 5 Section 6 #43	standard [1]
AKC	{{{akcgroup}}}	standard [2]
ANKC	Group 4 (Hounds)	standard [3]
CKC	Group 2 - Hounds	standard [4]
KC (UK)	Hound	standard [5]
NZKC	Hounds	standard [6]
UKC	Group 3 - Sighthounds and Pariahs	standard [7]

Dog (*Canis lupus familiaris*)

The **Basenji** is a breed of hunting dog that was bred from stock originating in central Africa. Most of the major kennel clubs in the English-speaking world place the breed in the Hound Group; more specifically, it may be classified as belonging to the sighthound type. The Fédération Cynologique Internationale places the breed in Group 5, Spitz and Primitive types, and the United Kennel Club (US) places the breed in the Sighthound & Pariah Group.

The Basenji produces an unusual yodel-like sound commonly called a "barroo", due to its unusually shaped larynx. This trait also gives the Basenji the nickname "Barkless Dog."

Basenjis share many unique traits with Pariah dog types. Basenjis, like dingos and some other breeds of dog, come into estrus only once annually, as compared to other dog breeds which may have two or more breeding seasons every year. Both dingos and Basenjis lack a distinctive odor, and are prone to howls, yodels, and other undulated vocalizations over the characteristic bark of modern dog breeds. One theory holds that the latter trait is the result of the selective killing of barkier dogs in the traditional Central African context because barking could lead enemies to humans' forest encampments. While dogs that resemble the basenji in some respects are commonplace over much of Africa, the breed's original foundation stock came from the old growth forest regions of the Congo Basin, where its structure and type were fixed by adaptation to its habitat, as well as use (primarily net hunting in extremely dense old-growth forest vegetation).

Characteristics

Appearance

Basenji are small, elegant-looking, short-haired dogs with erect ears, a tightly curled tail, and a graceful neck. Some people consider their appearance similar to that of a miniature deer. A basenji's forehead is wrinkled, especially when the animal is young or extremely old. Basenji eyes are typically almond shaped, which gives the dog the appearance of squinting seriously.

Dogs typically weigh 24 pounds (11 kg) and stand 16 inches (40.6 cm) at the withers. They are typically a square breed, which means that they are as long as they are tall. The basenji is an athletic dog and is deceptively powerful for its size. They have a graceful, confident gait like a trotting horse, and skim the ground in a double-suspension gallop, with their characteristic curled tail straightened out for greater balance, when running flat-out at their top speed.

The basenji is recognized in the following standard colorations: red, black, tricolor (black with tan in the traditional pattern), and brindle (black stripes on a background of red), all with white, by the FCI, KC, AKC, and UKC. There are additional variations, such as the "trindle", which is a tricolor with brindle points, and several other colorations exist in the Congo such as liver, shaded reds and sables, and "capped" tricolors (creeping tan).

Temperament

The Basenji is alert, affectionate, energetic, and curious and reserved with strangers. The Basenji is somewhat aloof, but can also form strong bonds with people and can become emotionally attached to a single human. Basenjis may not get along with non-canine pets. It is commonly patient, but does best with older considerate handlers. Basenjis dislike wet weather, like to climb, can easily get over chain wire fences, and are very clever at getting their own way. The Basenji has the unique properties of not barking (it makes a low, liquid ululation instead) and cleaning itself like a cat. It can be described as speedy, frisky, tireless at play, and teasing the owner into play. Most Basenji problems usually involve a mismatch between owner and pet. Basenjis often stand on their hind legs, somewhat like a meerkat, by themselves or leaning on something; the Basenji is also known to be able to jump over 6 feet vertically. This behavior is often observed when the dog is curious about something. Basenjis reveal their animal-of-prey nature by chasing after fast moving objects that cross their paths.

Health

There is apparently only one completed health survey of basenjis, a 2004 UK Kennel Club survey.

Many basenjis suffer from PRA (progressive retinal atrophy), which causes blindness, and Fanconi's syndrome, which can cause kidney failure. Besides Fanconi Syndrome and PRA, Basenjis also suffer from Hypothyroidism, IPSID (immunoproliferative systemic intestinal disease), and HA (Hemolytic Anemia). Basenjis are also sensitive to environmental and household chemicals which can cause liver problems.

Mortality

Basenjis in the 2004 UK Kennel Club survey had a medium longevity of 13.6 years (sample size of 46 deceased dogs), which is 1–2 years longer than the median longevity of other breeds of similar size. The oldest dog in the survey was 17.5 years. Most common causes of death were old age (30%), urologic (incontinence, Fanconi syndrome, chronic kidney failure 13%), behavior ("unspecified" and aggression 9%), and cancer. (9%).

Morbidity

Among 78 live dogs in the 2004 UKC survey, the most common health issues noted by owners were dermatologic and urologic (urologic issues in basenjis can be signs of Fanconi syndrome).

Fanconi Syndrome

Fanconi syndrome, an inheritable disorder in which the kidneys fail to reabsorb electrolytes and nutrients, is unusually common in basenjis. Symptoms include excessive drinking, excessive urination, and glucose in the urine, which may lead to a misdiagnosis of diabetes. Fanconi syndrome usually presents between 4 and 8 years of age, but sometimes as early as 3 years or as late as 10 years. Fanconi syndrome is treatable and organ damage is reduced if treatment begins early. Basenji owners are advised to test their dog's urine for glucose once a month beginning at the age of 3 years. Glucose testing strips designed for human diabetics are inexpensive and available at most pharmacies.

Fanconi DNA Linkage Test

In July 2007, Dr. Gary Johnson of the University of Missouri released the linked marker DNA test for Fanconi Syndrome in basenjis. It is the first predictive test available for Fanconi Syndrome. With this test, it is possible to more accurately determine the probability of a dog carrying the gene for Fanconi Syndrome.

Dogs tested using this "Linkage Test" will return one of the following statuses:

- **Probably Clear/Normal**

    Indicates the individual has most likely inherited normal DNA from both parents. It is unlikely that basenjis which test this way will produce affected puppies no matter which dog they are bred to.

- **Probably Carrier**

    Indicates the individual has most likely inherited normal DNA from one parent and DNA with the Fanconi syndrome mutation from the other parent. Although this basenji is unlikely to develop Fanconi syndrome, it could produce puppies that will develop Fanconi syndrome. To minimize the chances of this happening it is recommended carriers be bred only to those that test as Probably Clear/Normal for Fanconi Syndrome.

- **Probably Equivocal/Indeterminant**

    Indicates the individual's DNA contained features found in both "normal" and "carrier" basenjis. At present it cannot be predicted whether these basenjis are carriers or normal; however, it is unlikely that they will develop Fanconi syndrome. The safest strategy would be to treat them as "carriers" and only bred to those basenjis that test as Probably Clear/Normal for Fanconi Syndrome.

- **Probably Affected**

    Indicates the individual is likely to develop clinical Fanconi syndrome and is likely to produce puppies with Fanconi Syndrome if bred to basenjis other than those that test as Probably Clear/Normal for Fanconi Syndrome.

This linkage test is being provided as a tool to assist breeders whilst research continues towards the development of the direct fanconi test.

For more information about the linkage test visit: Basenji Health Endowment Fanconi Test FAQ [8].

Other basenji health issues

Basenjis sometimes carry a simple recessive gene which, when homozygous for the defect, causes genetic Hemolytic Anemia. Most 21st-century basenjis are descended from ancestors that have tested clean. When lineage from a fully tested line (set of ancestors) cannot be completely verified, the dog should be tested before breeding. As this is a non-invasive DNA test, a basenji can be tested for HA at any time.

Basenjis sometimes suffer from hip dysplasia, resulting in loss of mobility and arthritis-like symptoms. All dogs should be tested by either OFA or PennHIP prior to breeding.

Malabsorption, or immunoproliferative enteropathy, is an autoimmune intestinal disease that leads to anorexia, chronic diarrhea, and even death. A special diet can improve the quality of life for afflicted dogs.

The breed can also fall victim to progressive retinal atrophy (a degeneration of the retina causing blindness) and several less serious hereditary eye problems such as coloboma (a hole in the eye structure), and persistent pupillary membrane (tiny threads across the pupil).

History

The basenji is arguably one of the most ancient dog breeds. Originating on the continent of Africa, basenji-like dogs have lived with humans for thousands of years. Dogs resembling modern Basenjis can be seen on stelae in the tombs of Egyptian pharaohs, sitting at the feet of their masters, looking just as they do today, with pricked ears and tightly curled tails. Dogs of this type were originally kept for hunting small game by coursing.

Europeans first described the type of dog from which the basenji breed was derived in the Congo in 1895. These local dogs, which Europeans identified as a unique breed and called "basenji" were prized by locals for their intelligence, courage, speed, and silence. However an article published called The Intelligence of Dogs by Stanley Coren, Ph.D. questions this. It ranks the breed at #78 out of 79 which is the second to lowest rank in intelligence. Many question the qualifications of this article and whether it accurately evaluates each breed. In fact, Dr. Coren equated "intelligence" with "obedience", and the basenji is not the most obedient of breeds because of its intelligence. Therefore, the veracity of Dr. Coren's findings is questionable.

Basenjis were assistants to the hunt, chasing wild game into nets for their masters. The Azande and Mangbetu people from the northeastern Congo region describe basenjis, in the local Lingala language, as *mbwá na basɛ́nzi*. Translated, this means "dogs of the savages", or "dogs of the villagers". In the Congo, the basenji is also known as "dog of the bush." The dogs are also known to the Azande of southern Sudan as Ango Angari. The word *basɛ́nzi* itself is the plural form of *mosɛ́nzi*. In Swahili, another Bantu language, from East Africa, *mbwa shenzi* translates to "wild dog". Another local name is *m'bwa m'kube m'bwa wamwitu*, or "jumping up and down dog", a reference to their tendency to jump straight up to spot their quarry.

Several attempts were made to bring the breed to England, but the earliest imports succumbed to disease. In 1923, for example, Lady Helen Nutting brought six basenjis with her from Sudan, but all six died from distemper shots they received in quarantine. It was not until the 1930s that foundation stock was successfully established in England, and then to the United States by animal importer Henry Trefflich. So it is that nearly all the basenjis in the Western world are descended from these few original imports. The breed was officially accepted into the AKC in 1943. In 1990, the AKC stud book was reopened to fourteen new imports at the request of the Basenji Club of America. The stud book was reopened again to selected imported dogs from January 1, 2009 to December 31, 2013. An American led expedition collected breeding stock in villages in the Basankusu area of the Democratic Republic of Congo, in 2010. Basenjis are also registered with the UKC.

Although in the past it was speculated that Basenjis were somehow descended from jackals, modern genetic testing shows that Basenjis are related to all other dogs and are descended from the wolf, Canis lupus.

Basenjis in popular culture

- The title character of the 1954 novel *Good-bye, My Lady*, by James H. Street, is a basenji. It's the story of a young boy in Mississippi who takes in a most unusual stray. The book was made into a movie of the same name in 1956, with a cast that included Brandon De Wilde, Walter Brennan, and Sidney Poitier.

- Veronica Anne Starbuck's 2000 novel *Heart of the Savannah* features a basenji named Savannah. Savannah narrates this story about her adventures as an African-bred dog brought to America. Starbuck also wrote a sequel titled *August Magic*.

- Simon Cleveland wrote a novel titled *The Basenji Revelation*, published by Lulu Press in 2004, in which a government agent suffers amnesia and undergoes a change in personality after inheriting a basenji from his late mother. The book delivers insightful facts about the ancient origins of the breed.

- The true story of a basenji was featured in the episode *The Cat Came Back* on the radio program *This American Life*. The segment tells the story of a family who chose a basenji because they do not shed or slobber, but became frustrated with his aloofness and destructiveness. They eventually bring him to live on a farm away, but within a few days the tenacious dog found its way all the way back home.

- In Spike Milligan's War Diaries "Mussolini: His Part in My Downfall" (Sept 24, 1943) the following exchange takes place:

    ...we are bloody lost. Lt. Budden is looking studiously at his map, the wrong way up.
    "It's upside down, Sir."
    "I know that, I turned it upside down for a reason."
    "Sorry, Sir, only trying to help."
    "If you want to help, Milligan, act like a basenji."

- According to the webcomic *Achewood*, if Jesus Christ were a dog, he'd be a basenji.

- A man and his Basenji were featured on an episode of *LA Ink*. The basenji has an unusual marking of a diamond in the middle of his back. The owner has a replica tattooed on his own back during the episode.

- Basenjis are featured in an episode of the animated television series The Wild Thornberrys In episode 3.04 "Tyler Tucker, I Presume?". Nigel Thornberry encounters a group of tribesmen along with their Congolese hunting dogs. The series' director, Mark Risley owns several basenjis, and his dogs provided the recorded "voices" for their animated counterparts.

- The basenji was featured on CBS's early show during Dog Week: http://www.youtube.com/watch?v=B3FAU2a0Roc

- A Basenji CH JETHARD CIDEVANT was named Crufts Supreme Champion in 2001.

See also

- Pariah dog

External links

- Basenji [9] at the Open Directory Project

Basset Bleu de Gascogne

Basset Bleu de Gascogne

A Basset Bleu de Gascogne	
Other names	Blue Gascony Basset
Country of origin	France
Traits	
Classification and standards	
FCI Group 6 Section 1 #35	standard [1]
KC (UK) Hound	standard [2]
UKC Scenthounds	standard [3]
Dog (*Canis lupus familiaris*)	

The **Basset Bleu de Gascogne** also known as the **Blue Gascony Basset** is a long-backed, short legged breed of dog of the hound type. A breed with origins in the Middle Ages which descends from the Grand Bleu de Gascogne however it nearly went extinct around the early 1800s and its saviour was attributed to Alain Bourbon. A French native breed, it is rare outside of its homeland. It is recognized internationally by the Fédération Cynologique Internationale, in the UK by The Kennel Club, and by the United Kennel Club in the United States. The "bleu" of its name is a reference to its coat which has a ticked appearance.

Appearance

The color of their coat is predominantly white, ticked so as to give a bluish appearance, with brown spots and tan markings above the eyes and on the ears. They are a smooth-coated breed. Height at the withers is usually between (13–17 in) although the Kennel Club standard specifies (12–15 in). Their general appearance is usually not too heavy, and they weight between (35–40 lb). They have dark brown eyes and low-set ears that can reach at least the end of their muzzle. Because of their working nature as a hunting hound, effects of this work such as scars, nicks, notches on the ears and so on are not considered a fault in the show ring.

History

The Basset Bleu de Gascogne descended directly from the old breed of Grand Bleu de Gascogne. They have been recorded in paintings from the 14th century in Gascony, southwest France. The exact origin of the breed is debated, one theory is that it is a cross of the Grand Bleu with the Saintongeois Basset, another theory is that the Basset Bleu is a natural mutation of the Grand combined with selective breeding for shorter legs in order to slow down the breed. It is thought that Gaston III of Foix-Béarn kept a pack of these dogs to hunt wild boar and wolves. He is known as the writer of the Livre de chasse, considered the classic treatise on medieval hunting.

Prior to the French Revolution, hunting was reserved for the nobility who generally hunted on horseback. Following the French Revolution, hunting was opened up to the common people who would hunt on foot and found following a large hunting dog difficult. From this the slower, shorter legged Basset Bleu de Gascogne may have been created.

During the early 1800s the breed nearly went extinct with a declining popularity in hunting. However, the breed was saved and revived by the work of Alain Bourbon.

Recognition and categorisation

The Kennel Club of the UK recognizes the Basset Bleu De Gascogne in the imported breed register and in the Hound Group. The United Kennel Club recognised the breed in 1991, and both they and the Fédération Cynologique Internationale (FCI) list the Basset Bleu De Gascogne in the Scenthound Group. The breed is also known as the Blue Gascony Basset in the FCI. The Basset Bleu De Gascogne is not recognized by the American Kennel Club or the Canadian Kennel Club. In addition to the major registries, the Basset Bleu De Gascogne is also recognized by many minor registries and specialty registries, including as a rare breed under the American Rare Breed Association which uses the FCI standard.

See also

- Basset Hound
- Basset Fauve de Bretagne
- Grand Basset Griffon Vendéen
- Petit Basset Griffon Vendéen

Basset Fauve de Bretagne

Basset Fauve de Bretagne

Basset Fauve de Bretagne	
Other names	Fawn Brittany Basset
Country of origin	France
Traits	

Classification and standards		
FCI	Group 6 Section 1 #36	standard [1]
ANKC	Group 4 (Hounds)	standard [2]
KC (UK)	Hound	standard [3]
UKC	Scenthounds	[? standard]

Notes
The United Kennel Club (US) uses the Fédération Cynologique Internationale standard.
Dog (*Canis lupus familiaris*)

The **Basset Fauve de Bretagne** is a short legged hunting breed of dog of the scent hound type, originally from Brittany, a historical kingdom of France.

Appearance

The Basset Fauve de Bretagne is a smallish hound, built along the same lines as the Basset Hound, but lighter all through and longer in the leg. Wire-coated, the coat is very harsh to the touch, dense, red-wheaten or fawn. He measures 32 - 38cm in height and weighs between 36 - 40lbs but some become very tall like a Labrador. They have coarse, dense fur which may require stripping. The hair on the ears is shorter, finer and darker than that on the coat. The ears just reach the end of the nose rather than trailing on the ground and should be pleated. They should have dark eyes and nose and ideally no crook on the front legs. The French standard says these are the shortest backed of all the basset breeds so they generally do not appear as exaggerated as the British Basset.

Health

There is apparently only one completed health survey of Basset Fauve de Bretagnes, a 2004 UK Kennel Club survey with a small sample size. The French Basset Fauve de Bretagne kennel club, Club du Fauve de Bretagne (http://fauvedebretagne.free.fr/- in French), is currently (as of July 15, 2007) conducting a health survey, but the questionnaire asks owners about all of their dogs collectively (rather than each individual dog) and does not ask about longevity.

Mortality

Based on a small sample size of 15 deceased dogs, Basset Fauve de Bretagnes in the 2004 UK Kennel Club survey had a median longevity of 10.4 years (maximum 13.9 years), which is a typical median longevity for purebred dogs, but a little low compared to other breeds of similar size. Most common causes of death were road traffic accidents, cancer, heart failure, and kidney failure. The high incidence of road traffic accidents may be perhaps blamed on this dog's love of the scent. Many pet Fauves go AWOL when they find a scent and this character trait is something an owner must never forget. Fauves can be trained very well in a controlled environment but training is rapidly forgotten once a fresh rabbit trail is found.

Morbidity

Among 84 live dogs in the 2004 UKC survey, the most common health issues noted by owners were reproductive, aural (otitis media and otitis externa), and ocular (corneal ulcers and cataracts).

History

The breed was developed in France as a hunting dog from the larger Grand Fauve de Bretagne, a breed that is now extinct. There was a rumour that the Basset Fauve de Bretagne was also close to extinction after the Second World War, and the breed was recreated using the remaining examples of the breed and crossing in Petit Basset Griffon Vendéen and standard wirehaired Dachshunds. However, the French club denies this, and says that Basset Fauve numbers were never so low. The middle breed, the Griffon Fauve de Bretagne, still exists but it is certainly rarer than the Basset. The breed in the UK is mainly seen as a show dog and family pet, finally coming off the Kennel Club's rare breed register in 2007. It can also be found in other parts of Europe where it is used to scent trail and also as a family pet. They are loving, happy, outgoing dogs and are good with children, but it must be remembered that they are scent hounds and do retain their love of the hunt so may not suit every family. In the UK the breed has no hereditary faults; however, epilepsy has been identified in some breeding lines in France and other parts of Europe. Some Fauves are born with black in the coat; this may or may not go with maturity. It is less common to see them with white patches but when they do occur it is generally confined to the chest and top of the head. However, even though the black ticking and white patches are not accepted colours, of course it does not interfere with their hunting ability, which is their prime job, and so these colour Fauves are still seen and occur fairly often in litters. The correct colour for a Fauve is anything from fawn to red but it should be solid with darker shaded ears.

Good Info

The Basset Fauve de Bretagne is a neat looking hound, free from exaggeration and lively and friendly; as a scenthound, though, he has the usual failing of becoming absorbed with what he's scenting. He is agile enough to trouble any rabbit he scents. The Fauve de Bretagne was probably developed from crosses of the Griffon Fauve de Bretagne and Brittany Bassets. The Griffon was used to guard flocks and hunt down predators, whilst the Brittany hunted in small packs of four hounds. Where the Basset Fauve de Bretagne is still used for hunting it is either singly or in pairs. The Basset Fauve de Bretagne became established as a distinct breed early in the 19thC and were introduced to the UK in 1983, and their cheerful disposition has earned them a good many friends. Overall a very sound dog they do not appear to suffer from any particular hereditary defects. However, like all hounds they are of an independent turn of mind, and early training in puppyhood will reap dividends later. It is never realistic to expect a hound to be obedient, as they have their own agenda much of the time, but they should become fairly co-operative. The coat is easy to care for; a regular brush will keep it smart, but, like a terrier he will need stripping two or three times a year. This is not a difficult task though you may prefer to leave it to a grooming parlour. A cheerful and equable breed, the Basset Fauve de Bretagne is of a size to make a handy housedog, though he has a great taste for exercise and thoroughly enjoys getting out into the fields. Most Basset Fauve de Bretagne's can be understood because their eyes are very clear and their ears turn out when they're nervous or unsure.

See also

- Basset Bleu de Gascogne
- Grand Basset Griffon Vendéen
- Petit Basset Griffon Vendéen
- Basset Hound
- Coat (dog)
- Rare breed (dog)

Basset Hound

Basset Hound

7 year old purebred lemon and white Basset	
Nicknames	Basset
Country of origin	France
Traits	

Classification and standards		
FCI	Group 6 Section 1 #163	standard [1]
AKC	Hound	standard [2]
ANKC	Group 4 (Hounds)	standard [3]
CKC	Group 2 - Hounds	standard [4]
KC (UK)	Hound	standard [5]
NZKC	Hounds	standard [6]
UKC	Scenthound	standard [7]

Dog (*Canis lupus familiaris*)

The **Basset Hound** is a short-legged breed of dog of the hound family. They are scent hounds, bred to hunt rabbits by scent. Their sense of smell for tracking is second only to that of the Bloodhound. The name *Basset* is derived from the French word *bas*, meaning "low", with the attenuating suffix *-et*, together meaning "rather low". Basset hounds are commonly brown and black and most often spotted, but also exist in a variety of colors.

Description

Appearance

Build:	Short-legged; proportionally heavier in bone than any other breed of dog
Weight:	(23–29 kg)
Height:	(30–38 cm)
Coat:	Short, hard and shiny, sheds.
Color:	Any recognized hound colour is acceptable (tri-Color, red & white, honey/lemon & white, Blue/Gray, and black & tan)
Head:	Large and well proportioned, prominent occiput on males.
Teeth:	Scissors or even bite
Eyes:	Brown, soft, sad, and slightly sunken, showing a prominent haw
Ears:	Extremely long, velvety in texture, hanging in loose folds, low set, and when drawn forward, fold well over the end of the nose
Tail:	Slightly curved, erect when walking. White tip aids in tracking. Never docked.
Limbs:	Short, powerful, heavy
Feet:	Massive, very heavy with tough heavy pads
Life span:	Median 10–12 years

These dogs are around 1-foot in height at the withers. They usually weigh between . They have smooth, short-haired coats but a rough haired hound is possible. Although any hound colour is considered acceptable by breed standards, Bassets are generally tricolor (black, tan, and white), open red and white (red spots on white fur), closed red and white (a solid red color with white feet and tails), Honey And White (honey coloured back, light brown spotty nose and legs, light brown tails with white tip) and lemon and white. Some Bassets are also classified as gray or blue; however, this colour is considered rare and undesirable. They have long, downward ears and powerful necks, with much loose skin around their heads that forms wrinkles. Their tails are long and tapering and stand upright with a curve. Tails usually have white tips so the dogs are more easily seen when hunting/tracking through large bushes or weeds. The breed is also known for its hanging skin structure, which causes the face to occasionally look sad; this, for many people, adds to the breed's charm. The dewlap, seen as the loose, elastic skin around the neck, and the trailing ears, help trap the scent of what they are tracking.

The Basset Hound is a large dog with short legs. They were originally bred to have osteochondrodysplasia, known as dwarfism. Their short stature can be deceiving; Bassets are surprisingly long and can reach things on table tops that dogs of similar heights cannot. However, because Bassets are so heavy and have such short legs, they are not able to hold themselves above water for very long, and should never be made to swim.

Temperament

The Basset Hound is seen as an especially friendly breed. For this reason they are an excellent pet for children. Many Bassets "forget" the training when a reward is not present. Bassets should be on a leash when out on walks.

Bassets are known to be a vocal breed. Bassets might howl or bark when they want something or to suggest that they think something is wrong (like a storm is coming). They also use a low, murmuring whine to get attention, which sounds to many owners as though their Bassets are "talking." This whine is also used by the hound to beg (for food or treats) and varies in volume depending on the nature of the individual hound and length of time it has been begging.

Hunting with Bassets

The Basset Hound was bred to hunt. Its keen nose and short stature are suited to small-game hunting on foot, although many Bassets have lost their age-old skills. There are a few groups that promote hunting with bassets. The American Hunting Basset Association [8] and the Basset Hound Club of America [9] has been the most active in promoting the use of Bassets for rabbit hunting.

Hunting with Basset Hounds when with an organization such as the American Hunting Basset Association or the Basset Hound Club of America do not involve the killing of any animals. These organizations are merely testing the Basset Hound's skills at tracking/trailing a rabbit's scent. Each organization is different in how it functions. With the AHBA, a group of 4 to 6 hounds (cast) are given one hour to find their own rabbit and judged based upon a standard set of rules while in the BHCA two dogs are paired and then put on a rabbit track and then judged. Typically the BHCA hunting lasts a few minutes per brace, the basset pair. With both organizations, the winning dog in each brace for the BHCA or cast for the AHBA go on to compete against the other winning dogs.

Hunting with Basset Hounds as a pack is common in the Mid-Atlantic States of Maryland, Virginia, New Jersey, and Pennsylvania. Several private and membership packs exist in these states. Hunting for cotton tails and hare is the quarry of preference. There were a number of Basset Hound packs in its original home of England when the hunting of hares (see Beagling) was made illegal by the Hunting Act 2004.

Hunting a hound pack requires a staff which consists of a Huntsman and the Whipper-Ins who are responsible for order and discipline of the pack. A Field Master is in charge of the field (members of the hunt and guests) that follows behind observing the hounds work the covert. Most clubs will hunt in traditional attire of a green jacket and brush pants. Recognized clubs offer those members who have supported the pack the opportunity to wear colors on the collar to indicate rank in the club.

These packs are typically of English and French hound blood lines with a mix of AKC blood lines in some packs. The National Beagle Club hosts spring and fall field trials for basset hounds. The competition held over a 4-day period with participating packs hunting in the traditional manner in braces of up to 1 hour and 15 minutes. The pack size for each competition varies, from 3 to 7 couple.

Health

Because of the extremely long ears of Bassets they are prone to ear disease. If their ears are allowed to dangle on the ground or in food on a daily basis they are capable of developing chronic and potentially fatal ear diseases. The only recent mortality and morbidity surveys of Basset Hounds are from the UK: a 1999 longevity survey with a small sample size of 10 deceased dogs and a 2004 UK Kennel Club health survey with a larger sample size of 142 deceased dogs and 226 live dogs.

In addition to ear problems, basset hounds may also have eye issues. Because of their droopy eyes, the area under the eyeball will collect dirt and become clogged with a mucus. It is best to wipe their eyes every day with a damp cloth. This helps to lessen the build up and eye irritation.

Basset Hounds can be on the lazy side and can become overweight on their own if allowed to. They need plenty of exercise and a good diet.

Basset hounds are also prone to yeast infections in the folds around the mouth, where drool can collect without thoroughly drying out. Wiping the area with a clean, dry towel and applying talcum powder can minimize this risk.

Mortality

Median longevity of Basset Hounds in the UK is about 11.4 years, which is a typical median longevity for purebred dogs and for breeds similar in size to Basset Hounds. The oldest of the 142 deceased dogs in the 2004 UK Kennel Club survey was 16.7 years. Leading causes of death in the 2004 UK Kennel Club survey were cancer (31%), old age (13%), GDV (bloat/torsion), (11%), and cardiac (8%).

Morbidity

Among 226 live Basset Hounds in the 2004 UKC survey, the most common health issues noted by owners were dermatologic (e.g., dermatitis), reproductive, musculoskeletal (e.g., arthritis and lameness), and gastrointestinal (e.g. GDV and colitis).

Basset Hounds are also prone to epilepsy, glaucoma, luxating patella, thrombopathia, Von Willebrand disease, hypothyroidism, hip dysplasia, and elbow dysplasia.

Training

Training Basset Hounds can be difficult. Trainers must be persistent with this breed in order to achieve a well mannered dog. Bassets have a tendency to listen to their noses and not with their ears. While this can lead to stubbornness, it also means that they are highly motivated by food. They tend to respond well to treat-based positive reinforcement methods. Owners need to make the training process lively and entertaining to allow the Basset to learn more efficiently. Training is an on-going process with Basset Hounds.

Popular culture

In February 27 1928, *Time* magazine featured a Basset Hound on the front cover. The accompanying story was about the 52nd annual Westminster Kennel Club Dog Show at Madison Square Garden as if observed by the Basset Hound puppy. This prestige is often seen as the event which made the Basset Hound a popular part of American popular culture.

Basset Hounds have had prominent roles in movies and television. Some Bassets have been featured in comic strips and cartoons. Examples include cartoon character Droopy, originally created in 1943 by Tex Avery, and Fred Basset, the main character in the comic strip *Fred Basset*, created by Alex Graham in 1963. Basset Hounds playing more minor roles include Rosebud the Basselope from Berke Breathed's comic strip *Bloom County*, Byron Basset in *Tiny Toon Adventures*, Toby, from *The Great Mouse Detective*, and Lafayette, from the 1970 Disney film *The Aristocats*. The notable webcomic PvP by Scott Kurtz occasionally features the author's pet Basset Hounds. In the children's novel *Lunchbox and the Aliens* (2006 Henry Holt), by Bryan W. Fields, a basset hound named Lunchbox is abducted by a pair of misfit aliens and accidentally made intelligent. Rodney Dangerfield voices a Basset Hound in the animated feature film, *Rover Dangerfield*.

Basset Hounds in films include Fred, the companion of Cledus in the 1977 movie *Smokey and the Bandit* and its two sequels. A basset, Gabriel, appears as Batou's Basset Hound in *Ghost in the Shell 2: Innocence*. Gabriel is in fact director Mamoru Oshii's real life pet, and is included in many of his animated films including the 2001's *Avalon*. In a scene most likely referencing Smokey and the Bandit, a truck driver has a Basset Hound beside him in *American Pie 2*. Basset Hounds are featured prominently in off-beat roles as well—one gets hit by a car and survives in *The Rage: Carrie 2*, and in the film *Monkeybone* a basset has its own nightmarish dream sequence. In *The Cassandra Crossing* a basset is airlifted by helicopter off a doomed train allowing officials to identify a deadly plague (and thus becomes one of the few survivors of the all-star cast disaster film). Finally, bassets appear in such other mainstream films as *The Lost Treasure of Sawtooth Island* (where it prominently appears alongside star Ernest Borgnine on the film poster/DVD cover); *An American Werewolf in Paris*, *Nanny McPhee*, *Spider-Man 2* and *Kit Kittredge: An American Girl*.

Television programs have used Basset Hounds as characters as well. In the early days of television, Elvis Presley famously sang "Hound Dog" to a Basset Hound named Sherlock on "The Steve Allen Show" on July 1, 1956. One of the most famous Bassets on television was Flash, the dog owned by Sheriff Rosco P. Coltrane in the 1980s TV series "The Dukes of Hazzard". A life-sized replica named "Flush" was used in dangerous situations. Other Bassets on television include Cleo, the doggie *femme fatal* from "The People's Choice", which starred Jackie Cooper; Pokey, a canine friend of Lassie early (1954-57) in the "Lassie" television series ; the Basset Hound named simply "Dog" from "Columbo", Henry from "Emergency!", Governor from "The Governor & J.J.", Quincey, from "Coach", Sam from "That's So Raven", Chips from "EastEnders", Arthur in "Our House" and Socrates in "Judging Amy".

Basset Hounds have also been featured in advertising. The logo for Hush Puppies brand shoes prominently features a Basset Hound whose real name is *Jason*. Basset Hounds are occasionally referred to as "Hush Puppies" for that reason. A Basset Hound also serves as the companion to the lonely Maytag Man in Maytag appliance advertisements. Tidewater Petroleum advertised its Flying A Gasoline using a Basset Hound named Axelrod. In the 1990s, a handsome red/white Basset Hound called SIGMUND featured in a several advertisements including one for Domestos bleach.

In June 2007, a realistic life-size Basset Hound mascot began to make appearances at various nightclubs and music festivals in the UK and across Europe. Ulysses the Basset Rave Hound was photographed with festival goers and famous DJ's at the Renaissance "Wild in the Country" festival, The Big Chill 2008 festival and famous Ibiza super-clubs Pacha, Space and Amnesia. Ulysses has his own fan page on the social networking website Facebook entitled "We love Ulysses".

Real Radio in the UK uses a basset hound in advertising. 'Barry' is used in TV ads, newspaper ads, and is referred by presenters on Real Radio itself.

History

Basset Hounds are a cross between the Bloodhound, the Regular Artisien Normand, and the Basset Artésien Normand. The first application of the word "Basset" to a breed of dog can be traced to *La Vénerie,* an illustrated text on hunting written by Jacques du Fouilloux in 1561. Fouilloux illustrates wire-haired bassets resembling the modern Basset Fauve de Bretagne. In Fouilloux's treatise, bassets are used to pursue foxes and badgers to ground, after which the quarry is dug from its burrow and so reduced to possession.

Other early French Bassets closely resembled the Basset Artésien Normand, which is still a breed today. The Basset Artesian Normand is one of the two recognized French Basset breeds. Originating in Artois and Normandy, it dates back to the 1600s. The Basset Artesian Normand looks like a Basset Hound, but lighter in weight. A short, straight legged hound, its body is twice as long as it is high. Its head is dome-shaped and powerful with hairy cheeks. The neck is slightly dewlap and the muscles are smooth with a moderate amount of wrinkles. The chest is round with clearly visible sternum. The coat is very short, bicolor: tan and white, or tricolor: tan, black and white. Breeders prefer white feet.

By the turn of the 20th century, the Basset Artesian Normand was developing into two distinct lines, straight-legged hunters and crocked-legged, droopy-eared companion and show dogs. French breeder Leon Verrier developed today's standard, which blends attributes of both varieties. The Artesian Basset needed straight legs that would neither hinder his speed nor drain his energy in order to work in unruly terrain, brush and briar. The breed was recognized in 1911.

Because many short-legged dogs from this time were called *Basset* and record-keeping from this time was sparse, it is difficult to speculate which of these breeds have bloodlines in common with today's Basset Hounds. It is commonly believed that Marquis de Lafayette brought Basset Hounds to the United States as a gift to George Washington.

In France, basset hounds achieved noticeable public cultural popularlity during the reign of Emperor Napoleon III (r. 1852-1870). In 1853, Emmanuel Fremiet, "the leading sculptor of animals in his day" exhibited bronze sculptures of Emperor Napoleon III's basset hounds at the Paris Salon. Ten years later, in 1863, the Basset Hound reached international fame at the Paris Dog Show. At that time there were two common Bassets, those with a rough coat (*Basset Griffon*) and those with smooth (*Basset Français*). The dogs were further classified by the length of their legs. The two popular Basset breeders at this time were *M. Lane* and the *Count Le Couteulx*.

In 1866, Lord Galway imported a pair of *Le Couteulx* Bassets to England, but it was not until 1874 that Basset Hounds were widely introduced there by Sir Everett Millais. The Kennel Club accepted the breed in 1882 and the English Basset Hound Club was formed in 1884. The American Kennel Club first recognized Basset Hounds as a breed in 1885. In 1935, the Basset Hound Club of America was organized in the United States. The current American breed standard was adopted in 1964.

Civic events

In North America, Basset Hound picnics and waddles are traditions in many regions and draw impressive crowds and participations from hundreds or even thousands of Bassets and their owners. Most events are held to raise funds for local and regional Basset rescue groups. For example, The Allentown Basset Picnic [10] thrived for seven years before becoming Tri-State's Basset Freedom Fest in 2003. Other major annual basset hound events, including the Buffalo Basset Bash, the New Orleans Basset Boogie, the Washington (state) Basset Rescue's Basset Blast in Spokane, the Woodinville, Washington Annual Basset Bash and parade and the Michigan Basset Waddle, share many similarities with North American community or food festivals and even "crown" king and queen bassets in a manner reminiscent of other civic festival crownings of event "royalty". Other traditions and competitions, such as deciding which basset has the best waddle, longest ears, best bay, or can keep a towel on its head the longest, are generally unique to basset hound picnics and waddles. These events also feature a wide variety of custom-made items depicting basset hounds and play an important role in raising money for basset hound rescue organizations. Often featured at shows and festivals is a world-famous pack of performing basset hounds known as "The Happy Basset Hounds." The trio consist of Eleanor, Annabel and Buster, and they make their home in Texarkana, Ark. The act was formerly headlined by the celebrated Ernest T. Basset, now deceased.

External links

- Basset Hound [11] at the Open Directory Project - An active listing of Basset Hound links.
- American Kennel Club [12]

Bavarian Mountain Hound

Bavarian Mountain Hound

A hound on the trail of game.	
Other names	Bavarian Mountain Scenthound Bayerischer Gebirgsschweißhund
Country of origin	Germany
Traits	

Classification and standards		
FCI	Group 6 Section 2 #217	standard [1]
KC (UK)	Hounds	standard [2]
UKC	Scenthound Breeds	[? standard]

Notes
The UKC currently do not have their own breed standards, the UKC currently uses the FCI standard.
Dog (*Canis lupus familiaris*)

The **Bavarian Mountain Hound** is a breed of dog from Germany. It is a scent hound and has been used in Germany since the Middle Ages to trail wounded game. It is a cross between the Bavarian Hound, and the Hanover Hound.

Characteristics

Appearance

The Bavarian Mountain Hound's head is strong and elongated. The skull is relatively broad and slightly domed. It has a pronounced stop and a slightly curved nosebridge. The muzzle should be broad with solid jaws, and its lips fully covering mouth. Its nose is black or dark red with wide nostrils. Its ears are high set and medium in length. They are broader at the base and rounded at the tips, hanging heavily against the head. Its body is slightly longer than it is tall and slightly raised at the rump. The neck medium in length, strong, with a slight dewlap. Topline sloping slightly upward from withers to hindquarters. Chest well-developed, long, moderately wide and well let-down with a slight tuck-up. It has a long, fairly straight croup and solid back. While its tail is set on high, medium in length and hanging to the hock, carried level to the ground or hanging down.

Size

Bavarian Mountain Hounds weigh between 20 to 25 kg, males are 47 to 52 cm (18.5 - 20.5 in) high, while females are 44 to 48 cm (17-19 in).

Coat and color

The coat is short, thick and shiny, lying very flat against the body and moderately harsh. It is finer on the head and ears, harsher and longer on the abdomen, legs and tail. Its coat can come in all shades of black-masked fawn or brindle.

Temperament

Bavarian Mountain Hounds are calm, quiet, poised and very attached to their masters and family. When hunting, they are hard, single-minded and persistent. Courageous, spirited, fast and agile, they are at ease on a rugged terrain, with a superb nose and powerful hunting instinct. They need a patient, experienced trainer.

Care

The Bavarian Mountain is not suited for city life. It is in regular need of space and exercise and also requires regular brushing. They are not dogs for the casual hunter. Most are owned and used by foresters and game wardens.

Beagle

Beagle

Other names	English Beagle
Traits	

Classification and standards		
FCI	Group 6 Section 1 #161	standard [1]
AKC	Hound	standard [2]
ANKC	Group 4 (Hounds)	standard [3]
CKC	Group 2 – Hounds	standard [4]
KC (UK)	Hound	standard [5]
NZKC	Hounds	standard [6]
UKC	Scenthound	standard [7]
Dog (*Canis lupus familiaris*)		

The **Beagle** is a breed of small to medium-sized dog. A member of the Hound Group, it is similar in appearance to the Foxhound but smaller, with shorter legs and longer, softer ears. Beagles are scent hounds, developed primarily for tracking hare, rabbit, and other game. They have a keen sense of smell and tracking instinct that sees them employed as detection dogs for prohibited agricultural imports and foodstuffs in quarantine around the world. They are popular as pets because of their size, even temper, and lack of inherited health problems. These characteristics also make them the dog of choice for animal testing.

Although beagle-type dogs have existed for over 2,000 years, the modern breed was developed in Great Britain around the 1830s from several breeds, including the Talbot Hound, the North Country Beagle, the Southern Hound, and possibly the Harrier.

Beagles have been depicted in popular culture since Elizabethan times in literature and paintings, and more recently in film, television and comic books. Snoopy of the comic strip *Peanuts* has been promoted as "the world's most famous beagle".

History

Early beagle-type dogs

Dogs of similar size and purpose to the modern Beagle can be traced in Ancient Greece back to around the 5th century BC. Xenophon, born around 433 BC, in his *Treatise on Hunting* or *Cynegeticus* refers to a hound that hunted hares by scent and was followed on foot. Small hounds are mentioned in the Forest Laws of Canute which exempted them from the ordinance which commanded that all dogs capable of running down a stag should have one foot mutilated. If genuine, these laws would confirm that beagle-type dogs were present in England before 1016, but it is likely the laws were written in the Middle Ages to give a sense of antiquity and tradition to Forest Law.

In the 11th century, William the Conqueror brought the Talbot hound to Britain. The Talbot was a predominantly white, slow, deep-throated, scent hound derived from the St Hubert Hound which had been developed in the 8th century. At some point the English Talbots were crossed with Greyhounds to give them an extra turn of speed. Long extinct, the Talbot strain probably gave rise to the Southern Hound which, in turn, is thought to be an ancestor of the modern day Beagle.

From medieval times, *beagle* was used as a generic description for the smaller hounds, though these dogs differed considerably from the modern breed. Miniature breeds of beagle-type dogs were known from the times of Edward II and Henry VII, who both had packs of Glove Beagles, so named since they were small enough to fit on a glove, and Queen Elizabeth I kept a breed known as a Pocket Beagle, which stood 8 to 9 inches (20 to 23 cm) at the shoulder. Small enough to fit in a "pocket" or saddlebag, they rode along on the hunt. The larger hounds would run the prey to ground, then the hunters would release the small dogs to continue the chase through underbrush. Elizabeth I referred to the dogs as her *singing beagles* and often entertained guests at her royal table by letting her Pocket Beagles cavort amid their plates and cups. Nineteenth-century sources refer to these breeds interchangeably and it is possible that the two names refer to the same small variety. In George Jesse's *Researches into the History of the British Dog* from 1866, the early 17th century poet and writer Gervase Markham is quoted referring to the Beagle as small enough to sit on a man's hand and to the:

```
Standards for the Pocket Beagle were drawn up as late as 1901; these
genetic lines are now extinct, although modern breeders have attempted
to recreate the variety.
```

Eighteenth century

By the 1700s two breeds had been developed for hunting hare and rabbit: the Southern Hound and the North Country Beagle (or Northern Hound). The Southern Hound, a tall, heavy dog with a square head, and long, soft ears, was common from south of the River Trent and probably closely related to the Talbot Hound. Though slow, it had stamina and an excellent scenting ability. The North Country Beagle, possibly a cross between an offshoot of the Talbot stock and a Greyhound, was bred chiefly in

Yorkshire and was common in the northern counties. It was smaller than the Southern Hound, less heavy-set and with a more pointed muzzle. It was faster than its southern counterpart but its scenting abilities were less well developed. As fox hunting became increasingly popular, numbers of both types of hound diminished. The beagle-type dogs were crossed with larger breeds such as Stag Hounds to produce the modern Foxhound. The beagle-size varieties came close to extinction but some farmers in the South ensured the survival of the prototype breeds by maintaining small rabbit-hunting packs.

Development of the modern breed

Reverend Phillip Honeywood established a Beagle pack in Essex in the 1830s and it is believed that this pack formed the basis for the modern Beagle breed. Although details of the pack's lineage are not recorded it is thought that North Country Beagles and Southern Hounds were strongly represented; William Youatt suspected that Harriers formed a good majority of the Beagle's bloodline, but the origin of the Harrier is itself obscure. Honeywood's Beagles were small, standing at about at the shoulder, and pure white according to John Mills (writing in *The Sportsman's Library* in 1845). Prince Albert and Lord Winterton also had Beagle packs around this time, and royal favour no doubt led to some revival of interest in the breed, but Honeywood's pack was regarded as the finest of the three.

Although credited with the development of the modern breed, Honeywood concentrated on producing dogs for hunting and it was left to Thomas Johnson to refine the breeding to produce dogs that were both attractive and capable hunters. Two strains were developed: the rough- and smooth-coated varieties. The rough-coated Beagle survived until the beginning of the 20th century, and there were even records of one making an appearance at a dog show as late as 1969, but this variety is now extinct having probably been absorbed into the standard Beagle bloodline.

In the 1840s, a standard Beagle type was beginning to develop: the distinction between the North Country Beagle and Southern Hound had been lost, but there was still a large variation in size, character, and reliability among the emerging packs. In 1856, "Stonehenge" (the pseudonym of John Henry Walsh, editor of *The Field*), writing in the *Manual of British Rural Sports* was still dividing Beagles into four varieties: the medium Beagle; the dwarf or lapdog Beagle; the fox Beagle (a smaller, slower version of the Foxhound); and the rough-coated or terrier Beagle, which he classified as a cross between any of the other varieties and one of the Scottish terrier breeds. Stonehenge also gives the start of a standard description:

By 1887 the threat of extinction was on the wane: there were 18 Beagle packs in England. The Beagle Club was formed in 1890 and the first standard drawn up at the same time. The following year the Association of Masters of Harriers and Beagles was formed. Both organisations aimed to further the best interests of the breed, and both were keen to produce a standard type of Beagle. By 1902 the number of packs had risen to 44.

Export

Beagles were in the United States by the 1840s at the latest, but the first dogs were imported strictly for hunting and were of variable quality. Since Honeywood had only started breeding in the 1830s, it is unlikely these dogs were representative of the modern breed and the description of them as looking like straight-legged Dachshunds with weak heads has little resemblance to the standard. Serious attempts at establishing a quality bloodline began in the early 1870s when General Richard Rowett from Illinois imported some dogs from England and began breeding. Rowett's Beagles are believed to have formed the models for the first American standard, drawn up by Rowett, L. H. Twadell, and Norman Ellmore in 1887. The Beagle was accepted as a breed by the American Kennel Club (AKC) in 1884. In the 20th century the breed has spread worldwide.

Popularity

On its formation, the Association of Masters of Harriers and Beagles took over the running of a regular show at Peterborough that had started in 1889, and the Beagle Club in the UK held its first show in 1896. The regular showing of the breed led to the development of a uniform type, and the Beagle continued to prove a success up until the outbreak of World War I when all shows were suspended. After the war, the breed was again struggling for survival in the UK: the last of the Pocket Beagles was probably lost during this time, and registrations fell to an all-time low. A few breeders (notably Reynalton Kennels) managed to revive interest in the dog and by World War II, the breed was once again doing well. Registrations dropped again after the end of the war but almost immediately recovered. In 1959 Derawunda Vixen won "Best in Show" at Crufts.

As purebred dogs, Beagles have always been more popular in the United States and Canada than in their native country. The National Beagle Club of America was formed in 1888 and by 1901 a Beagle had won a Best in Show title. As in the UK, activity during World War I was minimal, but the breed showed a much stronger revival in the U.S. when hostilities ceased. In 1928 it won a number of prizes at the Westminster Kennel Club's show and by 1939 a Beagle – Champion Meadowlark Draughtsman – had captured the title of top-winning American-bred dog for the year. On 12 February 2008, a Beagle, K-Run's Park Me In First (Uno), won the Best In Show category at the Westminster Kennel Club show for the first time in the competition's history. In North America they have been consistently in the top-ten most-popular breeds for over 30 years. From 1953 to 1959 the Beagle was ranked No. 1 on the list of the American Kennel Club's registered breeds; in 2005 and 2006 it ranked 5th out of the 155 breeds registered. In the UK they are not quite so popular, placing 28th and 30th in the rankings of registrations with the Kennel Club in 2005 and 2006 respectively.

Name

According to the Oxford English Dictionary, the first mention of the beagle by name in English literature dates from ca. 1475 in the *Esquire of Low Degree*. The origin of the word "beagle" is uncertain, although it has been suggested that the word derives from the French *begueule* (meaning "open throat" from *bayer* "open wide" and *gueule* "mouth") or from an Old English, French, or the Gaelic word *beag*, meaning "little." Other possibilities include the French *beugler* (meaning "to bellow") and the German *begele* (meaning "to scold").

It is not known why the black and tan Kerry Beagle, present in Ireland since Celtic times, has the *beagle* description, since at 22 to 24 inches (56 to 61 cm) it is significantly taller than the modern day Beagle, and in earlier times was even larger. Some writers suggest that the Beagle's scenting ability may have come from cross-breeding earlier strains with the Kerry Beagle. Originally used for hunting stags, it is today used for hare and drag hunting.

Description

Appearance

The general appearance of the Beagle resembles a Foxhound in miniature, but the head is broader and the muzzle shorter, the expression completely different and the legs shorter in proportion to the body. This is because beagles were trained to use their sense of smell often, and they would bend down a lot. They are generally between high at the withers and weigh between , with females being slightly smaller than males on average.

They have a smooth, somewhat domed skull with a medium-length, square-cut muzzle and a black (or occasionally liver), gumdrop nose. The jaw is strong and the teeth scissor together with the upper teeth fitting perfectly over the lower teeth and both sets aligned square to the jaw. The eyes are large, hazel or brown, with a mild hound-like pleading look. The large ears are long, soft and low-set, turning towards the cheeks slightly and rounded at the tips. Beagles have a strong, medium-length neck (which is long enough for them to easily bend to the ground to pick up a scent), with little folding in the skin but some evidence of a dewlap; a broad chest narrowing to a tapered abdomen and waist and a short, slightly curved tail (known as the "stern") tipped with white. The white tip, known as the "flag" has been selectively bred for, as it allows the dog to be easily seen when its head is down following a scent. The tail does not curl over the back, but is held upright when the dog is active. The Beagle has a muscular body and a medium-length, smooth, hard coat. The front legs are straight and carried under the body while the rear legs are muscular and well bent at the stifles.

Colouring

Beagles appear in a range of colours. Although the tricolour (white with large black areas and light brown shading) is the most common, Beagles can occur in any hound colour.

Tricoloured dogs occur in a number of shades, from the "Classic Tri" with a jet black saddle (also known as "Blackback"), to the "Dark Tri" (where faint brown markings are intermingled with more prominent black markings), to the "Faded Tri" (where faint black markings are intermingled with more prominent brown markings). Some tricoloured dogs have a broken pattern, sometimes referred to as *pied*. These dogs have mostly white coats with patches of black and brown hair. Tricolour Beagles are almost always born black and white. The white areas are typically set by eight weeks, but the black areas may fade to brown as the puppy matures. (The brown may take between one and two years to fully develop.) Some Beagles gradually change colour during their lives, and may lose their black markings entirely.

Two-colour varieties always have a white base colour with areas of the second colour. Tan and white is the most common two-colour variety, but there is a wide range of other colours including lemon, a very light tan; red, a reddish, almost orange, brown; and liver, a darker brown, and black. Liver is not common and is not permitted in some standards; it tends to occur with yellow eyes. Ticked or mottled varieties may be either white or black with different coloured flecks (*ticking*), such as the blue-mottled or bluetick Beagle, which has spots that appear to be a midnight-blue colour, similar to the colouring of the Bluetick Coonhound. Some tricolour Beagles also have ticking of various colours in their white areas.

Sense of smell

Alongside the Bloodhound, the Beagle has one of the best developed senses of smell of any dog. In the 1950s, John Paul Scott and John Fuller began a 13 year study into canine behaviour. As part of this research, they tested the scenting abilities of various breeds by putting a mouse in a field and timing how long it took the dogs to find it. The Beagles found it in less than a minute, while Fox Terriers took 15 minutes and Scottish Terriers failed to find it at all. Beagles are better at ground-scenting (following a trail on the ground) than they are at air-scenting, and for this reason they have been excluded from most mountain rescue teams in favour of collies, which use sight in addition to air-scenting and are more biddable. The long ears and large lips of the Beagle probably assist in trapping the scents close to the nose.

Variations

Breed varieties

The American Kennel Club recognizes two separate varieties of Beagle: the 13-inch for hounds less than , and the 15-inch for those between . The Canadian Kennel Club recognizes a single type, with a height not exceeding . The Kennel Club (UK) and FCI affiliated clubs recognize a single type, with a height of between .

English and American varieties are sometimes mentioned. However, there is no official recognition from any Kennel Club for this distinction. Beagles fitting the American Kennel Club standard – which disallows animals over – are smaller on average than those fitting the Kennel Club standard which allows heights up to .

Pocket Beagles are sometimes advertised for sale but the bloodline for this variety is extinct, and, although the UK Kennel Club originally specified a standard for the Pocket Beagle in 1901, the variety is not now recognised by any Kennel Club. Often, small Beagles are the result of poor breeding or dwarfism.

A strain known as Patch Hounds was developed by Willet Randall and his family from 1896 specifically for their rabbit hunting ability. They trace their bloodline back to Field Champion Patch, but do not necessarily have a patchwork marking.

Crossbreeds

In the 1850s, Stonehenge recommended a cross between a Beagle and a Scottish terrier as a retriever. He found the crossbreed to be a good worker, silent and obedient, but it had the drawback that it was small and could barely carry a hare. More recently the trend has been for "designer dogs" and one of the most popular has been the Beagle/Pug cross known as a Puggle. Less excitable than a Beagle and with a lower exercise requirement, these dogs are suited to city dwelling.

Temperament

The Beagle has an even temper and gentle disposition. Described in several breed standards as "merry", they are amiable and generally neither aggressive nor timid. They enjoy company, and although they may initially be standoffish with strangers, they are easily won over. They make poor guard dogs for this reason, although their tendency to bark or howl when confronted with the unfamiliar makes them good watch dogs. In a 1985 study conducted by Ben and Lynette Hart, the Beagle was given the highest excitability rating, along with the Yorkshire Terrier, Cairn Terrier, Miniature Schnauzer, West Highland White Terrier and Fox Terrier. Beagles are intelligent, but as a result of being bred for the long chase are single-minded and determined, which can make them hard to train. They are generally obedient but can be difficult to recall once they have picked up a scent and are easily distracted by smells around them. They do not generally feature in obedience trials; while they are alert, respond well to food-reward training, and are eager to please, they are easily bored or distracted. They are ranked 72nd in Stanley Coren's *The Intelligence of Dogs*, as Coren places them among the group with the lowest degree of working/obedience intelligence. Coren's scale, however, does not assess understanding, independence or creativity.

Beagles are excellent with children and this is one of the reasons they have become popular family pets, but they are pack animals, and can be prone to separation anxiety. Not all Beagles will howl, but most will bark when confronted with strange situations, and some will bay (also referred to as "speaking", "giving tongue", or "opening") when they catch the scent of potential quarry. They also generally get along well with other dogs. They are not demanding with regard to exercise; their inbred stamina means they do not easily tire when exercised, but they also do not need to be worked to exhaustion before they will rest, though regular exercise helps ward off the weight gain to which the breed is prone.

Health

The median longevity of Beagles is 12–15 years, which is a typical lifespan for a dog of their size.

Beagles may be prone to epilepsy, but this can be controlled with medication. Hypothyroidism and a number of types of dwarfism occur in Beagles. Two conditions in particular are unique to the breed: Funny Puppy, in which the puppy is slow to develop and eventually develops weak legs, a crooked back and although normally healthy, is prone to a range of illnesses; Hip dysplasia, common in Harriers and in some larger breeds, is rarely considered a problem in Beagles. Beagles are considered a chondrodystrophic breed, meaning that they are prone to types of disk diseases.

In rare cases, Beagles may develop immune mediated polygenic arthritis (where the immune system attacks the joints) even at a young age. The symptoms can sometimes be relieved by steroid treatments.

Their long floppy ears can mean that the inner ear does not receive a substantial air flow or that moist air becomes trapped, and this can lead to ear infections. Beagles may also be affected by a range of eye problems; two common ophthalmic conditions in Beagles are glaucoma and corneal dystrophy. "Cherry eye", a prolapse of the gland of the third eyelid, and distichiasis, a condition in which eyelashes grow into the eye causing irritation, sometimes exist; both these conditions can be corrected with surgery. They can suffer from several types of retinal atrophy. Failure of the nasolacrimal drainage system can cause dry eye or leakage of tears onto the face.

As field dogs they are prone to minor injuries such as cuts and sprains, and, if inactive, obesity is a common problem as they will eat whenever food is available and rely on their owners to regulate their weight. When working or running free they are also likely to pick up parasites such as fleas, ticks, harvest mites and tapeworms, and irritants such as grass seeds can become trapped in their eyes, soft ears or paws.

Beagles may exhibit a behaviour known as reverse sneezing, in which they sound as if they are choking or gasping for breath, but are actually drawing air in through the mouth and nose. The exact cause of this behaviour is not known, but it is not harmful to the dog.

Working life

Hunting

Beagles were developed primarily for hunting hare, an activity known as beagling. They were seen as ideal hunting companions for the elderly who could follow on horseback without exerting themselves, for young hunters who could keep up with them on ponies, and for the poorer hunters who could not afford to maintain a stable of good hunting horses. Before the advent of the fashion for foxhunting in the 19th century, hunting was an all day event where the enjoyment was derived from the chase rather than the kill. In this setting the tiny Beagle was well matched to the hare, as unlike Harriers they would not quickly finish the hunt, but because of their excellent scent-tracking skills and stamina they were almost guaranteed to eventually catch the hare. The Beagle packs would run closely together ("so close that they might be covered with a sheet") which was useful in a long hunt, as it prevented stray dogs from obscuring the trail. In thick undergrowth they were also preferred to spaniels when hunting pheasant.

With the fashion for faster hunts, the Beagle fell out of favour for chasing hare, but was still employed for rabbit hunting. In *Anecdotes of Dogs*, Jesse says:

In the United States they appear to have been employed chiefly for hunting rabbits from the earliest imports. Hunting hare with Beagles became popular again in Britain in the mid-19th century and continued until it was made illegal in Scotland by the Protection of Wild Mammals (Scotland) Act 2002 and in England and Wales by the Hunting Act 2004. Under this legislation Beagles may still pursue rabbits with the landowner's permission. Drag hunting is popular where hunting is no longer permitted or for those owners who do not wish to participate in blood sports but still wish to exercise their dog's innate skills.

The traditional foot pack consists of up to 70 Beagles, marshalled by a Huntsman who directs the pack and who is assisted by a variable number of whippers-in whose job is to return straying hounds to the pack. The Master of the Hunt is in overall day-to-day charge of the pack, and may or may not take on the role of Huntsman on the day of the hunt. Beagles may also be employed individually or in a brace (a pair).

As hunting with Beagles was seen as ideal for young people, many of the British public schools traditionally maintained Beagle packs. Protests were lodged against Eton's use of Beagles for hunting as early as 1902 but the pack is still in existence today, and a pack used by Imperial College in Wye, Kent was stolen by the Animal Liberation Front in 2001. School and university packs are still maintained by Eton, Marlborough, Wye, Radley, the Royal Agricultural College and Christ Church,

Oxford.

Beagles have been used for hunting a wide range of game including Snowshoe Hare, Cottontail rabbits, game birds, Roe Deer, Red Deer, Bobcat, Coyote, Wild Boar and foxes, and have even been recorded as being used to hunt Stoat. In most of these cases, the Beagle is employed as a gun dog, flushing game for hunter's guns.

Quarantine

Beagles are used as detection dogs in the Beagle Brigade of the United States Department of Agriculture. These dogs are used to detect food items in luggage being taken into the United States. After trialling several breeds, Beagles were chosen because they are relatively small and unintimidating for people who are uncomfortable around dogs, easy to care for, intelligent and work well for rewards. They are also used for this purpose in a number of other countries including by the Ministry of Agriculture and Forestry in New Zealand, the Australian Quarantine and Inspection Service, and in Canada, Japan and the People's Republic of China. Larger breeds are generally used for detection of explosives as this often involves climbing over luggage and on large conveyor belts, work for which the smaller Beagle is not suited.

Testing

Beagles are the dog breed most often used in animal testing, due to their size and passive nature. Of the 8,018 dogs used in testing in the UK in 2004, 7,799 were Beagles (97.3%). In the UK, the Animals (Scientific Procedures) Act 1986 gave special status to primates, equids, cats and dogs and in 2005 the Animal Procedures Committee (set up by the act) ruled that testing on mice was preferable, even though a greater number of individual animals were involved. In 2005 Beagles were involved in less than 0.3% of the total experiments on animals in the UK, but of the 7670 experiments performed on dogs 7406 involved Beagles (96.6%). Most dogs are bred specifically for the purpose, by companies such as Harlan. In the UK companies breeding animals for research must be licensed under the Animals (Scientific Procedures) Act.

Testing of cosmetic products on animals is banned in the member states of European Community, although France protested the ban and has made efforts to have it lifted. It is permitted in the United States but is not mandatory if safety can be ascertained by other methods, and the test species is not specified by the Food and Drug Administration (FDA). When testing toxicity of food additives, food contaminants, and some drugs and chemicals the FDA uses Beagles and mini-pigs as surrogates for direct human testing.

Anti-vivisection groups have reported on abuse of animals inside testing facilities. In 1997 footage secretly filmed by a freelance journalist inside Huntingdon Life Sciences in the UK showed staff punching and screaming at Beagles. Consort Kennels, a UK-based breeder of Beagles for testing, closed down in 1997 after pressure from animal rights groups.

Medical research

In the United States where the breeds of dog used are not specified (although Beagles feature heavily in published research papers) the number of tests performed each year on dogs dropped by two-thirds, from 195,157 to 64,932, over the period from 1972 to 2004. In Japan the laws on animal experimentation do not require reporting on the types or number of animals used, and in France the proportion of inspectors to testing facilities means the regulatory environment is essentially one of trust.

Beagles are used in a range of research procedures: fundamental biological research, applied human medicine, applied veterinary medicine, and protection of man, animals or the environment.

Other roles

Although bred for hunting, Beagles are versatile and are nowadays employed for various other roles in detection, therapy, and as family pets. Beagles are used as sniffer dogs for termite detection in Australia, and have been mentioned as possible candidates for drug and explosive detection. Because of their gentle nature and unimposing build, they are also frequently used in pet therapy, visiting the sick and elderly in hospital. In June 2006, a trained Beagle assistance dog was credited with saving the life of its owner after using his owner's mobile phone to dial an emergency number. In the aftermath of the 2010 Haiti Earthquake, a Beagle search and rescue dog with a Colombian rescue squad was credited with locating the owner of the Hôtel Montana, who was subsequently rescued after spending 100 hours buried in the rubble.

In popular culture

Beagles have been featured across a wide range of media. References to the dog appear before the 19th century in works by such writers as William Shakespeare, John Webster, John Dryden, Thomas Tickell, Henry Fielding and William Cowper, and in Alexander Pope's translation of Homer's *Iliad*.

Beagles appeared in comic strips and animated cartoons from the 1950s with the *Peanuts* character Snoopy (billed as "the world's most famous Beagle"), Odie from the comic strip Garfield, Walt Disney's Beagle Boys and Beegle Beagle, the constant companion of Hanna-Barbera's Grape Ape.

They have appeared in numerous films, taking a central role in *Cats and Dogs*, and the title roles in the adaptation of Phyllis Reynolds Naylor's book *Shiloh* and the live-action version of *Underdog*. They have played supporting roles in films including *Audition*, *The Monster Squad* and *The Royal Tenenbaums*, and on television in *Star Trek: Enterprise*, *EastEnders*, *The Wonder Years*, and *To the Manor Born* among others.

Bagel, one of Barry Manilow's two Beagles, appeared on several of his album covers. Former US President Lyndon Baines Johnson had several Beagles, and caused an outcry when he picked up one of them by its ears during an official greeting on the White House lawn.

The ship on which Charles Darwin made his voyage which provided the material for his travel book *The Voyage of the Beagle* and much of the inspiration for *On the Origin of Species* was named HMS *Beagle* after the breed, and, in turn, lent its name to the ill-fated British Martian lander *Beagle 2*.

Notes

a. In this article "Beagle" (with a capital B) is used to distinguish the modern breed from other beagle-type dogs.

b. Youatt states that the Southern Hound may have been native to the British Isles and used on hunts by the Ancient Britons.

c. The Harts posed the following question to a panel of 96 experts, half of which were veterinary surgeons and the other half dog obedience trial judges:

d. The specific references in each of the author's works are as follows:

Shakespeare: "*Sir Toby Belch*: She's a beagle, true-bred, and one that adores me: what o' that?" *Twelfth Night* (c.1600) Act II Scene III

Webster: "*Mistress Tenterhook*': You are a sweet beagle" *Westward Ho* (1607) Act III Scene IV:2

Dryden: "The rest in shape a beagle's whelp throughout, With broader forehead and a sharper snout" *The Cock and the Fox*, and again: "About her feet were little beagles seen" in *Palamon and Arcite* both from *Fables, Ancient and Modern* (1700)

Tickell: "Here let me trace beneath the purpled morn, The deep-mouth'd beagle, and the sprightly horn" *To a Lady before Marriage* (published posthumously in 1749)

Fielding: "'What the devil would you have me do?' cries the Squire, turning to Blifil, 'I can no more turn her, than a beagle can turn an old hare.'" *The History of Tom Jones, a Foundling* (1749) Chapter 7.

Cowper: "For persevering chase and headlong leaps, True beagle as the staunchest hound he keeps" *The Progress of Error* (1782)

Pope: "Thus on a roe the well-breath'd beagle flies, And rends his hide fresh-bleeding with the dart" *The Iliad of Homer* (1715–20) Book XV:697–8

External links

- Beagle [8] at the Open Directory Project
- Beagle clubs [9] at the Open Directory Project
- Dog Breed Profile - Beagle [10]

Black and Tan Coonhound

Black and Tan Coonhound

Other names	American Black and Tan Coonhound
Country of origin	United States
Traits	

Classification and standards		
FCI	Group 6 Section 1 #300	standard [1]
AKC	Hound	standard [2]
CKC	Group 2 - Hounds	standard [3]
UKC	Scenthound Breeds	standard [4]

Dog (*Canis lupus familiaris*)		

The **Black and Tan Coonhound** is a breed of dog used principally for trailing and treeing raccoon. It's a cross between the Bloodhound, and the Black And Tan Virginia Foxhound. The Black and Tan Coonhound runs its game entirely by scent. The courage of the Coonhound also make it proficient on the hunt for deer, bear, cougar and other big game, although many US states are restricting the hunting of antlered animals with dogs. The general impression is that of power, agility and alertness, with the ability to cover ground swiftly with powerful rhythmic strides. Each hound has its own distinctive voice which is often recognizable to its owners from great distance.

Description

Appearance

Black and Tan Coonhound overview	
Weight:	(29–59 kg)
Height:	(58–69 cm)
Coat:	Short, dense and glossy
Litter size:	~8 puppies
Life span:	10–12 years

The breed standard for Black and Tan Coonhounds is as follows:

- Eyes are hazel to brown
- Ears are extremely long, wide, and thin, set low and far back on the dog's head, hanging well down the neck.
- Their black and tan markings are similar to the Doberman Pinscher and the Rottweiler but have key distinguishing differences from these breeds. The most prominent are the long tails and ears, and their loud, baying bark.
- Legs are long in proportion to the body length, muscular and finely modelled.
- The tail is set slightly below the natural line of the back, strongly tapered, and carried at a right angle, when the dog is alert or excited.
- 23 to 27 inches (58 to 69 cm) at the shoulder
- 8 to 10 inches (20 to 25 cm) head (back of skull to tip of nose)
- 65 to 130 pounds (29 to 59 kg)
- Males are typically larger and heavier boned than females.

Health

Generally healthy, but there is some risk of hip dysplasia, ear cancer and other ear infections, and eye problems.

Temperament

The Black and Tan Coonhound is a gentle, adaptable, and lovable dog. Many are easygoing and people-friendly, and the Black and Tan Coonhound is happiest when performing the work it has been bred for. Easily distracted by their incredible sense of smell, these dogs require patient handling and encouragement. Though most are trusting and sweet-natured, Black and Tan puppies require a fair amount of encouragement to boost their confidence, especially when living indoors as pets. Black and Tan Coonhounds are happy to be couch-potatoes when given plenty of exercise, and they enjoy the company of their human family. Black and Tans may seem cautious or nervous around strangers or unfamiliar dogs, but will socialize well with time, as they are bred to hunt and work in packs. They don't become senior citizens until about ten years old, and will be active, fun-loving buddies for their first decade.

The Black and Tan is best known as a raccoon hunter, the breed has also been used very successfully to hunt other types of game such as bear, stag, oppossum, deer and mountain lion - even on difficult terrain. It withstands well the rigors of winter as well as intense heat. Some of the Black and Tan Coonhound talents include hunting, tracking, watchdogging, and agility. Black and Tan Coonhounds are the only breed officially recognized as Coonhounds by the American Kennel Club.

This breed drools and slobbers, a trait that can be troublesome. This breed is not well-suited for someone who is looking for a quiet dog; Black and Tan Coonhounds, like all coonhounds, are quite vocal and will bark and howl often.

Black and Tan Coonhounds are effective at warning their owners when a stranger enters the yard. Their bark sounds threatening to strangers, but they are unlikely to actually bite unless they sense danger or they or their pack are threatened.

Though not seen frequently in urban areas, they enjoy popularity in rural areas. It is said that coonhounds are found on the porch of more rural homes in the United States than any other breed. While that is not a statistical fact, their place on the AKC registered breeds list ranks them as one of the more popular breeds.

History

The Black and Tan Coonhound is descended from the Talbot hound, found in medieval England after the eleventh century. Its ancestry is then traced through the Bloodhound and the Foxhound to the Virginia Foxhound, commonly called the "black and tan".

In 1945, the Black and Tan became the only one of the six varieties of Coonhound to be recognized in the Hound Group by the American Kennel Club. The Redbone Coonhound and the Plott Hound have since been recognized in the Miscellaneous Class. The other three varieties of Coonhound are the Bluetick Coonhound, the English Coonhound, and the Treeing Walker Coonhound.

External links

- American Black And Tan Coonhound Association [5]
- American Black And Tan Coonhound Rescue [6]

Bloodhound

Bloodhound

Bloodhound	
Other names	Chien de Saint-Hubert St. Hubert Hound Sleuth hound
Country of origin	Belgium / France or England/Scotland
Traits	
Classification and standards	
FCI	Group 6 Section 1 #084 standard [1]
AKC	Hound standard [2]
ANKC	Group 4 (Hounds) standard [3]
CKC	Group 2 - Hounds standard [4]
KC (UK)	Hound standard [5]
NZKC	Hounds standard [6]
UKC	Scenthounds standard [7]
Dog (*Canis lupus familiaris*)	

A **bloodhound** (also known as the **St. Hubert hound** and **Sleuth Hound**) is a large breed of dog that was bred originally to hunt deer and wild boar, later specifically to track human beings by scent. It is famed for its ability to follow scents hours or even days old over great distances. Its extraordinarily keen nose is combined with a strong and tenacious tracking instinct, producing the ideal scenthound, and it is used by police and law enforcement the world over to track escaped prisoners, missing persons, and even missing animals.

Appearance

Bloodhounds weigh from 33 to 50 kg (80 to 110 lb), although some individuals can weigh as much as 72 kg (160 lb). They stand 58 to 69 cm (23 to 27 inches) high at the withers. According to the AKC standard of the breed, larger dogs are to be preferred by conformation judges. The acceptable colors for bloodhounds are black and tan, liver and tan, or red. Bloodhounds possess an unusually large skeletal structure with most of their weight concentrated in their bones, which are very thick for their length. The coat is typical for a scenthound: hard and composed of fur alone, with no admixture of hair.

Temperament

This breed is a gentle dog which is nonetheless tireless in following a scent. Because of its strong tracking instinct, it can be willful and somewhat difficult to obedience train. Bloodhounds have an affectionate, gentle, and even-tempered nature, so they make excellent family pets. However, like any large breed, they require supervision when around small children.

Health

Illnesses

Compared to other purebred dogs, bloodhounds have an unusually high rate of gastrointestinal ailments, with bloat being the most common type of gastrointestinal problem. The breed also suffers an unusually high incidence of eye, skin, and ear ailments; thus these areas should be inspected frequently for signs of developing problems. Owners should be especially aware of the signs of bloat, which is both the most common illness and the leading cause of death of bloodhounds. The thick coat gives the breed the tendency to overheat quickly.

Lifespan and mortality

Bloodhounds in a 2004 UK Kennel Club survey had a median longevity of 6.75 years, which makes them one of the shortest-lived of dog breeds. The oldest of the 82 deceased dogs in the survey died at the age of 12.1 years. Bloat took 34% of the animals, making it the most common cause of death and the bloodhound the breed to lose the most to the condition. The second leading cause of death in the study was cancer, at 27%; this percentage is similar to other breeds, but the median age of death was unusually young (median of about 8 years).

History

Chien de St Hubert

The St Hubert was, according to legend, first bred ca. 1000 AD by monks at the Saint-Hubert Monastery in Belgium; its origins are likely in France, home of many of modern hounds.

From ca. 1200 the monks of the Abbey of St Hubert annually sent several pairs of black hounds as a gift to the King of France. They were not always highly thought of in the royal pack. Charles IX 1550-74, preferred the larger Chien-gris, and wrote that the St Huberts were suitable for people with gout to follow, but not for those who wished to shorten the life of the hunted animal. He described them as pack-hounds of medium stature, and long in the body, not well sprung in the rib and of no great strength. Writing in 1561 Jaques de Fouilloux describes them as strong of body, but with low, short legs. He says they have become mixed in breeding, so that they are now of all colours and widely distributed. Both writers thought them only useful as leash hounds.

They appear to have been more highly thought of during the reign of Henry IV (1553-1610), who presented a pack to James I of England. By the end of the reign of Louis XIV (1715), they were already rare. In 1788, D'Yauville who was master of the Royal hounds says those sent by the St Hubert monks, once much prized, had degenerated, and scarcely one of the annual gift of six or eight was now kept.

Upon the French Revolution of 1789 the gifts ceased, and hunting in France went into a decline till the end of the Napoleonic wars. When it recovered during the 19th Century, huntsmen, with many breeds to choose from, seem to have had little interest in the St Hubert. An exception was Baron Le Couteulx de Canteleu, who tried to find them. He reported that there were hardly any to be found in France and those to be met with in the Ardennes had been so much crossed that they had not preserved the characteristics of the breed.

It was generally agreed among writers on the bloodhound in the last two centuries that the original St Hubert strain died out in the nineteenth century, and that the European St Hubert owes its present existence to the development of the bloodhound.

Bloodhound

References to the bloodhound begin to appear in English writing in the mid 14th century, in contexts which suggest it was well established by then. It is often claimed that its ancestors were brought over from Normandy by William the Conqueror, but there is no actual evidence for this. That the Normans brought hounds from Europe during the post-Conquest period is a virtual certainty, but whether they included the bloodhound itself, rather than ancestors from which the bloodhound was subsequently developed, is a matter of dispute which is probably not resolvable on the basis of surviving evidence.

In Medieval hunting the typical use of the bloodhound was as a 'limer', or 'lyam-hound', that is a dog handled on a leash or 'lyam', to find the hart or boar before it was hunted by the pack hounds (raches). It was prized for its ability to hunt the cold scent of an individual animal, and, though it did not usually take part in the kill, it was given a special reward from the carcase.

It also seems that from the earliest times the bloodhound was used to track people. There are stories written in Medieval Scotland of Robert the Bruce (in 1307), and William Wallace (1270-1305) being followed by 'sleuth hounds'. Whether true or not, these stories show that the sleuth hound was already known as a man-trailer, and it later becomes clear that the sleuth hound and the bloodhound were the same animal.

In the 16th century, John Caius, in unquestionably the most important single source in the history of the bloodhound, describes its hanging ears and lips, its use in game parks to follow the scent of blood, which gives it its name, its ability to track thieves and poachers by their foot scent, how it casts if it has lost the scent when thieves cross water, and its use on the Scottish borders to track cross-border raiders, known as Border Reivers. This links it to the sleuth hound, and from Caius also comes the information that the English bloodhound and the sleuth hound were essentially the same, though the bloodhound was slightly bigger, with more variation in coat colour.

The picture on the right was published in Zurich in 1563, in Conrad Gesner's *Thierbuch* (a compendium of animals) with the captions: 'Englischen Blüthund' and 'Canis Sagax Sanguinarius apud Anglos' (English scent hound with associations of blood), and sent to Gesner among drawings to illustrate his descriptions of British dogs for European readers. It is thus the earliest known picture published specifically to demonstrate the appearance of the bloodhound. We are told it was done from life, and detail such as the soft hang of the ear indicates it was carefully observed. Fully accurate or not, it suggests changes between the bloodhound of then and today. The collar and long coiled rope reflect the bloodhound's typical functions as a limer or leashed man-trailer in that period.

The earliest known report of a trial of the bloodhound's trailing abilities comes from the scientist Robert Boyle[8], who described how a bloodhound tracked a man seven miles along a route frequented by people, and found him in an upstairs room of a house.

With the rise of fox-hunting, the decline of deer-hunting, and the extinction of the wild boar, as well as a more settled state of society, the use of the bloodhound diminished. It was kept by the aristocratic owners of a few deer-parks and by a few enthusiasts, with some variation in type, until its popularity began to increase again with the rise of dog-showing in the 19th Century. Numbers, however, have remained low in Britain. Very few survived the Second World War, but the gene-pool has gradually been replenished with imports from America. Nevertheless, because of UK quarantine restrictions, importing was expensive and difficult, throughout the 20th century, and in the post-war period exports to the USA, and to Europe where the population had also been affected by the war, considerably exceeded imports.

During the later 19th century numbers of bloodhounds were imported from Britain by French enthusiasts, who regretted the extinction of the ancient St Hubert. They wished to re-establish it, using the bloodhound, which, despite its developments in Britain, they regarded as the St Hubert preserved unchanged. Many of the finest specimens were bought and exhibited and bred in France as Chiens de

St Hubert, especially by Le Couteulx de Canteleu, who himself bred over 300. Whatever few original St Huberts remained either died out or were absorbed into the new population. As a result, the bloodhound became known on parts of the Continent as the Chien de Saint Hubert, and is recognised under that name by the Federation Cynologique Internationale. Its country of origin is given by the FCI as Belgium, while the UK Kennel Club regards it as a native British breed, though accepting the European St Huberts as bloodhounds.

In Le Couteulx' book of 1890 we read that 'Le Chien de St Hubert actuel' is very big, from 0m,69 to 0m,80 (27½-31½in) high. This does not accord with the 16th century descriptions of the St Hubert given above, nor with the FCI standard, but the idea that the St Hubert is much bigger (up to 0.915m, 36 in) than the bloodhound persisted well into the 20th century, among some St Hubert enthusiasts.

When the first bloodhounds were exported to the USA is not known. Bloodhounds were used to track runaway slaves before the American Civil War, but it has been questioned whether the dogs used were genuine bloodhounds. However, in the later part of the 19th century, and in the next, more pure bloodhounds were introduced from Britain, and bred in America, especially after 1888, when the English breeder, Edwin Brough, brought three of his hounds to exhibit at the Westminster KC show in New York City. He went into partnership with Mr J L Winchell, who with other Americans, imported more stock from Britain. Bloodhounds in America have been more widely used in tracking lost people and criminals - often with brilliant success - than in Britain, and the history of the bloodhound in America is full of the man-trailing exploits of outstanding bloodhounds and their expert handlers, the most famous hound being Nick Carter. Law enforcement agencies have been much involved in the use of bloodhounds, and there is a National Police Bloodhound Association, originating in 1962.

In Britain there have been instances from time to time of the successful use of the bloodhound to track criminals or missing people. However man-trailing is enjoyed as a sport by British bloodhound owners, through national working trials, and this enthusiasm has also spread to Europe. In addition while the pure bloodhound is used to hunt singly there are also several bloodhound packs which use bloodhounds with some degree of foxhound outcrossing to hunt the human scent.

Meanwhile the bloodhound has become widely distributed internationally, though numbers are small in most countries, with more in the USA than anywhere else. Following the spread of the bloodhound from Britain in the nineteenth and twentieth centuries, imports and exports and, increasingly, artificial insemination, are maintaining the world population as a common breeding stock, without a great deal of divergence in type in different countries.

Bloodhounds are now coloured red, black and tan or liver and tan; however, until Elizabethan times they also occurred in other solid colours, including white, and all other hound colours. It is possible that the Talbot, now extinct, was a white bloodhound, but this is uncertain.

During the late 19th century, bloodhounds were frequent subjects for artists such as Edwin Landseer and Briton Riviere; the dogs depicted are close in appearance to modern bloodhounds, indicating that the essential character of the bloodhound predates modern dog breeding. However, the dogs depicted by Landseer show less wrinkle and haw than modern dogs.

Breed standards

Descriptions of the desirable physical qualities of a hunting hound go back to Medieval books on hunting. All dogs used in the hunting field were 'gentle', that is of good breeding (not necessarily pure breeding), and parents were carefully chosen to maintain and improve conformation. In 1896, making some use of wording found in earlier descriptions, Edwin Brough and Dr J Sidney Turner published *Points and Characteristics of the Bloodhound or Sleuth-Hound*. This was adopted by the newly-formed Association of Bloodhound Breeders, and ultimately became, with very little change, the 'official' breed standard of the KC and the AKC. Meanwhile, the Belgian or Dutch Comte Henri de Bylandt, or H A graaf van Bylandt, published *Races des Chiens* in 1897, a huge and very important illustrated compilation of breed descriptions, or standards. In this French edition the Bloodhound appears as the Chien de St Hubert, although the hounds illustrating the standard are all British Bloodhounds, many of them those of Edwin Brough. The book was revised and reprinted in four languages in 1904, and in this edition the English text of the standard is that of the Association of Bloodhound Breeders, while the French text is closely based on it. However, the present FCI standard uses a quite different layout and wording. The AKC standard has hardly been altered from the original of 1896, the principal change being that the colours, 'black and tan', 'red and tan', and 'tawny', have been renamed as 'black and tan', 'liver and tan', and 'red', but the British KC[9] has made considerable changes. Some of these were simply matters of presentation and did not affect content. However, responding to the view that the requirements of some breed standards were potentially detrimental to the health or well-being of the animal, changes have been made affecting the required eye-shape and the loose skin, the most recent revision being 2008-9.

Derivation of name

Most recent accounts will say that the etymological meaning is 'hound of pure or noble blood'. This derives from an original suggestion of Le Couteulx de Canteleu in the nineteenth century, which has been enthusiastically and uncritically espoused by later writers, perhaps because it absolved this undoubtedly good-natured dog from suggestions of bloodthirstiness. Neither Le Couteulx nor anyone since has offered any historical evidence to support this view. Before that the word had been taken to mean, roughly, 'blood seeking hound'. This was the explanation put forward by John Caius, who was one of the most learned men of his time, and had an interest in etymology, in the sixteenth century. It is supported by considerable historical linguistic evidence, which can be gleaned from such sources as the *Oxford English Dictionary* (*OED*): the fact that first uses of the word 'blood' to refer to good breeding in an animal post date the first use of 'bloodhound'; that other comparable uses, as in 'blood-horse' and 'blood-stock' appear many centuries later; and that derogatory uses of the word 'bloodhound', which any suggestion of noble breeding would sadly weaken, appear from as early as c1400. Other early sources tell us that hounds were supposed to have an interest in blood, and that the bloodhound was used to follow the trail of a wounded animal. In the absence of anything in early usage, or any historical evidence whatsoever, to support the modern explanation, the older must be regarded as correct.

See also

Northern and Southern Hounds

Dog type

Hugh Dalziel *British Dogs* Ch IX, on line [10]

Scenting ability

The bloodhound's physical characteristics account for its ability to follow a scent trail left several days in the past. Under optimal conditions, a bloodhound can detect as few as one or two cells. The bloodhound's nasal chambers(where scents are identified) are larger than those of most other breeds. The large, long pendent ears serve to prevent wind from scattering nearby skin cells while the dog's nose is on the ground; the folds of wrinkled flesh under the lips and neck—called the shawl—serve to catch stray scent particles in the air or on a nearby branch as the bloodhound is scenting, reinforcing the scent in the dog's memory and nose.

Voice

A common misconception is that bloodhounds are employed in packs; while this is sometimes the case in Britain, in North America bloodhounds are used as solitary trackers. When they are on a trail, they are usually silent and do not give voice as other scenthounds. The original use of the bloodhound as a leash-hound, to find but not disturb animals, would require silent trailing.

Nevertheless, the bloodhound bay is among the most impressive of hound voices. When hunting in a pack they are expected to be in full cry. They are more likely to 'give tongue, 'throw their tongue' or 'speak' when hunting in a pack than when hunting singly, and more when hunting free than when on the leash. The quality of 'speaking to the line', that is giving tongue when on the correct scent while remaining silent when off it, is valued in British bloodhound circles, on aesthetic grounds and because it makes it very easy to 'read' the hound's tracking behaviour. As a result special trophies for speaking to the correct line are on offer at British working trials (where hounds hunt singly), although rarely awarded.

Bloodhound Packs

The Medieval bloodhound was not primarily a pack hound, but a leash hound, though there may have been packs in different places or at different times. Up to the nineteenth century, a single hound or a brace was used on deer-parks, to find deer for the gun. However, mid century two packs appeared, that of Thomas Neville, who hunted in the New Forest area, and who preferred very black hounds, and that of Lord Wolverton. Both these hunted semi-domesticated deer ('carted deer'), which were recaptured on being brought to bay, and returned home. It was said of Lord Wolverton's hounds that he found it difficult to get them to hunt as a pack, because each liked to follow the scent on his own. Eventually many were sold to Le Couteulx de Canteleu and taken to France. At the turn of the century several packs existed briefly, following either deer, or the 'clean boot' - individual human scent without any enhancement such as animal blood or aniseed. Since the second world war there have been several packs, perhaps most notably that of Eric Furness, who introduced a cross to a Dumfriesshire foxhound into his Peak bloodhounds. Generally Masters of Bloodhounds since then have followed the practice of maintaining a level of outcross breeding in their packs to improve speed and agility, while retaining bloodhound type. These packs hunt the clean boot and are followed by a field on horseback.

Noteworthy bloodhounds

Grafton was the bloodhound in Landseer's famous painting *Dignity and Impudence*[11] (1839). Both dogs in the picture belonged to Jacob Bell.

Mr T A Jennings' Ch Druid, known as 'Old Druid' was the first bloodhound champion. Born in 1857 he was later bought by Emperor Napoleon III for his son, Prince Eugene Louis Jean Joseph, and taken to France. Photographs of him, of another famous hound, Cowen's Druid, and a bitch named Countess, appear in a rare book from 1865 in the British Library[12], and may be the oldest photographs of bloodhounds to have survived.

A bloodhound named Nick Carter is frequently cited as the archetype of the trailing bloodhound and the extensive publicity this dog received may be the source of much bloodhound-related folklore. Born in 1900, Nick Carter was owned and handled by Captain G.V. Mullikin of Lexington, Kentucky; he is credited with more than 650 finds, including one that required him to follow a trail 105 hours old.

Ch. Heathers Knock on Wood, known as "Knotty", is one of the most awarded bloodhounds of all time; he has received more Best-in-Shows than any other bloodhound and is the first liver-and-tan bloodhound ever to win a Best-in-Show. Knotty was awarded the Best-in-Show at the Eukanuba Tournament in 2005 and won the Hound Group in the Westminster Kennel Club Show in that same year. Knotty's offspring have also proven to be able showdogs and as a result of a very high amount of his puppies being awarded the title of "Champion" by the AKC, Knotty was inducted into the AKC's Stud Dog Hall of Fame shortly before his death in Spring of 2008.

On the popular 1960's sitcom Beverly Hillbillies, veteran canine actor Stretch portrayed Jed's bloodhound Duke.

Fictional bloodhounds

- Pluto, pet of Mickey Mouse, from The Chain Gang
- Ol' Red, from the George Jones (later remade by Blake Shelton) song of the same name.
- Ladybird from King of the Hill
- Copper from the film and novel *The Fox and the Hound*
- Beaureguard in *Pogo*
- Pedro, the bloodhound owned and used by the English detective, Sexton Blake.
- Henry, a bloodhound used in a popular series of British TV dog food commercials, with Clement Freud.
- Trusty in "Lady and the Tramp" and "Lady and the Tramp 2"
- Snuffles in *Quick Draw McGraw*
- Napoleon from *The Aristocats*
- Duke, Jed's bloodhound from the *Beverly Hillbillies*
- Hubert from *Best in Show*
- Bobby Lee and others from Virginia Lanier's bloodhound series
- Buddy, in Cats and Dogs
- Bruno in Cinderella (1950 film)
- The Bumpuses' hounds in A Christmas Story
- Woofer and Whimper in Clue Club
- McGruff the Crime Dog
- Jasper T. Jowls at *Chuck E. Cheese's*
- 2nd book in the Provost's Dog trilogy or Beka Cooper series by Tamora Pierce
- General Pepper from *Star Fox (series)*
- Bear & Bryant in Sweet Home Alabama
- Pommes Frites, faithful and remarkable companion of Michael Bond's culinary detective, Monsieur Pamplemousse
- Old Towser in "One Hundred and One Dalmatians"
- Waylon and Floyd in The Fox and the Hound 2"
- Sniffer in Air Buddies and Santa Buddies
- Laughing Dog from *Duck Hunt*
- Bayard Hamar from Alice in Wonderland (2010 film)
- B.H. (Calcutta) Failed : a bloodhound which had lost its sense of smell, in The Perishers, cartoon strip published in *The Daily Mirror*.

Further reading

Boitard, Jean-Pierre, Le Chien de Saint-Hubert, éditions Artémis 2002. ISBN 2-84416-155-3

External links

- Canadian Bloodhound Club [13]
- American Bloodhound Club [14]
- The Bloodhound Club (UK) [15]
- Search Dog Association [16]
- French bloodhound [17]
- Lithuanian bloodhound [18]
- American Kennel Club [19]
- Vladivostok Bloodhound Club [20]

Bluetick Coonhound

Bluetick Coonhound

Bluetick Coonhound (female)	
Country of origin	United States
Traits	
Classification and standards	
AKC Hound (FSS)	standard [1]
The AKC Foundation Stock Service [3] (FSS) is an optional recording service for purebred dogs that are not yet eligible for AKC registration.	
ANKC Group 4 (Hounds)	standard [2]
NZKC Hounds	standard [3]
UKC Scenthounds	standard [4]
Dog (*Canis lupus familiaris*)	

The **Bluetick Coonhound** is a breed of dog. It is a type of coonhound and typically bred in the southern United States.

Description

Appearance

The overall body style of the Bluetick Coonhound is muscular and speedy, not chunky or clumsily built. The head is carried well up and the tail carried over the back, without signs of fear or nervousness. The Bluetick coat should be moderately coarse and glossy. The Bluetick Coonhound gets its "blue" coloring from black/white mottling which gives the impression of a navy blue color. This mottling covers the body and can be interspersed with variously-shaped black spots on the back, ears and sides. Preference runs to more blue than black on the body. Black should predominate on the head and ears. Bluetick Coonhounds should have tan dots over the eyes and on the cheeks with dark red ticking on the feet and lower legs below the body line, on the chest, and below the tail. Red can be eliminated, as well as the tan head coloring. Blue mottling on the body is preferred to lighter ticking. Blue ticking should be predominant over white in the body coat. Off colors are not allowed, but almost solid black with just some ticking on the feet and chest is permitted. Also most blue ticks can have gray at the end of the tail.

The Bluetick Coonhound has low-set ears which reach at least to the nose. The muzzle should be square, not narrow or snipey, and slightly shorter than the depth of skull. There should be a prominent stop, and the skull should be slightly domed. The lips and flews should well cover the lower jaw. The blueticks eyes should be large and set wide apart. Coloring light brown to dark brown, with a close fitting eylid. The neck of the Bluetick should be arched and muscular, of moderate length and without excessive dewflap.

Male coonhounds should be 22 to 27 inches at the shoulder and weigh approximately 55 to 80 pounds. Females are considerably smaller, being 21 to 25 inches at the shoulder and weighing between 45 to 65 pounds. The body should be higher at the shoulder than the hips, and when measured from the withers to the base of tail it should be slightly longer than tall. Blueticks (as they are known by fanciers) should have a deep chest with well sprung ribs, curving into the belly rather than having an extreme tucked up look.

Feet should be cat-like, rounded with well-arched toes. Their paws are larger than nearly all other breeds of dogs. Rear legs should have a moderate bend at the hocks. All legs should be straight when viewed from the front or rear.

Gascon blues are larger than standard blueticks, with males a minimum of 27 inches and a maximum of 30 inches. See the American Blue Gascon Coonhound Association's breed standard: http://www.abgha.org/standard.htm

Temperament

Bluetick Coonhounds are gentle with children and loyal, loving pets, but they can be challenging to train. They are the breed least likely to be aggressive to people, but they should not be trusted around cats or other small animals. They are, like their hound counterparts, very intelligent breeds, with an uncanny knack for problem-solving. This can be particularly problematic if they are confined to a household or too small a yard, and one should give this breed plenty of space. Once trained, the breed is very mindful of its owner. Breed will drool occasionally and salivate heavily when exposed to "human" foods. They are very loud, constant, and howling barkers. They are bred to be working hunting dogs and can be a challenge to lazy pet owners.

In normal conditions the dog is excellent around families and children. Once trained, they are mindful, friendly dogs. However, their noses will keep them in trouble, so food and garbage should not ever be left out unattended. Often mistaken for aggressiveness, the breed will "greet" strangers with its signature howl and will sniff the subject until satisfied. Usually this is just the way the breed gets to know its subjects. Since Blueticks are driven by their strong sense of smell, they make excellent hunting/tracking dogs. They will tree any animal that is small and handle the best of the coon hound breeds.

History

The Bluetick Coonhound, which originated in Louisiana, was developed from the Bleu de Gascogne hound of southwest France, as well as the English Foxhound, the cur dog, the American Foxhound, and the Black And Tan Virginia Foxhound. Originally, Bluetick Coonhounds were registered in the United Kennel Club under the English Foxhound and Coonhound, but were recognized by the club as a separate breed in 1946. Bluetick Coonhounds are also recognized by the Australian National Kennel Council and the New Zealand Kennel Club. Breeders have started the process of obtaining recognition from the American Kennel Club, and Blueticks are now eligible to compete in AKC coonhound events. The American Blue Gascon is a subgroup of bluetick coonhounds that is larger, heavier, and more "houndy" looking than the standard bluetick. American Blue Gascons are often referred to as "old-fashioned" blueticks. This is due to their appearance and "colder" nose, or slower style of tracking, compared to other modern coonhound breeds. The picture here appears to be of a female American Blue Gascon.

Famous Bluetick Coonhounds

A Bluetick Coonhound named "Smokey" is the official athletic mascot of the University of Tennessee.

A Bluetick Coonhound named Tet was the companion of Stringfellow Hawke, the main character of popular 1980s television show Airwolf.

Neil Young has stated that his song "Old King" is a tribute to a deceased Bluetick Coonhound he once owned.

An unnamed Bluetick Coonhound is featured in Blake Shelton's hit single, "Ol' Red". The song relates an escape plan of a man convicted of a crime of passion when he murdered his wife and her lover. He devises a plan to have a female Bluetick lure the prison's male Bloodhound Ol' Red away from Shelton instead of tracking him as he heads in the opposite direction. The closing lines of the song are: "Now there's red-haired Blueticks all in the South, / Love got me in there and love got me out."

Coonhounds are featured in the book Where the Red Fern Grows. However, the two main dogs are Redbone Coonhounds.

Emmylou Harris sings about her friend Lillian's "Bluetick hound dog, Gideon" in her song Red Dirt Girl.

Charlie Daniels mentions that he's "kinda like my old Bluetick hound/I like to lay around in the shade" in his song "Long Haired Country Boy."

David Allan Coe mentions a Bluetick hound in his song "Cum Stains on the Pillow."

A Bluetick was featured in a Miracle Whip television commercial. After making a sandwich, the dog discovers the owner is out of Miracle Whip. (Jeff Gorman Films - Man's Best Friend Makes a Sandwich; Animal Makers animation)

Ken Kesey, in his novel, "One Flew Over the Cuckoos Nest", used a Bluetick Coonhound as a symbol for his main character Chief Bromden.

In Savage Sam, the sequel to Old Yeller, the title character is a Bluetick Coonhound. He is meant to be the son of Old Yeller, despite Old Yeller having been a Blackmouth Cur.

Justin Moore's song "Backwoods" features a line "Bluetick coonhound you know where I'm found out in the..."

In Chappelle's Show the dog in the opening credits is a Bluetick Coonhound.

External links

- Bluetick Breeders and Coonhunters Association [5]
- Bluetick Coonhound Breeders of America [6]
- American Blue Gascon Hounds Association [7]

Borzoi

Borzoi

A female Borzoi	
Other names	Barzoï Russian Wolfhound Russkaya Psovaya Borzaya Psovoi
Traits	

Classification and standards		
FCI	Group 10 Section 1 #193	standard [1]
AKC	Hound	standard [2]
ANKC	Group 4 (Hounds)	standard [3]
CKC	Group 2 - Hounds	standard [4]
KC (UK)	Hound	standard [5]
NZKC	Hound	standard [6]
UKC	Sighthound and Pariah	standard [7]

Dog (*Canis lupus familiaris*)

The **borzoi** () is a breed of domestic dog (*Canis lupus familiaris*) also called the **Russian wolfhound** and descended from dogs brought to Russia from central Asian countries. It is similar in shape to a greyhound, and is also a member of the sighthound family.

The system by which Russians over the ages named their sighthounds was a series of descriptive terms, not actual names. "Borzói" is the masculine singular form of an archaic Russian adjective that means "fast". "Borzáya sobáka" ("fast dog") is the basic term used by Russians, though the word "sobáka" is usually dropped. The name "Psovaya" derived from the word Psovina, meaning "wavy, silky coat", just as "Hortaya" (as in Hortaya Borzaya) means shorthaired. In Russia today the breed we know as borzoi is therefore officially called "Russkaya Psovaya Borzaya". Other Russian sighthound breeds are

"Stepnaya Borzaya" (from the steppe), called "Stepnoi"; and "Krimskaya Borzaya" (from the Crimea), called "Krimskoi". In Russian criminal lingo the word *borzoi* means "insolent".

The plural "borzois" may be found in dictionaries. However, the Borzoi Club of America asserts "borzoi" is the preferred form for both singular and plural (in Russian, the plural is actually "borzýe"). At least one manual of grammatical style rules that the breed name should not be capitalized except at the beginning of a sentence; again, breed fanciers usually differ, and capitalize it wherever found.

Description

Appearance

Borzoi are large Russian sighthounds which look similar to a number of central Asian breeds such as the Afghan hound, Saluki and the Kyrgyz Taigan. As a general approximation, "long-haired greyhound" is a useful description. Borzoi can come in almost any color or color combination.The long top-coat is silky and quite flat, with varying degrees of waviness or curling. The soft undercoat thickens in winter or cold climates, but is shed in hot weather to prevent overheating. In its texture and distribution over the body, the borzoi coat is unique.

Borzoi males frequently reach in excess of 100 pounds (45kg), ~120 pounds. Males should stand at least 30 inches (about 80 centimeters) at the shoulder, while females shouldn't be less than 26 inches (about 66 centimeters). Despite their size, the overall impression is of streamlining and grace, with a curvy shapeliness and compact strength.

Temperament

The borzoi is a quiet but athletic and independent dog. Most borzoi are almost silent, barking only very rarely. They do not have strong territorial drives and cannot be relied on to raise the alarm upon sighting a human intruder. They are gentle and highly sensitive dogs with a natural respect for humans, and as adults they are decorative couch potatoes with remarkably gracious house-manners. Borzois should never display dominance or aggression towards people. Typically however, they are rather reserved and sensitive to invasion of their personal space; this can make them nervous around children unless they are brought up with them from an early age. Despite their size they adapt very well to suburban living, provided they have a spacious yard and regular opportunities for free exercise.

A common misunderstanding about the intelligence of breeds in the Hound group stems from their independent nature, which conflicts with the frequent confusion between the concepts of "intelligence" and "obedience" in discussions of canine brainpower. Stanley Coren's survey of canine obedience trainers, published in the book The Intelligence of Dogs, reported that borzoi obeyed the first command less than 25% of the time. Coren's test however was by his own admission heavily weighted towards the "obedience" interpretation of intelligence and based on a better understanding of "working" breeds than hounds. Unfortunately the publicity given to this report has led to unfair denigration of breeds which are under-represented in obedience clubs and poorly understood by the average obedience trainer. "Work" for hound breeds is done out of hearing and often out of sight of the human companion; it is an activity for which the dogs are "released", rather than an activity which is "commanded". In obedience terms, borzoi are selective learners who quickly become bored with repetitive, apparently pointless, activity, and they can be very stubborn when they are not properly motivated. For example, food rewards, or "baiting", may work well for some individuals, but not all. Nevertheless, borzoi are definitely capable of enjoying and performing well in competitive obedience and agility trials with the right kind of training. Like other sighthounds they do not cope well with harsh treatment or training based on punishment, and will be extremely unhappy if raised voices and threats are a part of their daily life. However like any intelligent dog, borzoi respond extremely well to the guidance, support, and clear communication of a benevolent human leadership.

Borzoi were bred to pursue, or "course", game and have a powerful instinct to chase things that run from them. Built for speed and endurance, they can cover long distances in a very short time. A fully-fenced yard is an absolute necessity for keeping any sighthound. They are highly independent and will range far and wide without containment, with little regard for road traffic. For off-lead exercise, a borzoi needs a very large field or park, either fully fenced or well away from any roads, to ensure its safety.

Borzoi are born with specialized coursing skills, but these are quite different from the dog-fighting instincts seen in some breeds. It is quite common for borzoi at play to course (run down) another dog, seize it by the neck and hold it immobile. Young pups do this with their littermates, trading off as to who is the prey. It is a specific hunting behavior, not a fighting or territorial domination behavior.

Borzoi can be raised very successfully to live with cats and other small animals provided they are introduced to them at a young age. Some, however, will possess the hunting instinct to such a degree that they find it impossible not to chase a cat that is moving quickly. The hunting instinct is triggered by movement and much depends on how the cat behaves.

Health

Life expectancy is 7 to 10 years. Exceptional individuals have lived to be more than 14 years of age. Dogs that are physically fit and vigorous in their youth through middle age are more vigorous and healthy as elderly dogs, all other factors being equal. In the UK various cancers, followed by cardiac problems, seem to be the most frequent causes of premature death [8].

Like its native relative the Hortaya Borzaya, the borzoi is basically a very sound breed. OCD, hip and elbow dysplasia have remained almost unknown, as were congenital eye and heart diseases before the 1970s. However, in some countries modern breeding practices have introduced a few problems.

As with other very deep-chested breeds, gastric torsion is the most common serious health problem in the borzoi. Also known as bloat, this life-threatening condition is believed to be anatomical rather than strictly genetic in origin. Many borzoi owners recommend feeding the dog from a raised platform instead of placing the food-dish on the ground, and making sure that the dog rests quietly for several hours after eating, as the most reliable way to prevent bloat.

Less common are cardiac problems including cardiomyopathy and cardiac arrhythmia disorders. A controversy exists as to the presence of progressive retinal atrophy in the breed. A condition identified as Borzoi Retinopathy is seen in some individuals, usually active dogs, which differs from progressive retinal atrophy in several ways. First, it is unilateral, and rarely seen in animals less than 3 years of age; second, a clear cut pattern of inheritance has not been demonstrated; and finally, most affected individuals do not go blind.

Correct nutrition during puppyhood is also debatable for borzoi. These dogs naturally experience enormous growth surges in the first year or two of their lives. It is now widely accepted that forcing even faster growth by feeding a highly concentrated, high-energy diet is dangerous for skeletal development, causing unsoundness and increased tendency to joint problems and injury. Being built primarily for speed, borzoi do not carry large amounts of body fat or muscle, and therefore have a rather different physiology to other dogs of similar size (such as the Newfoundland, St. Bernard or Alaskan Malamute). Laboratory-formulated diets designed for a generic "large" or "giant" breed are unlikely to take the needs of the big sighthounds into account.

The issues involved in raw feeding may be particularly relevant to tall, streamlined breeds such as the borzoi. It is interesting to note that the Hortaya Borzaya, undoubtedly a very close relative, is traditionally raised on a meager diet of oats and table scraps. The Hortaya is also said to be intolerant of highly concentrated kibble feeds. Basically, a lean body weight in itself is nothing to be concerned about, and force-feeding of healthy young borzoi is definitely not recommended.

History

It was long thought that Saluki type sighthounds were originally brought to Russia from Byzantium in the South about the 9th and 10th centuries and again later by the Mongol invaders from the East. However, now that the archeological archives and research results of the former USSR are open to scientists, it has become quite clear that the primal sighthound type evolved between the Kyrgyzstan, the lower Kazakhstan part of Altai and the Afghan plains, and that the earliest actual sighthound breeds were the plains Afghan hounds and the Kyrgyz Taigan.

These ancient breeds then migrated South (founding the Tazi/Saluki branch) and West (founding the Stepnaya, Krimskaya and Hortaya branches) to develop into breeds adapted to those regions. This was a slow process which happened naturally through normal spreading of trade, with the silk and spice trade via the Silk Road being the prime vector.

The more modern Psovaya Borzaya was founded on Stepnaya, Hortaya and the Ukrainian-Polish version of the old Hort. There were also imports of Western sighthound breeds to add to the height and weight. It was crossed as well with the Russian Laika specifically and singularly to add resistance against Northern cold and a longer and thicker coat than the Southern sighthounds were equipped with.

All of these foundation types - Tazi, Hortaya, Stepnaya, Krimskaya and Hort - already possessed the instincts and agility necessary for hunting and bringing down wolves.

The Psovoi was popular with the Tsars before the 1917 revolution. For centuries, Psovoi could not be purchased but only given as gifts from the Tsar. The most famous breeder was Grand Duke Nicholas Nicolaievich of Russia, who bred countless Psovoi at Perchino, his private estate.

The Russian concept of hunting trials was instituted during the era of the Tsars. As well as providing exciting sport, the tests were used for selecting borzoi breeding stock; only the quickest and most intelligent hunting dogs went on to produce progeny. For the aristocracy these trials were a well-organized ceremony, sometimes going on for days, with the borzoi accompanied by mounted hunters and Foxhounds on the Russian steppe. Hares and other small game were by far the most numerous kills, but the hunters especially loved to test their dogs on wolf. If a wolf was sighted, the hunter would release a team of two or three borzoi. The dogs would pursue the wolf, attack its neck from both sides, and hold it until the hunter arrived. The classic kill was by the human hunter with a knife. Wolf trials are still a regular part of the hunting diploma for all Russian sightdog breeds of the relevant type, either singly or in pairs or trios, in their native country.

In the 1917 Revolution, large numbers of native Psovoi were destroyed by the revolutionaries. The Tsars had turned them into a symbol of affluence and tyranny, and they were not welcomed into the new world of the Soviet Union. Some noblemen took it upon themselves to shoot their own dogs rather than allow them to fall into the hands of militants. However, the Psovoi survived along with the other borzaya variants in the Russian countryside.

In the late 1940s a Soviet soldier named Constantin Esmont made detailed records of the various types of borzoi dogs he found in the Cossack villages. Esmont's amazing pictures were recently published and can be viewed by clicking on the link below.

Esmont was concerned that the distinct types of borzaya were in danger of degenerating without a controlled system of breeding. He convinced the Soviet government that borzoi were a valuable asset to the hunters who supported the fur industry and henceforth, their breeding was officially regulated. To this day short-haired Hortaya Borzaya are highly valued hunting dogs on the steppes, while the long-haired Psovaya Borzaya, still carrying some of the stigma of its association with the old White Russia, has become more common as a decorative companion.

Exports of borzoi to other countries were extremely rare during the Soviet era. However enough had been taken to England, Scandinavia, Western Europe and America in the late 19th century for the breed to establish itself outside its native country.

Art

In 2004, the UK Kennel Club held its 4th temporary exhibition entitled 'The Borzoi in Art'. The exhibition offered a unique insight into the borzoi and how the breed has been depicted in art throughout the 19th and 20th Centuries. The exhibition included paintings, bronzes and porcelain which had previously never before been available for the public viewing. The exhibition ran from September 27 to December 3. The borzoi may frequently be found in art deco period works.

Famous borzoi

- The borzoi is the symbol of Alfred A. Knopf publishing house.
- *Tasha*, a female borzoi belonging to the noted vet Buster Lloyd-Jones (founder of Denes natural pet foods), was born in the UK during the Second World War and is the pedigree ancestor of most British borzoi bloodlines.
- *Ben* was the white male borzoi, beloved of E.J. Smith, Captain of the Titanic. There exists a photo of the Captain and his dog outside his cabin on the ship. The Dog was not however on the maiden voyage.
- *Kolchak* Has been the mascot of the 27th Infantry Regiment since the Regiment participated in the Siberia Campaign. The 27th Infantry has been nicknamed 'The Wolfhounds' in recognition of their endurance during battles in Siberia.

In popular culture

- "Mademoiselle Nobs" from Pink Floyd: Live at Pompeii who "sings" a song with the band.
- The book *War and Peace* contains a wolf hunting scene with borzois in book 7, chapters 3 to 6.
- The 1968 film version *War and Peace* contains a hunting scene with borzoi from the kennel of Ekhaga, Sweden.
- The 1999 film, *Onegin* has a couple of scenes with borzoi in a Russian landowner's country mansion a) being led through snowy inner courtyard by one of the servants b) lounging next to enormous hearth/ fireplace next to their master.
- Uncle Zeke starred as "Digger" in the 2000 Disney film, *102 Dalmatians*
- The borzoi brothers, Rocket, Missile, and Jet in *Ginga Densetsu Weed*
- Boris in Walt Disney's film *Lady and the Tramp*
- D'or's Prince Igor owned by Barbara Todd (Zcerlov) and bred by Andre Legere appears in the film, *Hello Dolly!*
- Lyndell Ackerman's "Nessie" CH Windyglens Finesse in the TV show *Wings*.
- Borzoi can also been seen in cameo roles in the films *Love at First Bite*, *Legends of the Fall* ("Notchee Boy")[9], *Excalibur*, *Bride of Frankenstein*, *Easter Parade*, *Wolfen*, *Ziegfeld Follies*, *Gangs of New York* (2002), *Chaplin*, *The Avengers* (TV series), *JAG*, *Maverick* (1994), *Sleepy*

Hollow, *Last Action Hero*, and *A Knights Tale* (on the DVD deleted scenes).

- In the book *Dark Symphony* by Christine Feehan, Byron gives his lifemate, Antonietta, a black borzoi named "Celt".
- In an SCTV parody commercial for fictional Poochare dog food, a borzoi dog is seen being taken for a walk by Eugene Levy.

References

- *The Borzoi Handbook* Winifred E. Chadwick. London: Nicholson & Watson 1952. Including a translation of *The Perchino Hunt By His Excellency Dmitri Walzoff (1912).*
- http://ru.wiktionary.org/wiki/%D0%B1%D0%BE%D1%80%D0%B7%D1%8B%D0%B9

External links

- Borzoi Russia [10]
- Borzoi Canada [11]
- Borzoi Club of America, inc. [12]
- A collection of historical articles on the Borzoi breed, some dating as far back as 1891 [13]
- some breed history: standards/description, hunting, coursing etc [14]
- Constantin Esmont and his historic photographs [15]
- Article: The Borzoi Coat [16]
- Article: The Modern Borzoi [17]
- Historical artistic and cultural album dedicated to the Borzoi. English, German and French language [18]
- Information including Breeders, Shows, Studdogs [19]

Cirneco dell'Etna

Cirneco dell'Etna

A male Cirneco dell'Etna	
Nicknames	Cirneco
Country of origin	Sicily, Italy

Traits	

Classification and standards		
FCI	Group 5 Section 7 #199	standard [1]
AKC	Hound (FSS)	[? standard]
	The AKC Foundation Stock Service [3] (FSS) is an optional recording service for purebred dogs that are not yet eligible for AKC registration.	
KC (UK)	Hound	standard [2]

Notes	
The UK K.C. currently only carries an Interim breed standard. (as of December 2007)	
Dog (Canis lupus familiaris)	

The **Cirneco dell'Etna** (plural *Cirnechi*) is a small breed of dog originally from Sicily. This hound was historically used to hunt rabbits and can work for hours without food or water. The breed also has a keen sense of smell and is primarily built for endurance over harsh terrain such as that of Mount Etna. It is the smallest of the Mediterranean island hunting hounds, the others being the Pharaoh Hounds and Ibizan Hounds. Cirnechi were believed, most likely correctly, to have been brought to Sicily over 3000 years ago by the Phoenician traders.

Today they are increasingly kept for the sport of conformation showing and as pets, due to their low coat maintenance and friendly nature, although as an active hound they do need regular exercise. A Cirneco should measure from 43-51 cm (17-20in) and weigh between 10–12 kg (22-26lb). As with other breeds, those from hunting stock can lie outside these ranges.

External links

- The Cirneco dell'Etna Club of America [3]
- The Cirneco dell'Etna Club of United Kingdom [4]
- Cirneco dell'Etna UK breeder [5]
- Cirneco dell'Etna UK owners [6]
- Cirneco dell'Etna United Kingdom Breed Club [7]
- Cirneco dell'Etna information [8]
- Official gun dog, scent hound, field trial description [9]

Dachshund

Dachshund

A red, short-haired, standard-sized dachshund	
Nicknames	Doxie (US), Dackel or Teckel (GER, FR), wiener dog/hotdog (US), sausage dog (UK/US/AUS/NZ), Worshond, Weenie Dog (US) (S.A.), Bassotto (ITA)
Country of origin	Germany

Traits	
Litter size	4-8
Life span	12-16

Classification and standards		
FCI	Group Section 1 #148	standard [1]
AKC	Hound	standard [2]
ANKC	Group 4 – (Hounds)	[miniature wire-haired [3] standard]
NZKC	{{{nzkcgroup}}}	[long-haired [4] smooth-haired [5] wire-haired [6] miniature long-haired [7] miniature smooth-haired [8] miniature wire-haired [9] standard]
UKC	Scenthound Breeds	standard [10]

Dog (*Canis lupus familiaris*)		

The **dachshund** is a short-legged, elongated dog breed, of the hound family. The standard size was developed to scent, chase, and flush badgers and other burrow-dwelling animals, while the miniature was developed to hunt smaller prey, like rabbits. In the American West, they have also been used to hunt prairie dogs.

The name "dachshund" is of German origin and literally means "badger dog", from *Dachs* ("badger") and *Hund* ("dog"). The pronunciation varies widely in English: variations of the first syllable include , and of the second syllable . In German it is pronounced []. Because of their long, narrow build, they are sometimes nicknamed **hot dog dog**, **wiener dog** or **sausage dog**. Although "dachshund" is a German word, in modern German they are also commonly known by the name *Dackel*; in the case of the formally certified hunting and tracking rank, the name *Teckel* is used.

While classified in the hound group or scent hound group in the United States and Great Britain, there are some who consider this classification to be arguable, speculating that it arose from the fact that the word *Hund* is similar to the English word *hound* – and the word "Dachshund" has even been anglicized as "Dash Hound". Many dachshunds, especially the wire-haired subtype, may exhibit behavior and appearance that are similar to that of the terrier group of dogs. An argument can be made for the scent (or hound) group classification because the breed was developed to utilize scent to trail and hunt animals, and probably descended from scent hounds, such as bloodhounds, pointers, Basset Hounds, or even Bruno Jura Hounds; but with the dogged and persistent personality and love for digging that probably developed from the terrier, it can also be argued that they could belong in the terrier, or "earth dog", group. In the Fédération Cynologique Internationale (World Canine Federation), or FCI, the dachshund is actually in its own group, Group 4, which is the dachshund group. Part of the controversy is because the dachshund is the only certifiable breed of dog to hunt both above and below ground.

Characteristics

Appearance

The typical dachshund is long-bodied and muscular, with short and stubby legs. Its paws are unusually large and paddle-shaped, for efficient digging. It has skin that is loose enough not to tear while tunneling in tight burrows to chase prey. The dachshund has a deep chest to allow enough lung capacity to keep going when hunting. Its snout is long with an increased nose area that absorbs odors.

There are three types, classified by their coats: short-haired, called "smooth"; long-haired; and wire-haired.

Size

Dachshunds come in three sizes: standard, miniature, and *kaninchen*, which means *rabbit*. Although the standard and miniature sizes are recognized almost universally, the rabbit size is not recognized by clubs in the United States and the United Kingdom, but is recognized by all of the clubs within the Fédération Cynologique Internationale (World Canine Federation) (FCI), which contain kennel clubs from 83 countries all over the world..

A full-grown standard dachshund averages to , while the miniature variety normally weighs less than . The kaninchen weighs to . According to kennel club standards, the miniature (and kaninchen, where recognized) differs from the full-size only by size and weight, thus offspring from miniature parents must never weigh more than the miniature standard to be considered a miniature as well. While many kennel club size divisions use weight for classification, such as the American Kennel Club, other kennel club standards determine the difference between the miniature and standard by chest circumference; some kennel clubs, such as in Germany, even measure chest circumference in addition to height and weight.

H. L. Mencken said that "A dachshund is a half-dog high and a dog-and-a-half long," although they have been referred to as "two dogs long". This characteristic has led them to be quite a recognizable breed, and they are featured in many a joke and cartoon, particularly *The Far Side* by Gary Larson.

Coat and color

Dachshunds exhibit three coat varieties: smooth coat (short hair), long hair, and wire-hair. Wirehaired is the least commonly seen coat in the US (it is the most common in Germany) and the most recent coat to appear in breeding standards.

Dachshunds have a wide variety of colors and patterns. They can be single-colored, single-colored with spots ("dappled"-called "merle" in other dog breeds), and single-colored with tan points plus any pattern. Dachshunds also come in piebald. The piebald has a white background with various shades of brown. The dominant color is red, the most common along with black and tan. Isabella is a silver/gray all over color with light translucent brown points or no distinct points at all. Two-colored dogs can be black, wild boar, chocolate, fawn, with tan "points", or markings over the eyes, ears, paws, and tail, of tan or cream. A two-colored dachshund would be called by its dominant color first followed by the point color, such as "black and tan" or "chocolate and cream". Other patterns include piebald, in which a white pattern is imposed upon the base color or any other pattern, and a lighter "boar" red. The reds range from coppers to deep rusts, with or without somewhat common black hairs peppered along the back, tail, face, and ear edges, lending much character and an almost burnished appearance; this is referred to among breeders and enthusiasts as a "stag" or an "overlay" or "sable". True sable is a dachshund with each single hair banded with three colors: light at the base of the hair, red in the middle, black at the end. An additional, striking coat marking is the brindle pattern. "Brindle" refers to dark stripes over a solid background, usually red; if a dachshund is brindled on a dark coat and has tan points, you will see brindling on the tan points only. Even one single, lone stripe of brindle is brindle. If a dachshund has one single spot of dapple, it is a dapple.

Solid black and solid chocolate dachshunds occur and, even though dogs with such coloration are often considered handsome, the colors are nonstandard, that is, the dogs are frowned upon in the conformation ring in the US and Canada. Chocolate is commonly confused with dilute red. Additionally, according to the conformation judges of the Dachshund Club of America (DCA) and the American Kennel Club (AKC) the piebald pattern is nonstandard. However, the piebald dachshund can still be shown; the only disqualifying fault in Dachshunds is knuckling over. While some judges choose to dismiss a dog of color, many choose to judge them and those who are actually judging the dog will look past the cosmetic color of a dog and judge the conformation of the dog first. There were several piebald dachshunds that became AKC Champions in 2008. All things being equal between the dogs in the ring, the traditional colors which are listed in the Official AKC Standard (governed by DCA) should be visibly listed.

Light-colored dachshunds can sport amber, light brown, or green eyes; however, kennel club standards state that the darker the eye color, the better. They can also have eyes of two different colors; however, this is only found in dapple and double dapple dachshunds. Dachshunds can have a blue and a brown eye. Blue eyes, partially blue eyes, or a blue eye and a brown eye are called "wall" coloring, and are considered a non-desirable trait in kennel club standards. Dappled eyes are also possible. The standard was changed by the DCA in 2007 to exclude the wording double-dapple from the standard and strictly use the wording dapple. The reason is that the double dapple gene is linked to blindness and deafness. Wall-eye is permissible. Piebald-patterned dachshunds will never have blue in their eyes, unless the dapple pattern is present.

Breeders may also breed a piebald dapple brindle; and though these are increasing popularity due to their unique markings, they are not considered standard and are not allowed to show.

Temperament

Dachshunds are playful, but can be stubborn, and are known for their propensity for chasing small animals, birds, and tennis balls with great determination and ferocity. Many dachshunds are stubborn, making them a challenge to train. Several quotes have been recorded regarding the training of dachshunds; one is from E. B. White:

> "Being the owner of dachshunds, to me a book on dog discipline becomes a volume of inspired humor. Every sentence is a riot. Some day, if I ever get a chance, I shall write a book, or warning, on the character and temperament of the dachshund and why he can't be trained and shouldn't be. I would rather train a striped zebra to balance an Indian club than induce a dachshund to heed my slightest command. When I address Fred I never have to raise either my voice or my hopes. He even disobeys me when I instruct him in something he wants to do."

They have a loud bark and without proper training they can become nuisance barkers. Dachshunds are known for their devotion and loyalty to their owners, though they can be standoffish towards strangers. If left alone, many dachshunds will whine until they have companionship. Like many dogs if left alone too frequently, some dachshunds are prone to separation anxiety and may chew objects in the house to relieve stress. They rank 49th in Stanley Coren's *Intelligence of Dogs*, being of average working and obedience intelligence.

Dachshunds can be difficult to housebreak, and patience and consistency is often needed in this endeavor.

According to the American Kennel Club's breed standards, "the dachshund is clever, lively and courageous to the point of rashness, persevering in above and below ground work, with all the senses well-developed. Any display of shyness is a serious fault." Their temperament and body language give the impression that they do not know or care about their relatively small size. Like many small hunting dogs, they will challenge a larger dog. Indulged dachshunds may become snappy or extremely obstinate.

Many dachshunds do not like unfamiliar people, and many will growl or bark at them. Although the dachshund is generally an energetic dog, some are sedate. This dog's behavior is such that it is not the dog for everyone. A bored, untrained dachshund will become destructive. If raised improperly and not socialized at a young age, dachshunds can become aggressive or fearful. They require a caring owner who understands their need for entertainment and exercise.

Dachshunds may not be the best pets for small children. Like any dog, dachshunds need a proper introduction at a young age. Well trained Dachshunds and well behaved children usually get along fine. Otherwise, they may be aggressive and bite an unfamiliar child, especially one that moves quickly around them or teases them. However, many Dachshunds are very tolerant and loyal to children within their family, but these children should be mindful of the vulnerability of the breed's back and not carry them around roughly.

A 2008 University of Pennsylvania study of 6,000 dog owners who were interviewed indicated that dogs of smaller breeds were more likely to be "genetically predisposed towards aggressive behaviour". Dachshunds were rated the most aggressive, with 20% having bitten strangers, as well as high rates of attacks on other dogs and their owners. The study noted that attacks by small dogs were unlikely to cause serious injuries and because of this were probably under-reported.

Health

The breed is known to have spinal problems, especially intervertebral disk disease (IVDD), due in part to an extremely long spinal column and short rib cage. The risk of injury may be worsened by obesity, jumping, rough handling, or intense exercise, which place greater strain on the vertebrae.

Treatment consists of combinations of crate confinement and courses of anti-inflammatory medications (steroids and non-steroidal anti-inflammatory drugs like carprofen and meloxicam), or chronic pain medications, like tramadol. Serious cases may require surgery to remove the troublesome disk contents. A dog may need the aid of a cart to get around if paralysis occurs.

A new minimally invasive procedure called "percutaneous laser disk ablation" has been developed at the Oklahoma State University Veterinary Hospital. Originally, the procedure was used in clinical trials only on dachshunds that had suffered previous back incidents. Since dachshunds are prone to back issues, the goal is to expand this treatment to dogs in a normal population.

In addition to back problems, the breed is also prone to patellar luxation which is where the kneecap can become dislodged.

In some double dapples, there are varying degrees of vision and hearing loss, including reduced or absent eyes. Not all double dapples have problems with their eyes and/or ears, which may include degrees of hearing loss, full deafness, malformed ears, congenital eye defects, reduced or absent eyes, partial or full blindness, or varying degrees of both vision and hearing problems; but heightened problems can occur due to the genetic process in which two dapple genes cross, particularly in certain breeding lines. Dapple genes, which are dominant genes, are considered "dilution" genes, meaning whatever color the dog would have originally carried is lightened, or diluted, randomly; two dominant "dilution" genes can cancel each other out, or "cross", removing all color and producing a white recessive gene, essentially a white mutation. When this happens genetically within the eyes or ears, this white mutation can be lethal to their development, causing hearing or vision problems.

Other dachshund health problems include hereditary epilepsy, granulomatous meningoencephalitis, dental issues, Cushing's syndrome, thyroid problems, various allergies and atopies, and various eye conditions including cataracts, glaucoma, progressive retinal atrophy, corneal ulcers, nonucerative corneal disease, sudden acquired retinal degeneration, and cherry eye. Since the occurrence and severity of these health problems is largely hereditary, breeders are working to eliminate these characteristics.

History

Some writers and dachshund experts have theorized that the early roots of the dachshund go back to ancient Egypt, where engravings were made featuring short-legged hunting dogs. Recent discoveries by the American University in Cairo of mummified dachshund-like dogs from ancient Egyptian burial urns may lend credibility to this theory. In its modern incarnation, the dachshund is a creation of German breeders and includes elements of German, French, and English hounds and terriers. Dachshunds have been kept by royal courts all over Europe, including that of Queen Victoria, who was particularly enamored of the breed. They were originally bred for hunting badgers by trailing scent.

The first verifiable references to the dachshund, originally named the "**Dachs Kriecher**" ("badger crawler") or "**Dachs Krieger**" ("badger warrior"), came from books written in the early 1700s. Prior to that, there exist references to "badger dogs" and "hole dogs", but these likely refer to purposes rather than to specific breeds. The original German dachshunds were larger than the modern full-size variety, weighing between , and originally came in straight-legged and crook-legged varieties (the modern dachshund is descended from the latter). Though the breed is famous for its use in exterminating badgers and badger-baiting, dachshunds were also commonly used for rabbit and fox hunting, for locating wounded deer, and in packs were known to hunt game as large as wild boar and as fierce as the wolverine.

There are huge differences of opinion as to when dachshunds were specifically bred for their purpose of badger hunting, as the American Kennel Club states the dachshund was bred in the 15th century, while the Dachshund Club of America states that foresters bred the dogs in the 18th or 19th century.

Double-dapple dachshunds, which are prone to eye disease, blindness, or hearing problems, are generally believed to have been introduced to the United States between 1879 and 1885.

The flap-down ears and famous curved tail of the dachshund have deliberately been bred into the dog. In the case of the ears, this is so that grass seeds, dirt, and other matter do not enter the ear canal. The curved tail is dual-purposed: to be seen more easily in long grass and, in the case of burrowing dachshunds, to help haul the dog out if it becomes stuck in a burrow. The smooth-haired dachshund, the oldest style, may be a cross between the German Shorthaired Pointer, a Pinscher, and a Bracke (a type of bloodhound), or to have been produced by crossing a short Bruno Jura Hound with a pinscher. Others believe it was a cross from a miniature French pointer and a pinscher; others claim that is was developed from the St. Hubert Hound, also a bloodhound, in the 1700s, and still others believe that they were descended from Basset Hounds, based upon their scent abilities and general appearance.

What is clear, however, is that no one seems to know for sure. According to William Loeffler, from *The American Book of the Dog (1891)*, in the chapter on Dachshunds:"The origin of the Dachshund is in doubt, our best authorities disagreeing as to the beginning of the breed." What can be agreed on, however, is that the short haired dachshund gave rise to both the long-haired and the wire-haired varieties.

There are two theories regarding how the standard longhair dachshund came about. One theory is that smooth Dachshunds would occasionally produce puppies which had slightly longer hair than their parents. By selectively breeding these animals, breeders eventually produced a dog which consistently produced longhair offspring, and the longhair dachshund was born. Another theory is that the standard longhair dachshund was developed by breeding smooth dachshunds with various land and water spaniels. The long-haired dachshund may be a cross among any of the small dog breeds in the spaniel group, including the German Stoberhund, and the smooth-haired dachshund.

The wire-haired dachshund, the last to develop, was created in late nineteenth century. There is a possibility the wire-haired dachshund was a cross between the smooth dachshund and various hard-coated terriers and wire-haired pinschers, such as the Schnauzer, the Dandie Dinmont Terrier, the German Wirehaired Pointer, or perhaps the Scottish Terrier.

Symbol of Germany

Dachshunds have traditionally been viewed as a symbol of Germany. Political cartoonists commonly used the image of the dachshund to ridicule Germany. During World War I the dachshunds' popularity in the United States plummeted because of this association and there are even anecdotes such as a Dachshund being stoned to death on the high street of Berkhamsted, England at this time because of its association with the enemy. As a result they were often called "liberty hounds" by their owners similar to "liberty cabbage" becoming a term for sauerkraut. The stigma of the association was revived to a lesser extent during World War II, though it was comparatively short-lived. German Field Marshal Erwin Rommel was known for keeping dachshunds.

Due to the association of the breed with Germany, the dachshund was chosen to be the first official mascot for the 1972 Summer Olympics in Munich, with the name Waldi.

Sports

Some people train and enter their dachshund to compete in dachshund racing, such as the Wiener Nationals. Several races across the United States routinely draw several thousand attendees, including races in Buda, Texas; Davis, California; Phoenix, Arizona; Los Alamitos, California; Findlay, Ohio; Milwaukee, Wisconsin; Oklahoma City, Oklahoma; Kansas City, Kansas; Palo Alto, California; and Shakopee, Minnesota. There is also an annual dachshund run in Kennywood, located in Pittsburgh, Pennsylvania, called the Wiener 100, and in Huntington, West Virginia called the Dachshund Dash.

Despite the popularity of these events, the Dachshund Club of America opposes "wiener racing", as many greyhound tracks use the events to draw large crowds to their facilities. The DCA is also worried about potential injuries to dogs, due to their predisposition to back injuries. Another favorite sport is earthdog trials, in which dachshunds enter tunnels with dead ends and obstacles attempting to locate an artificial bait or live but caged and protected rats.

Dackel versus *Teckel*

In Germany, dachshunds are widely called *Dackel* (both singular and plural). To be classified as a full *Teckel*, these dogs must undergo blood tracking tests. Classically, any dog of *Dackel* heritage is given an official tattoo upon one ear. After suitable training, the dog must then follow a blood trail that is at least 48 hours old successfully to its conclusion. Once this is completed, another tattoo is marked on the other ear to denote full *Teckel* rank. *Teckel*, whether tattooed or not, are bred for hunting purposes, and they tend to be visibly larger in their chests than their *Dackel* counterparts, though marginally shorter in length.

Popularity

Dachshunds are one of the most popular pets in the United States, ranking seventh in the 2008 AKC registration statistics. They are popular with urban and apartment dwellers, ranking among the top ten most popular breeds in 76 of 190 major US cities surveyed by the AKC. One will find varying degrees of organized local dachshund clubs in most major American cities, including New York, New Orleans, Los Angeles, and Chicago. The breed is popular in Germany, Austria, France, Switzerland, Hungary, Poland, the Czech Republic, Slovakia, Argentina, Chile, Brazil, Canada, Guatemala, Finland and Japan.

Famous Dachshunds and owners

- Rodolfo Cebolinha was the star of publicity campaign Cofap (a Brazilian company in the automotive parts) in the 90's. This Dachshund turned the name Cofap into a synonym of the breed, in Brazil.
- William Randolph Hearst was an avid lover of dachshunds. When his own dachshund Helena died, he eulogized her in his "In The News" column.
- Fred, E.B. White's dachshund, appeared in many of his famous essays.
- Lump, the pet of Pablo Picasso, who was thought to have inspired some of his artwork. (Pronounced: loomp; German for "Rascal") Picasso & Lump: A Dachshund's Odyssey tells the story of Picasso and Lump.
- Kevin Smith has a dachshund named Shecky.
- Jack Ruby, the killer of Lee Harvey Oswald, had a dachshund named Sheba, which he often referred to as his wife. At the time he committed his infamous murder, he had four of them—although he once had as many as ten.
- Andy Warhol had a pair of dachshunds, Archie and Amos, whom he depicted in his paintings and mentioned frequently in his diaries.
- Stanley and Boodgie, immortalized on canvas by owner David Hockney, and published in the book *David Hockney's Dog Days*.
- Wadl and Hexl, Kaiser Wilhelm II's famous ferocious pair. Upon arriving at Archduke Franz Ferdinand's country seat, château Konopiště, on a semi-official visit, they promptly proceeded to do away with one of the Austro-Hungarian heir presumptive's priceless golden pheasants, thereby almost causing an international incident.
- Senta, Kaiser Wilhelm II's companion during World War I and his exile to Huis Doorn. Senta died in 1927 at age 20 and is buried in the park of Huis Doorn, near the Kaiser's grave.
- Joe, owned by General Claire Lee Chennault and the mascot of Chennault's Flying Tigers of World War II.
- Queen Margrethe II of Denmark and her husband own and have owned a large array of dachshunds, both smooth- and wirehaired.
- Harry Mulisch, one of the three famous Dutch postwar writers, owns a dachshund. He once said his dog is more intelligent than a lot of people.
- Japanese singer Namie Amuro owns two Miniature Long-haired Dachshund, named Koto and Gat-chan.
- Belle Constantine Chappy, [Katakana: ベルコンスタンティンチャピー], nicknamed Belle, was the name of the long-haired miniature Dachshund owned by Japanese artist Gackt.
- Former Secretary of Defense Donald Rumsfeld was asked, in 2003, whether he has duct tape, plastic sheeting, and a three-day supply of bottled water at home. He replied, "I would like to say I did. I don't believe we do. But I do have a miniature dachshund named Reggie who looks out for us."
- Jepha Howard from *The Used* has a Long Haired Miniature named Zelda

- In Zelenogorsk, Russia, is a Dachshund monument near which passes a parade of Dachshunds on City Day, July 25.
- Late British reality television star Jade Goody owned a short-haired miniature Dachshund aptly named 'Batman'.

Dachshunds in fiction

- A collection of Gary Larson's *Far Side* cartoons was published in the 1990 book *Wiener Dog Art*. A special section was inserted that chronicled the presence and influence of dachshunds throughout the history of art.
- Dack in Vladimir Nabokov's Ada
- Howie in the Bunnicula books
- Hot Dog in *Krypto the Superdog*
- Schatzi (German for "little treasure") in *That '70s Show*
- Itchy Itchiford in *All Dogs Go to Heaven*
- Boots in *Emergency!*
- Dennis the Dachshund, a German sausage dog in the BBC's Children's Hour radio serial Toy Town, a scheming ne'er do well who spoke English with a German accent.
- Little Dog in *2 Stupid Dogs*
- Slinky in *Toy Story*, *Toy Story 2* and *Toy Story 3*
- Buster in *Toy Story 2* and *Toy Story 3*
- Wiener Dog, the name of Norm Henderson's dachshund on *The Norm Show*
- Mr. Weenie in *Open Season* and *Open Season 2*
- Jorge in *Clifford's Puppy Days*
- Pretzel in *Pretzel* by H.A. and Margret Rey
- Hundley in *Curious George* by H.A. and Margaret Rey
- Weenie, the pet of Oswald the Octopus in *Oswald*
- Oscar, in the comic strip *Liberty Meadows*.
- Schnitzel von Krumm, in the *Hairy Maclary* series of children's picture books by Lynley Dodd.
- Danke and her three puppies Wilhelmina, Chloe, and Heidi in *The Ugly Dachshund*
- Willie from the books by Ezra Jack Keats
- Oliver in the anime series *Ginga: Nagareboshi Gin*
- Bodo in Hausmeister Krause (a German sitcom)
- Origami in *Raising Helen*
- Fritz in *National Lampoon's Van Wilder: The Rise of Taj*
- The children's book *The Hallo-Wiener* by Dav Pilkey
- Rufus "The Red" (of Morehead, Kentucky). Credited for saving 4 children from a burning daycare in Kentucky. Has appeared on many talk shows.

- In the early Mickey Mouse comics, Mickey had a dachshund named Weenie.
- When Cap Toys resurrected Stretch Armstrong in the 1990s, they also created Stretch's dog, a dachshund named Fetch Armstrong.
- Shadow and Duke from the Shadow Adventures by Mavis Duke Hinton.
- Petey from *Searching For A Starry Night* by Christine Verstraete.
- Schultzie from *Lady and the Tramp* trying to tunnel out the Dog Pound while the dog quartet sings.
- Cheerio from *Hank Zipzer*
- Wally, the dachshund in the *Drabble* comic
- Blitzkrieg (lightning war), a mean dachshund from The Suite Life of Zack & Cody that belongs to Mr. Moseby's business rival.
- Marv's dog Sizzles on the children's TV show *Charlie and Lola*.
- In the film comedy *Mon Oncle* a dachshund unwittingly locks his owners in the garage.
- In the comedy *Hitch*, Will Smith uses a red, long-haired dachshund to lure a pet of a woman, a smooth tan dachshund, into the street, so his client will look like a hero and meet the girl.
- Marty in *Kenny the Shark*.
- In the film *Bolt*, a dachshund asks if Bolt wants to sniff first his back when he arrives in New York.
- Zero (the ghost dog of Jack Skellington) in the movie *Nightmare Before Christmas*.
- Dinah the Dachshund

See also

- Badger-baiting
- Nintendogs: Dachshund and Friends

Further reading

- Dachshund Breed Standard [11] Russian Kennel Club 13.03.2001
- Dachshund Breed Standard [12] Poland Kennel Club 09.05.2001
- Dachshund Breed Standard [13] American Kennel Club

External links

- Dachshund [14] at the Open Directory Project
- Dachshund Club of America, Inc. [15]

Drever

Drever

Drever	
Other names	Swedish Dachsbracke
Country of origin	Sweden
Traits	
Classification and standards	
FCI Group 6:Scenthounds Section 1.3:Small-sized Hounds #130	standard [1]
CKC Canadian Kennel Club Group 2	standard [2]
UKC Scenthound	standard [3]
Dog (*Canis lupus familiaris*)	

The **Drever** (Swedish Dachsbracke) is a breed of dog, a short-legged scenthound from Sweden used for hunting deer and other game. The Drever is descended from the Westphalian Dachsbracke, a type of German hound called *Bracke*. The breed name Drever was chosen through a contest in 1947.

Appearance

The Drever's most noticeable characteristic are its long body and short legs, inherited from the Westphalian Dachsbracke, but as a working dog these features are not exaggerated. It has short fur, and is of any color with white markings (but not all white, which has been linked to deafness.) The breed has the typical drop (hanging) ears of a hound, and a long tail. The maximum height of a Drever is 38 cm (15 ins) at the withers, which is about 15 cm (approx. 6 ins) shorter than a long legged hunting hound with the same size body. The Westphalian Dachsbracke is about 2 cm (less than an inch) shorter than the Drever.

Hunting

Most breeds with similar physical traits are bred for a single purpose, but the Drever has been bred to hunt all sizes of game, both hares and roe deer, and is also used to hunt fox and red deer. The Drever has a lot of stamina, and has become a popular hunting hound for deer hunters in northern Norway, Sweden, and Finland (in Finland drevers are not allowed in deer hunting yet, but it is used for hare and fox hunting). Roe deer are nervous quarry, and the hounds which are used to hunt them must move slowly, especially in areas where heavy snow can be expected in late autumn. This is given as the reason for breeding of a dog with a medium-sized body but short legs.

The Drever in Sweden is usually kept as a hunting hound and is not usually found as a pet.

History and recognition

The Drever is a Swedish breed originating with the Westphalian Dachsbracke (a small hound for tracking deer), brought from Germany to Sweden around 1910, and crossbred with other hounds to adjust "to Swedish terrain and game." By the 1940s there were two distinctive sizes of the Dachsbracke, and a newspaper contest was held in 1947 to choose the new name for the slightly larger variety; *Drever* was chosen, from the Swedish word *drev*, referring to a type of hunt where the dogs drive the game towards the hunter. The Drever was then recognised by the Swedish Kennel Club as a separate breed in 1947. The breed is recognised internationally by the Fédération Cynologique Internationale, in Group 6 *Scenthounds and related breeds*, Section 1.3, *Small-sized Hounds*.

The Drever was recognized by the Canadian Kennel Club in 1956 in the Hound Group, and in 1996 by the United Kennel Club in its Scenthound Group. The breed is also recognized by a long list of minor registries, rare breed groups, hunting clubs, and internet registry businesses, and is promoted in North America as a rare breed pet. It is not currently recognized by The Kennel Club (UK), the Australian National Kennel Council or the New Zealand Kennel Club, or the American Kennel Club.

Health

Specific health problems or claims of extraordinary health have not been documented for this breed. According to the breed standard, the Drever should be alert and self-possessed, with an affable, even temperament, and should not be aggressive or shy.

See also

- Westphalian Dachsbracke and the closely related Deutsche Bracke
- Dachshund a short legged Bracke
- Hunting dog
- Hound

External links

- Drever information on Canada Dogs [4]
- The Swedish Drever Club (in Swedish) [5]
- The Finnish Drever Club (in Finnish) [6]
- Drever [7] at the Open Directory Project

English Foxhound

English Foxhound

Other names	Foxhound
Country of origin	Great Britain - England

Traits

Classification and standards

FCI	Group 6 Section 1 #159	standard [1]
AKC	Hounds	standard [2]
ANKC	Group 4 (Hounds)	standard [3]
CKC	Group 2 - Hounds	standard [4]
KC (UK)	Hound	standard [5]
NZKC	Hound	standard [6]
UKC	Scenthounds	standard [7]

Dog (*Canis lupus familiaris*)

The **English Foxhound** is one of the four foxhound breeds of dog. They are scent hounds, bred to hunt foxes by scent.

Description

Appearance

The English Foxhound is about 21-25 inches tall to the withers, and weighs anywhere between 65-75 pounds, although some English Foxhounds bred for the show ring can be considerably bigger, with some males weighing over 100 pounds. The skull is wide, the muzzle is long, and eyes carry a sweet expression. The legs are muscular, straight-boned, and the paws are rounded, almost cat-like.

Temperament

The English Foxhound was originally a pack hound, therefore, it gets along well with other dogs and enjoys human companionship. It gets along with horses, children, and other pets, as it is a gentle, social, and tolerant breed.

It is a very active breed that enjoys the hunt. Though it is slower than the American Foxhound, it enjoys running and will run all day with very few breaks in between.

Health and lifespan

There are very few health problems in this breed. Occasionally seen are chronic hip dysplasia, renal disease, and epilepsy. The breed's lifespan is typically 10-13 years, although British hunts would routinely put working hounds down after 6-7 years hunting.

History

The English Foxhound was created in the late 1500s, as a result of the perception of the depletion of deer in England. Nobles and Royalty had hunted deer for both food and sport, using the Deerhound or Staghound for this purpose. During the reign of Henry VIII, it was perceived that a new prey was needed, and the fox was selected. The English Foxhound was then created by a careful mixing of the Greyhound, for speed, the Fox Terrier, for hunting instinct, and the Bulldog, for tenacity in the hunt.

During the British Raj, English Foxhounds were imported to India for the purpose of jackal coursing, though due to the comparatively hotter weather, they were rarely long lived. Foxhounds were preferred for this purpose over greyhounds, as the former was not as fast, and could thus provide a longer, more sporting chase.

Studbooks for this breed were kept as early as the 1800s.

The dogs were meant to trail foxes and live around horses. They are still used for those purposes.

Exercise

The English Foxhound is a very energetic breed. It needs plenty of exercise. This breed needs area to run. If confined to a small area, the foxhound may become destructive. The apartment life is not one for the English Foxhound, but the breed can thrive in a suburban setting, given the proper exercise and attention.

Miscellaneous

The English Foxhound is the rarest breed of dog in the United States by AKC registration, with seventeen currently registered.

External links

- English Foxhound Photos [8] from DogFacts.org [9]

Finnish Spitz

Finnish Spitz

Other names	Suomenpystykorva
Country of origin	Finland

Traits

Classification and standards

FCI	Group 5 Section 2 #49	standard [1]
AKC	Non-sporting	standard [2]
ANKC	Group 4 (Hounds)	standard [3]
CKC	Group 2 - Hounds	standard [4]
KC (UK)	Hound	standard [5]
NZKC	Hounds	standard [6]
UKC	Northern Breed	standard [7]

Dog (*Canis lupus familiaris*)

A **Finnish Spitz** (Finnish language: *Suomenpystykorva*) is a breed of dog originating in Finland. The breed is thought to be an old one, bred as a hunting dog. It is a "bark pointer", indicating the position of game by barking to attract the hunter's attention. It has been used mostly to bark at game that flees into trees, such as squirrels, grouses, and capercaillies, but it serves well also to hunt moose and elk. Some individuals have been known to go after even a bear, despite the dog's small size. In its native country, the breed is still mostly used as a hunting dog, but as it is very friendly and loves children, in other countries it serves mainly as a house pet. The Finnish Spitz has been the national dog of Finland since 1979.

Descriptions

Appearance

The Finnish Spitz has a square build, meaning that the length of the body is the same, or slightly shorter than the height of the withers to the ground. It should look like a fox with a fluffier coat. The length of the body is measured from the point of the shoulder or forechest in front of the withers to the rump, giving a truly square dogs a short back. Females are usually a little longer in the back. Both dogs and females should appear slightly longer in the leg. The Finnish Spitz is a double coated breed but the outer coat should not exceed 2½ inches at the ruff. The undercoat is soft and lighter in color than the red/gold outer coat. The undercoat will shed twice a year, and if a Finnish Spitz is to be kept healthy, a good shedding of the undercoat when the dog is ready to "blow coat" is needed. Some exhibitors show dogs with undercoat that should be removed but that is the breeder, owner or handler's choice. Omission to shed undercoat is considered neglect by some judges who prefer a clean and combed coat. Dew claws can appear on front and/or back feet. If back claws appear, they should be removed by the breeder. The front dewclaws can be removed but since they are usually small, they generally are not removed. If the back dew claws are present, they look like toes. The front dew claws appear to have no purpose.

Coat

The Finnish Spitz has a typical double coat, which consists of a soft, dense undercoat and long, harsh guard hairs that can measure one to two inches long. The coat should be stiffer, denser, and longer on the neck, back, back of thighs, and plume of the tail, whilst shorter on the head and legs. Dogs should sport a slightly longer and coarser coat than the bitches, who are slightly more refined. However the plume of the tail is important to the overall look of the dog but should not be too long. Feathered long tail hairs without sustenance can give the dog an unkempt look. Additionally the tailset is important and the Finnish Spitz should be able to move its tail from one side to the other. Most Finnish Spitz have a preferred side and this is not incorrect.

Proper care of the coat is most important. The Finnish Spitz blows coat or loses its undercoat twice a year. It is imperative that owners brush out the old undercoat so the new coat can grow properly. Excessive undercoat can cause skin problems and although a dog may look fluffy and full, the undercoat may be causing serious skin problems.

In the show ring, the coat should be shown as completely natural; a brush through the coat is acceptable but no trimming is allowed, not even of whiskers. However, any excessive undercoat should be removed. Some exhibitors leave in the undercoat to make the dog's coat look bigger. However, most well trained judges see this problem. Another exception is the hair under the bottom of the feet. The hair under the feet as well as the toe nails should be nicely trimmed for show.

Color

Puppies are often described as looking similar to a red fox cub. They are born dark grey/black/brown or fawn with a vast amount of black. A fawn puppy or one with a large amount of white of the chest is not preferable. The color of the adult dog can be assessed by an experienced breeder at birth or cannot really be assessed by a novice until about four to six months, but even then the color may change. The adult color should be golden red. It can be of almost any shade, varying from pale honey to dark chestnut. There are no preferences over shades as long as the color is bright and clear with no hints of dullness, which is of most importance. The coat should never be of a solid color. It should be shaded and without any defined color changes. The coat is usually at its darkest shade on the back of the dog, gradually getting lighter around the chest and belly. The undercoat must always be lighter in color than the topcoat, but is never allowed to be white. A small patch of white, no more than 1.5 centimeters wide, is allowable on the chest, and white tips on the feet are acceptable, but not desired.

Pigmentation

The nose, lips, and rims of eyes should always be black.

Height and weight

* Height at withers

    Males, 16 to 19 inches (44–50 cm)

    Females, 14½ to 17 inches (39–45 cm)

* Weight

    Males, 47-53 lb (11–13 kg)

    Females, 40-47 lb (8–9 kg)

Temperament

Finnish Spitz are considered to interact well with people, including children. In the home, the Finnish Spitz is a happy member, playing gently with children, but may be rougher with other dogs. Some Finnish Spitz love other dogs while others are shy, passive, or aggressive around them. Left alone the Finnish Spitz will figure out if another canine is acceptable.

The breed is prone to barking at anything they perceive as being out of the ordinary. They can be trained to reduce the amount of barking, although the barking does make them good watchdogs.

Training

Because of their intelligence, Finnish Spitz are independent and strong-willed dogs and are best trained with a soft voice and touch. They will easily become bored with repetitive training. Finnish Spitz can be trained to be very obedient with a light touch and lots of positive reinforcement.

Finnish Spitz can excel in obedience, agility and rally as a companion dog.

Health

The Finnish Spitz is typically a very healthy breed, and health concerns are rare. Here is a short list of what is known to occur. However, you should consult your breeder and others who breed Finnish Spitz to understand the prevalence to this breed.

* Hip dysplasia
* Patellar luxation
* Elbow dysplasia
* Epilepsy

References

* The American Kennel Club official site [2]
* The Finnish Spitz club of America [8]
* The Finnish Spitz Directory [9]
* History, Breed information [10]
* FinnishSpitzOnline.com
    * Brief breed history [11]
    * Breed information [12]

Grand Basset Griffon Vendéen

Grand Basset Griffon Vendéen

Grand Basset Griffon Vendéen	
Other names	Basset Griffon Vendéen (Grand)
Country of origin	France
Traits	
Classification and standards	
FCI Group 6 Section 1 #33	standard [1]
AKC Hound (FSS)	standard [2]
The AKC Foundation Stock Service [3] (FSS) is an optional recording service for purebred dogs that are not yet eligible for AKC registration.	
KC (UK) Hound	standard [3]
UKC Scenthound Breeds	[? standard]
Notes	
The United Kennel Club (US) uses the Fédération Cynologique Internationale standard.	
Dog (*Canis lupus familiaris*)	

The **Grand Basset Griffon Vendéen** is a long-backed, short legged hunting breed of dog of the hound type, originating in the Vendée region of France. They are still used today to hunt boar, deer, and to track rabbit and hare, but are more commonly kept as a domestic pet.

They are pack dogs, so owners should either spend a lot of time with them or get a second dog or cat. They have a happy and confident personality, which can sometimes manifest itself as disobedience, but they are great companions.

Health

The UK Kennel Club conducted a health survey of Basset Griffon Vendéens (Petit and Grand varieties combined) in 2004. This is apparently the only completed health survey (as of July 16, 2007) that might include Grand Basset Griffon Vendéen, but it is unclear what proportion of dogs in the survey were Grand Basset Griffon Vendéens instead of the more common Petit.

Mortality

Average longevity of 76 deceased Basset Griffon Vendéens (varieties combined) in the 2004 UK Kennel Club survey was 12.1 years (maximum 17.3 years). Leading causes of death were cancer (33%), old age (24%), and cardiac (7%).

Compared to surveyed longevities of other breeds of similar size, Basset Griffon Vendéens have a typical or somewhat higher than average life expectancy.

Morbidity

Among 289 live Basset Griffon Vendéens (varieties combined) in the 2004 UKC survey, the most common health issues noted by owners were reproductive, dermatologic (dermatitis and mites), and aural (otitis externa, excessive ear wax, and ear mites).

References

"Grand Basset Griffon Vendéen" FCI-Standard N° 33 14February 2001 [1] [[Fédération Cynologique Internationale|World Canine Federation]

See also

- Petit Basset Griffon Vendéen
- Basset Fauve de Bretagne
- Basset Bleu de Gascogne
- Basset Hound

Grand Bleu de Gascogne

Grand Bleu de Gascogne

Grand Bleu de Gascogne	
Country of origin	France
Traits	
Classification and standards	
FCI Group 6:Scenthounds. Section 1.1:Large sized scenthounds #22	standard [1]
UKC Scenthound	standard [2]
Dog (*Canis lupus familiaris*)	

The **Grand Bleu de Gascogne** (FCI No.22) Is a breed of dog of the scenthound type, originating in France and used for hunting in packs. Today's breed is the descendant of a very old type of large hunting dog, and is an important breed in the ancestry of many other hounds.

Appearance

The Grand Bleu de Gascogne is an imposing large dog, a typical hunting pack hound of the oldest type, with a lean and muscular body, long legs, slightly domed head, long drop ears, and drooping lips. Size is 65 to 72 cm (25.6 to 28.3 ins) at the withers, females slightly smaller. Dogs of this breed should show an attitude of calm strength and nobleness.

The colour of the coat is white mottled with black, giving a slate blue overall appearance. There are black patches on either side of the head, with a white area on top of the head which has in it a small black oval. Tan "eyebrow" marks are over each eye. Faults are deviations in appearance that have an effect on the health and working ability of the dog, as well as an absence of expected features of colour, structure, and size, indicating that a dog with such faults should not be bred. Faults include aggression or fearfulness, anatomical malformation, and lack of type.

The Grand Bleu de Gascogne is noted for its focus on the hunt as well as a good nose and distinctive sonorous, deep howl. The breed is "instinctively a pack hound."

History

The Grand Bleu de Gascogne's ancestors were contemporary with the St. Hubert Hounds, and were hunted in packs by the 14th century Comte de Foix on wolves, bears and boars. This type and breed are found in the ancestry all of the breeds of scenthound with "du midi" in their name.

Although these are large dogs, "Grand" does not necessarily refer to the size of the dogs. "In most cases it is simply a label for a pack that is used for larger game". Today. the breed is used in hunting boar, deer, and other game. The Grand Bleu de Gascogne is a very large dog weighing 80-120lbs

Health and temperament

No unusual health problems or claims of extraordinary health have been documented for this breed. Temperament of individual dogs may vary, but in general dogs bred to be pack hunting dogs do not make good pets.

See also

- Anglo French and French Hounds
- Dog terminology
- Petit Bleu de Gascogne
- Griffon Bleu de Gascogne
- Basset Bleu de Gascogne

External links

- Search The Open Directory Project (DMOZ) links for clubs and information about the Grand Bleu de Gascogne [3]

Greyhound

Greyhound

Greyhound	
Other names	English greyhound
Country of origin	See History section

Traits		
Weight	Male	27 to 40 kilograms (60 to 88 lb)
	Female	27 to 34 kilograms (60 to 75 lb)
Height	Male	71 to 76 centimetres (28 to 30 in)
	Female	68 to 71 centimetres (27 to 28 in)
Coat	Fine, smooth	
Litter size	6-8 pups	
Life span	10-13 years	

Classification and standards		
FCI	Group 10 Section 3 #158	standard [1]
AKC	Hound	standard [2]
ANKC	Group 4 (Hounds)	standard [3]
CKC	Group 2 - Hounds	standard [4]
KC (UK)	Hound	standard [5]
NZKC	Hounds	standard [6]
UKC	Sighthounds and Pariahs	standard [7]
Dog (*Canis lupus familiaris*)		

The **greyhound** is a breed of hunting dog that has been primarily bred for coursing game and racing, but with a recent resurgence of popularity as a pedigree show dog and family pet. It is a gentle and intelligent breed that often becomes attached to its owner. A combination of long, powerful legs, deep chest, flexible spine and slim build allow it to reach average race speeds of in excess of 18 metres per second (59 feet per second) or .

Description

Appearance

Males are usually 71 to 76 centimetres (28 to 30 in) tall at the withers and weigh around 27 to 40 kilograms (60 to 88 lb). Females tend to be smaller with shoulder heights ranging from 68 to 71 centimetres (27 to 28 in) and weights from less than 27 to 34 kilograms (60 to 75 lb). Greyhounds have very short hair, which is easy to maintain. There are approximately thirty recognized color forms, of which variations of white, brindle, fawn, black, red and blue (gray) can appear uniquely or in combination.

Anatomy

The key to the speed of a greyhound can be found in its light but muscular build, largest heart, and highest percentage of fast-twitch muscle of any breed, the double suspension gallop and the extreme flexibility of the spine. "Double suspension rotary gallop" describes the fastest running gait of the greyhound in which all four feet are free from the ground in two phases, contracted and extended, during each full stride.

Temperament

Despite the greyhounds reputation for being fast racing dogs and being very athletic, they don't need much exercise as they are bred as sprinters. They are typically quiet and gentle when they are not racing. They are ideal for families with young children, if a child is taught to properly treat a greyhound a greyhound can live in a home with children. Greyhounds have a sensitive nature, and gentle commands work best. They are ideal apartment dogs as they do not need a lot of space and they sleep a lot.

The word "grey" in their name does not refer to their colour but comes from Old English and is thought to mean "fine".

Roles

Racing

Until the early twentieth century, greyhounds were principally bred and trained for coursing. During the 1920s, modern greyhound racing was introduced into the United States and England (Belle Vue, Manchester, July 1926), as well as Northern Ireland (Celtic Park, April 1927) and the Republic of Ireland (Shelbourne Park, Dublin). The greyhound holds the record for fastest recorded dog.

Aside from professional racing, many greyhounds enjoy success on the amateur race track. Organizations like the Large Gazehound Racing Association (LGRA) and the National Oval Track Racing Association (NOTRA) provide opportunities for greyhounds and other sighthound breeds to compete in amateur racing events all over the United States

Coursing

The original function of greyhounds, both in the British Isles and on the Continent of Europe was in the coursing of deer. Much later they specialised as competition hare coursing dogs. Some greyhounds still fulfill their live coursing function, although artificial lure sports like lure coursing and racing are far more common and popular.

However to many purest breeders of racing greyhounds, the sport of coursing is still vitally important. This is the case particularly in Ireland where many of the world's leading breeders are based. A bloodline that has produced a champion on the live hare coursing field is often crossed with track lines in order to keep the early pace (i.e. speed over first 100 yards) that greyhounds are renowned for prominent in the line. Many of the leading sprinters over 300 yards to 550 yards will have bloodlines that can be traced back through Irish sires within a few generations that won events such as the Irish Coursing Derby or the Irish Cup.

The majority of pure-bred greyhounds are whelped in the Republic of Ireland. Also any sample check on the back breeding on the greyhound data website will show coursing champions within a few generations in the pedigree of track racing champions. Just to give a few examples, 2005 Irish Oaks winner, Grayslands Pixie, is a granddaughter of Lady Tico, the dam of 1992 Irish Coursing Derby winner Newry Hill. The 2005 Irish Derby winner, He Said So, 2007 Irish Derby winner, Razldazl Billy, and 2009 Irish Derby winner, College Causeway, all have 1983 English Derby Winner, I'm Slippy, in their immediate pedigree, whose dam was coursing bitch Glenroe Bess. The current number one United States sire of greyhounds running between 0 and 503 meters is Dodgem By Design, who is descended from coursing bitch Ballyhenry Black in the fourth generation of his back breeding. The current top sires in Ireland and the UK, Top Honcho and Brett Lee, have the fully coursing-bred Supreme Fun (by Newdown Heather ex Top Note) in the 4th and 5th generations of their respective pedigrees.

In Ireland the ICC (Irish Coursing Club) oversees about 80 live hare coursing meetings per year. Both the American Kennel Club and the American Sighthound Field Association sponsor lure coursing events in North America.

Greyhounds as pets

Greyhound owners and adoption groups generally consider greyhounds to be wonderful pets. They are pack-oriented dogs, which means that they will quickly adopt humans into their pack as alpha. Retired racing greyhounds occasionally develop separation anxiety when re-housed or when their new owners have to leave them alone for a period of time (the addition of a second greyhound often solves this problem).

Greyhounds bark very little, which helps in suburban environments, and are usually as friendly to strangers as they are with their own family. The most common misconception concerning greyhounds is that they are hyperactive. In retired racing greyhounds it is usually the opposite. Young greyhounds that have never been taught how to utilize the energy they are bred with can be hyperactive and destructive if not given an outlet, and require more experienced handlers. Rescued greyhounds, however, have been taught to chase after small, furry things, and may be confused or need guidance on how to deal with small animals such as kittens, rabbits, and other small furry objects.

At the race track, greyhounds are housed in crates for upwards of 20 hours per day, and most know of no other way of life than to remain in a crate the majority of the day. Retired racers therefore make excellent pets, because crating them (even in small apartments) is usually quite easy.

Greyhound adoption groups generally recommend that owners keep their greyhounds on a leash whenever outdoors, except in fully enclosed areas. This is due to their prey-drive, their speed, and the assertion that greyhounds have no road sense. Due to their strength, adoption groups recommend that fences be between 4 and 6 feet, to prevent them being able to jump.

Greyhounds do shed, but do not have undercoats and therefore are less likely to trigger people's dog allergies (they are sometimes incorrectly referred to as "hypoallergenic"). The lack of an undercoat, coupled with a general lack of body fat, also makes greyhounds more susceptible to extreme temperatures, and most sources recommend that greyhounds be housed inside.

Greyhounds are very sensitive to insecticides. Many vets do not recommend the use of flea collars or flea spray on greyhounds unless it is a pyrethrin-based product. Products like Advantage, Frontline, Lufenuron, and Amitraz are safe for use on greyhounds and are very effective in controlling fleas and ticks.

It is often mistakenly believed that greyhounds need a large living space; in truth, however, they can thrive in small spaces. Due to their temperament, greyhounds can make better "apartment dogs" than some of the smaller hyperactive breeds .

There are currently two online databases to easily lookup or search for all past and present registered dogs: Greyhound-Data.com [8] and Rosnet2000.com [9] Dogs can be searched by their Bertillon number , race name, or other attributes. Data includes photos, race statistics, and pedigree.

Health and physiology

Greyhounds are typically a healthy and long-lived breed, and hereditary illness is rare. Some greyhounds have been known to develop esophageal achalasia, bloat (gastric torsion), and osteosarcoma. Because the greyhound's lean physique makes it ill-suited to sleeping on hard surfaces, owners of companion greyhounds generally provide soft bedding; without bedding, greyhounds are prone to develop painful skin sores. The typical greyhound lifespan is 10 to 13 years.

Due to the unique physiology and anatomy of greyhounds, a veterinarian who understands the issues relevant to the breed is generally needed when the dogs need treatment, particularly when anaesthesia is required. Greyhounds cannot metabolize barbiturate-based anesthesia as other breeds can because they have lower amounts of oxidative enzymes in their livers. Greyhounds demonstrate unusual blood chemistry, which can be misread by veterinarians not familiar with the breed; this can result in an incorrect diagnosis.

Greyhounds have higher levels of red blood cells than other breeds. Since red blood cells carry oxygen to the muscles, this higher level allows the hound to move larger quantities of oxygen faster from the lungs to the muscles. Greyhounds have lower levels of platelets than other breeds. Veterinary blood services often use greyhounds as universal blood donors.

History

The breed's origin is romantically reputed to be connected to ancient Egypt, where depictions of smooth-coated sighthound types have been found which are typical of saluki (Persian greyhound) or sloughi (tombs at Beni Hassan c. 2000 BC). However, analyses of DNA reported in 2004 suggest that the greyhound is not closely related to these breeds, but is a close relative to herding dogs. Historical literature on the first sighthound in Europe (Arrian), the *vertragus*, the probable antecedent of the greyhound, suggests that the origin is with the ancient Celts from Eastern Europe or Eurasia. All modern, pure-bred pedigree greyhounds are derived from the greyhound stock recorded and registered, firstly in the private 18th century, then public 19th century studbooks, which ultimately were registered with coursing, racing, and kennel club authorities of the United Kingdom.

Historically, these sighthounds were used primarily for hunting in the open where their keen eyesight is valuable. It is believed that they (or at least similarly named dogs) were introduced to the area now known as the United Kingdom in the 5th and 6th century BC from Celtic mainland Europe although the Picts and other hunter gatherer tribes of the northern area now known as Scotland were believed to have had large hounds similar to that of the deerhound before the 6th century BC.

The name "greyhound" is generally believed to come from the Old English *grighund*. "Hund" is the antecedent of the modern "hound", but the meaning of "grig" is undetermined, other than in reference to dogs in Old English and Norse. Its origin does not appear to have any common root with the modern word "grey" for color, and indeed the greyhound is seen with a wide variety of coat colors. It is known that in England during the medieval period, lords and royalty keen to own greyhounds for sport, requested they be bred to color variants that made them easier to view and identify in pursuit of their quarry. The lighter colors, patch-like markings and white appeared in the breed that was once ordinarily grey in color. The greyhound is the only dog mentioned by name in the Bible; the King James version names the greyhound as one of the "four things stately" in the Proverbs. However, some more recent translations have changed this to *strutting rooster*, which appears to be a more correct translation of the Hebrew term זַרְזִיר (*zarzir*).

According to Pokorny the English name "greyhound" does not mean "gray dog/hound", but simply "fair dog". Subsequent words have been derived from the Proto-Indo-European root ***g'her-** "shine, twinkle": English *gray*, Old High German *gris* "grey, old", Old Icelandic *griss* "piglet, pig", Old Icelandic *gryja* "to dawn", *gryjandi* "morning twilight", Old Irish *grian* "sun", Old Church Slavonic *zorja* "morning twilight, brightness". The common sense of these words is "to shine; bright".

In 1928, the very first winner of Best in Show at Crufts was Primeley Sceptre, a greyhound owned by H. Whitley.

Cultural references to greyhounds

Greyhound Bus

The Greyhound Bus Lines bus company, in keeping with their logo which sports a racing greyhound, occasionally airs television commercials starring a talking computer-generated greyhound. The greyhound in these commercial shorts is often noted for his dry, deadpan wit. In holiday season commercials, the greyhound also sings about fare discounts, the song being set to a Christmas carol.

Police Force

Andhra Pradesh(INDIA) police has a special ops force named Greyhounds.

Sports

The greyhound is often used as a mascot by sports teams, both professional and amateur, as well as many college and high school teams.

Professional

- Sault Ste. Marie Greyhounds (Ontario Hockey League)
- Ohio Valley Greyhounds (United Indoor Football)

College

- Assumption College (in Worcester, Massachusetts)
- University of Indianapolis
- Loyola University Maryland
- Eastern New Mexico University
- Moberly Area Community College (in Moberly, Missouri)
- Moravian College in Bethlehem, Pennsylvania
- Yankton College (Yankton, South Dakota)
- Athol Murray College of Notre Dame (Wilcox, Saskatchewan)

Other

- "Greyhound" was the name of several roller coasters in the United States and Canada. None of these rides operate today.
- In Australia, racing Greyhounds are commonly known in slang terminology as "dish lickers" (e.g., "I just won 50 bucks at the dish lickers").
- The main-character family of the animated television series *The Simpsons* have a greyhound named Santa's Little Helper.
- The cover art of the 1994 Britpop album "Parklife" by Blur features greyhounds.
- The M8 Light Armored Car, a US military vehicle, was nicknamed "Greyhound" by British armed forces during the Second World War.

See also

- Sighthound
- Lure coursing
- Coursing
- Greyhound racing
- Greyhound adoption
- Similar breeds:

    - Afghan Hound
    - Borzoi (Russian wolfhound)
    - Galgo Español (Spanish greyhound)
    - Hortaya borzaya (Russian shorthaired sighthound)
    - Italian greyhound
    - Lurcher (Not a breed, but a type of dog with Greyhound ancestry)
    - Magyar agár (Hungarian greyhound)
    - Saluki
    - Whippet

External links

- Clubs, Associations and Societies
    - Greyhound Club of America [10]
    - Greyhound Pets of America [11]
    - National Greyhound Association [12]
    - World Greyhound Racing Federation [13]
- Information
    - Comprehensive database of Greyhound pedigrees Greyhound-data [14]
    - "The greyhound in 1864: ..." Walsh 1864 [15]
    - "The greyhound, ..." Dalziel 1887 [16]
    - Of Greyhounds and of their nature, Chapter XV: "The Master of Game" Edward of York circa 1406 [17]
    - Example of the Double Suspension Gallop [18]
    - Community & Greyhound Pedigrees DataBase [19]

Hamiltonstövare

Hamiltonstövare

none	
Other names	Hamilton Hound Swedish Foxhound
Nicknames	Hamilton
Country of origin	Sweden

Traits

Classification and standards		
FCI	Group 6 Section 1 #132	standard [1]
ANKC	Group 4 (Hounds)	standard [2]
KC (UK)	Hound	standard [3]
NZKC	Hounds	standard [4]
UKC	Scenthound	[? standard]

Notes
The UKC does not have an official breed standard.
Dog (*Canis lupus familiaris*)

The **Hamiltonstövare** is a breed of dog, bred as a hunting hound. The breed was developed in Sweden by the founder of the Swedish Kennel Club, Count Adolf Hamilton. Its ancestry includes several German hounds as well as English Foxhounds and Harriers.

The breed is known by the white blaze on the head, down the neck, four white paws, and a white tail tip. He differs from an English Foxhound in that his frame is lighter.

General Appearance

Rectangular, well proportioned, giving impression of great strength and stamina. Tricoloured.

Characteristics

Handsome, upstanding dog of striking colouring. Hardy and sound.

Head and Skull

Head longish, rectangular, with slightly arched and moderately broad skull. Occiput not too prominent. Stop well defined but not over pronounced. Jowls not too heavy. Muzzle fairly long, large and rectangular. Bridge of nose straight and parallel to line of skull. Nose always black, well developed with large nostrils. Upper lips full but not too overhanging.

Eyes

Clear and dark brown with tranquil expression.

Ears

Set fairly high, when drawn alongside jaw, ears extend to approximately half-way along muzzle and should be raised only slightly above skull when responding to call. Soft with straight fall and fore edge not folded out.

Mouth

Jaws strong, with a perfect, regular and complete scissor bite, i.e. upper teeth closely overlapping lower teeth and set square to the jaws.

Neck

Long and powerful, merging well into shoulders, skin on neck supple and close fitting.

Forequarters

Shoulders muscular and well laid back. When viewed from front forelegs appear straight and parallel. Upper foreleg long and broad and set at a right angle to shoulder blade. Elbows set close in to body.

Body

Back straight and powerful. Strong, broad, muscular loin. Croup slightly inclined. Chest deep, ribs moderately sprung, back ribs proportionately long. Belly slightly tucked up.

Hindquarters

Strong and parallel when viewed from behind. Well angulated, muscle well developed and broad when seen from side.

Feet

Short and hard. Pads firm and pointing straight forward.

Tail

Set on low, in an almost straight continuation of line of back. In length reaches hock. Fairly wide at base and narrowing off towards tip. Held in straight position or curving slightly in sabre-like shape. Not carried above the backline when moving.

Coat

Coat consists of two layers. Undercoat short, close and soft, especially thick during winter. Upper coat strongly weather-resistant lying close to body. On underside of tail, ordinary hair quite long but not forming a fringe. Ample hair between pads.

Colour

Upper side of neck, back, sides of trunk and upper side of tail black. Head and legs, as well as side of neck, trunk and tail brown. White markings as follows: blaze on upper part of muzzle, underside of neck, breast and tip of tail, lower legs and feet.

A mixture of black and brown undesirable, as is a preponderance of any of the three permissible colours.

Gait/Movement

Free striding and long reaching. Hindlegs showing drive. Not moving close behind.

Temperament

A typical hound in temperament- sweet and friendly to all- the Hamiltonstovare is also a hardworking hunter. It is happy to be with its family, but it is also happy to be out hunting.

The Hamiltonstovare is its "own hound," and although it is friendly and gregarious, it naturally defers to doing what it wants rather than what might be requested of it. It takes enthusiasm and praise to persuade the Hamiltonstovare to comply with its owner's requests, but it'll do it if it's inspired.

Size

Dogs 53-61 cms (21-24 ins). The ideal size is 57 cms (22 ½ ins).

Bitches 49-57 cms (19 ¼ - 22 ½ ins). The ideal size is 53 cms (21 ins).

Faults

Any departure from the foregoing points should be considered a fault and the seriousness with which the fault should be regarded should be in exact proportion to its degree and its effect upon the health and welfare of the dog.

Harrier (dog)

This article is about the dog. For other uses, see Harrier (disambiguation).

Harrier

A tri-color Harrier		
Country of origin	United Kingdom	
Traits		
Classification and standards		
FCI	Group 6 Section 1 #295	standard [1]
AKC	Hound	standard [2]
ANKC	Group 4 (Hounds)	standard [3]
CKC	Group 2 (Hounds)	standard [4]
NZKC	Hound	standard [5]
UKC	Scenthound	standard [6]
Dog (*Canis lupus familiaris*)		

The **Harrier** is a small to medium sized dog breed of the hound class, used for hunting hares by trailing them. It resembles an English Foxhound but is smaller, though not as small as a Beagle.

Description

Appearance

The Harrier is similar to the English Foxhound, but smaller. They are one of the few truly medium-sized breeds of dogs. Harriers stand between 19 and 21 inches at the shoulder, and adults weigh between 45 and 60 lbs. They have short hair, hanging ears, and come in a variety of color patterns. A humorous, yet fairly accurate short-hand description of a Harrier is that of "a Beagle on steroids." It is a muscular hunting hound with a short, hard coat. It has large bones for stamina and strength. The Harrier is slightly longer than tall, with a level topline. The tail is medium-length, carried high, but is not curled over the back. The skull is broad with a strong square muzzle. The rounded ears are pendant, and the eyes are either brown or hazel. The wide nose is black. The expression is mellow when the dog is relaxed and alert when he is excited. The teeth should meet in a scissors or level bite. The feet are tight and cat-like, and the front toes may turn inward.

Temperament

The Harrier is cheerful, sweet-tempered, tolerant of people, and it is excellent with children. This pack dog is good with other dogs, but should be supervised with non-canine pets unless it is raised with them from puppyhood. It prefers life in a pack with people, dogs, or both. This active dog likes to go exploring, sniffing, and trailing, so be sure to keep it on a leash or in a safe enclosed area. Some Harriers like to bay.

Health

This breed's lifespan is generally 12-15 years. Hip dysplasia is known to occur in this breed.

Care

Exercise

The Harrier requires daily exercise, such as long vigorous walks or runs. Allowing them to play in open space (so long as it is enclosed and safe) makes exercise fun and easy. Without appropriate exercise, the Harrier can become hyperactive, overweight and/or destructive. This dog was bred to run and work all day long and cannot be satisfied by a sedentary lifestyle.

History

Sources have widely conflicting stories about the origins of this breed. According to one, the earliest Harrier types were crossed with Bloodhounds, the Talbot Hound, and even the Basset Hound. According to another, the breed was probably developed from crosses of the English Foxhound with Fox Terrier and Greyhound. And yet another, the Harrier is said to be simply a bred-down version of the English Foxhound. The first Harrier pack in England was established by Sir Elias de Midhope in 1260 and spread out as a hunting dog throughout the west of England and into Wales. Although there are many working Harriers in England, the breed is still not recognised in that country.

In any case, today's Harrier is between the Beagle and English Foxhound in size and was developed primarily to hunt hares, though the breed has also been used in fox hunting. The name, Harrier, reveals the breed's specialty. The Harrier has a long history of popularity as a working pack dog in England.

The Harrier is the most commonly used hound by clubs in Ireland, with nearly 130 different clubs spread throughout the country. More commonly in Ireland it is used to hunt both foxes and hares, with some clubs hunting mainly foxes.

External links

- Harrier Club of America [7]
- http://www.downhomeharriers.com/facts.html
- http://www.ridgecrest.ca.us/~auborn/harriers/harrier_info.html

Ibizan Hound

Ibizan Hound

Ibizan Hound.	
Other names	Ca Eivissenc Podenco Ibicenco Ibizan Warren Hound
Country of origin	Spain
Traits	
Classification and standards	
FCI Group 5 Section 7 #89	standard [1]
AKC Hound	standard [2]
ANKC Group 4 (Hounds)	standard [3]
CKC Group 2 - Hounds	standard [4]
KC (UK) Hound	standard [5]
NZKC Hounds	standard [6]
UKC Sighthounds and Pariahs	standard [7]
Dog (*Canis lupus familiaris*)	

The **Ibizan Hound**, pronounced "I-bee-zan" or "I-beeth-an", is a lean, agile dog of the hound family. There are two hair types of the breed: smooth and wire. The more commonly seen type is the smooth. Some consider there to be a third type, long, but most consider the longhair to be a variation of the wire.

Description

Appearance

The Ibizan Hound is an elegant and agile breed, with an athletic and attractive outline and a ground-covering springy trot. Though graceful in appearance, it has good bone girth and is a rugged/hardy breed. Its large upright ears - a hallmark of the breed - are broad at the base and frame a long and elegant headpiece. The neck is long and lean. It has a unique front assembly with well laid-back shoulders and straight upper arm. It comes in both smooth and wire-coated varieties. It is either red, white, or a combination of red and white. Its nose is flesh colored, as are its ears, eye rims, and pads of feet. Its eyes are a striking amber color and have an alert and intelligent expression. The Ibizan may range in height from 24 to 29 inches (61 to 74 cm) and weigh from 45 to 65 pounds (20 to 29 kg), males being larger than females.

Temperament

Ibizan Hounds are moderately intelligent, active, and engaging by nature. They rank 53rd in Stanley Coren's The Intelligence of Dogs, being of average working/obedience intelligence. They are true "clowns" of the dog world, delighting in entertaining their people with their antics. Though somewhat independent and stubborn at times, they do take well to training if positive methods are used, but will balk at punitive training methods. They are generally quiet, but will alarm bark if necessary, so they make good watch dogs. They are sensitive hounds, and very good around children and other dogs alike. They generally make good house dogs, but are active and athletic, therefore need a lot of daily exercise. They do not make good kennel dogs.

Ibizan Hounds are "escapologists": they are able to jump incredible heights from a stand still. As such, they need very tall fences. They also have been known to climb. They have a strong prey drive, therefore they cannot be trusted off lead unless in a safely enclosed area.

Health

The Ibizan Hound is typical of the Hound Group in that it rarely suffers from hereditary illness. Minor health concerns for the breed include seizures and allergies; very rarely, one will see axonal dystrophy, cataract, retinal dysplasia and deafness in the breed. Ibizan Hound owners should have their dogs' eyes tested by a veterinarian before breeding. Ibizan Hounds are sensitive to barbiturate anesthesia, and typically live between 12 and 14 years.

History & Use

This breed originates in the island of Eivissa and has been traditionally used in the Catalan-speaking areas of Spain and France to hunt rabbits and other small game. The Ibizan Hound is a fast dog that can hunt on all types of terrain, working by scent, sound and sight. Hunters run these dogs in mostly female packs, with perhaps a male or two, as the female is considered the better hunter.

The Ibizan Hound authority Miquel Rosselló has provided a detailed description of a working trial which characterises their typical hunting technique and action, strikingly illustrated with action photos by Charles Camberoque which demonstrate hunt behaviour and typical hunt terrain. While local hunters will at times use one dog or a brace, and frequently packs of 6-8 or as many as 15, the working trial requires an evaluation of one or two braces. A brace is called a *colla*. The couples should be tested on at least 2 to 5 rabbits (not hares), without the use of any other hunting aid. An inspection and evaluation of the exterior, fitness, character and obedience of the dogs is recommended prior to the hunt. The trial is qualified as having 5 parts. The dogs should show: (1) careful tracking and scenting of the rabbit, without being distracted in the least, 0-30 points; (2) correct signalling of the game, patient stand, strong jump into the air, obedience 0-10 points; (3) chase, giving tongue, speed, sureness, anticipation 0-30 points; (4) putting the game to cover at close quarters, listening, waiting, obedience, correct attack 0-10 point; and (5) good catch, or correct indication of the game's location, retrieval, obedience 0-20 points.

Individual dogs are expected to show a great degree of discipline, obedience and co-operation. They should be extremely agile, have good speed and a powerful vertical jump from a stationary position in rough and often heavily covered ground. They should have excellent scent-tracking abilities, give tongue at the right time when approaching the game closely, and otherwise be silent so that they can locate the game by sound.

The Ibizan Hound is similar in function and type to several breeds, such as the Pharaoh Hound, the Cirneco dell'Etna, the Portuguese Podengo, and the Podenco Canario. The Ibizan Hound is the largest of these breeds, classified by the Fédération Cynologique Internationale as primitive types.

This breed is considered by most experts one of the most ancient dog breeds. It is believed the Ibizan Hound evolves from the *tesem*, the ancient Egyptian hunting dog. Representations of this dog on the walls of ancient tombs show a striking similarity to the modern Ibizan Hound. These dogs would have been brought to the island of Eivissa by the Phoenicians, who founded settlements there as early as the VIII Century BC. A recent DNA analysis did not find support for this opinion and did not include the Ibizan Hound among their identified ancient dog breeds. A more recent article argues that continued trait selective breeding may be behind this lack of support. Heidi G. Parker, the lead author of the original study has stated recently that indeed their original findings do not imply that the Ibizan Hound is not an ancient breed and that with better tools they would in all likelihood be able to trace a continuous lineage of thousands of years for many dog breeds and add them to their group of ancient dogs.

The Ibizan Hound breed is recognized by the Fédération Cynologique Internationale, Continental Kennel Club, American Kennel Club, United Kennel Club, Kennel Club of Great Britain, Canadian Kennel Club, National Kennel Club, New Zealand Kennel Club, Australian National Kennel Council, America's Pet Registry, and American Canine Registry. It was fully recognized by the American Kennel Club in 1979.

In folk culture

According to journalist Norman Lewis, when an owner no longer wants to own one of these dogs (having too much of an appetite, for instance), it is considered very bad luck to kill the dog. Instead, they release the dog on the other side of the island, so that someone else might 'adopt' the animal.

External links

- Ibizan Hound Photos [8]
- Charles Camberoque: photos of Ibizans at work [9]
- Video: How Ibizans hunt [10]
- Ibizan Hound at Dog Breed Info [11]
- Ibizan Hound Club (Eivissa) [12]
- Norwegian Ibizan Hound Club [13]
- Swiss Ibizan Hound Club [14]
- German Ibizan Hound Club [15]
- Ibizan Hound Rescue in Spain [16]
- Ibizan Hounds in the UK [17]
- Additional information on the German language Wikipedia.(In German: "Podenco Ibicenco") [18]

Irish Wolfhound

Irish wolfhound

An Irish wolfhound	
Other names	Cú Faoil
Country of origin	Ireland

Traits

Classification and standards

FCI	Group 10 Section 2 #160	standard [1]
AKC	Hound	standard [2]
ANKC	Group 4 (Hound)	standard [3]
CKC	Group 2 (Hound)	standard [4]
KC (UK)	Hound	standard [5]
NZKC	Hound	standard [6]
UKC	Sighthounds and Pariahs	standard [7]

Dog (*Canis lupus familiaris*)

The **Irish wolfhound** (,) is a breed of domestic dog (*Canis lupus familiaris*), specifically a sighthound. The name originates from its purpose (wolf hunting) rather than from its appearance. If their connection to the Celtic dogs used at the sacking of Delphi during the Iron Age is accurate, then their name derives indeed from that of the earliest bohemian tribes from central Europe. Irish Wolfhounds are the tallest dog breed on average.

Appearance

Built like a very muscular greyhound, the Irish wolfhound male can attain the stature of a small pony. Its large, long head tapers to a medium point and is held high. Ears are small and stay close to the head except during moments of intensity. Strong shoulders, a muscular neck, a deep chest and a retracted abdomen give the dog its characteristic body shape. Paws are large and round. The tail is carried between the legs, curving slightly upward. The coat is rough, shaggy, wiry and especially bushy over the eyes and under the jaw. The Irish Wolfhound is graceful with an easy yet powerful gait. Historically these dogs had to possess not only speed, but also endurance, allowing them to follow their prey and hunt it down. They had to be hearty enough to withstand being injured whilst using their own brute force to bring the prey down. The modern representation of the breed appears to be a dog capable of doing just that. Generally breeders aim for a height range of 85 to 95 centimeters (34 to 38 inches) at the withers in males, 50 to 80 centimeters (30 to 35 inches) for females. Generally acceptable weight 46–70 kg (101–154 lbs). The recognized colors are gray, brindle, red, black, pure white, fawn or any other color that appears in the Deerhound.

Temperament

An easygoing animal, they are usually quiet by nature. Wolfhounds often create a strong bond with their family and can become quite destructive or morose if left for long periods. Despite the need for their own people, Wolfhounds generally are somewhat stand-offish with total strangers. They should not be territorially aggressive to other domestic dogs but are born with specialized skills and it is common for hounds at play to course another dog. This is a specific hunting behaviour, not a fighting or territorial domination behaviour. Most Wolfhounds are very gentle with children and are aware of their size and power. The Irish Wolfhound is relatively easy to train. They respond well to firm, but gentle, consistent leadership. However, historically these dogs were required to work at great distances from their masters and think independently when hunting rather than waiting for detailed commands and this can still be seen in the breed. The Wolfhound of today is far from the one that struck fear into the hearts of the Ancient Romans. Irish Wolfhounds are often favoured for their loyalty, affection, patience and devotion. Although at some points in history they have been used as watchdogs, unlike some breeds, the Irish Wolfhound is usually unreliable in this role as they are often friendly toward strangers, although their size can be a natural deterrent. That said, when protection is required this dog is never found wanting. When they or their family are in any perceived danger they display a fearless nature. Owenmore Wolfhound breeder Linda Glover believes the dogs' close affinity with humans makes them acutely aware and sensitive to ill will or malicious intentions leading to them excelling as a guardian rather than guard dog. J A McAleen, in praising them, wrote:

> No other dog can come so close to the understanding and kindly companionship That exists between humans as this dog can. A giant in structure, a lamb in disposition, a lion in courage; affectionate and intelligent, thoroughly reliable and dependable at all times, as a

companion and as a guard he is perfection

Health

Irish wolfhounds have a relatively short lifespan. Published lifespan estimations vary between 5 and 10 years. Dilated cardiomyopathy and bone cancer are the leading cause of death and like all deep-chested dogs, gastric torsion (bloat) is also common; the breed is also affected by hereditary intrahepatic portosystemic shunt.

In a privately funded study conducted under the auspices of the Irish Wolfhound Club of America and based on an owner survey, Irish wolfhounds in the United States from 1966 to 1986 lived to a mean age of 6.47 and died most frequently of bone cancer. A more recent study by the UK Kennel Club puts the average age of death at 7 years.

By the age of 8 months, Irish wolfhounds appear adult, and many owners start stressing them too much. Outstretched limbs and irreparable damage are the result. Wolfhounds need at least 18 months to be ready for lure coursing, running as a sport, and other strenuous activities. It takes almost two years for the wolfhound to fully grow.

Wolfhounds should not receive additional supplements when a good dog food is used. It is generally accepted that they should be fed a large breed puppy food until 18 months old and then change to a large breed adult food. Most breeders today recommend that they not be supplemented to slow their rapid growth.

Irish wolfhounds are one of the tallest of dog breeds so they are well suited to rural life, but their medium energy profile allows them to adjust fairly well to suburban and urban life as well, provided they receive appropriate exercise.

History

The breed is very old; there are suggestions it may have been brought to Ireland around 3500 BC by early settlers, further genetic testing may help clarify a point of origin. These dogs are mentioned, as cú (variously translated as hound, Irish hound, war dog, wolf dog, etc.) in Irish laws, which predate Christianity, and in Irish literature which dates from the 5th century or, in the case of the Sagas, from the old Irish period - AD600-900. The word "Cu" often became an added respected prefix on the names of warriors as well as kings denoting that they were worthy of the respect and loyalty of a Cu. Ancient wood cuts and writings have placed them in existence as a breed by 273 BC. However there is indication that they existed even as early as 600 BC when the Tectosages and Tolistobogii Celts sacked Delphi. Survivors left accounts of the fierce Celts and the huge dogs who fought with them and at their side. They were mentioned by Julius Caesar in his treatise, The Gallic Wars, and by 391 BC, they were written about by Roman Consul, Quintus Aurelius, who received seven of them as a gift to be used for fighting lions, bears, that in his words, "all Rome viewed with wonder.". Bred as war dogs by the ancients, who called them *Cú Faoil*. The Irish continued to breed them for this purpose, as well as to guard their homes and protect their stock. Regular references of Irish wolfhounds being used in dog fights are found in many historical sagas—Culain's favourite dog, Luath, was slain by a southern chief's hound, Phorp. Cúchulain, a name which translates literally as "hound of Culain", gained his name when as a child, known then as Setanta, he slew the ferocious guard dog of Culain forcing him to offer himself as a replacement.

While many modern texts state Irish wolfhounds were used for coursing deer, contemporary pre-revival accounts such as *Animated Nature* (1796) by Oliver Goldsmith are explicit that the original animal was a very poor coursing dog. Their astonishing size, speed, and intelligence made them ideal animals for both boar hunting and wolf hunting. They were perhaps too ideal, as the boar and wolf are now extinct in Ireland. Unlike the Russian wolfhound (Borzoi), who were bred to keep a wolf at bay until the hunter arrived, the Irish wolfhounds were bred not only to hunt the wolf down, but to go in for the kill. They killed wolves in the same way a cat kills a rat, by shaking it until its neck snapped. The Irish wolfhound has been recorded as being exhibited in ancient Rome to some excitement, and mention is made that they so amazed and terrified the Romans that it was seen fit to only transport them in cages. During the English conquest of Ireland, wolfhounds were trained by the Irish for war; their job was to catch armoured knights on horseback and separate them from their horses.

Only kings and the nobility were allowed to own the great Irish hound, the numbers permitted depending on position. They were much coveted and were frequently given as gifts to important personages and foreign nobles. Like the nobility they served, the hounds were often bejeweled with chains and collars studded with precious gem stones and metals. Wolfhounds were the companions of the regal, and housed themselves alongside them. King John of England, in about 1210 presented an Irish hound to Llewellyn, a prince of Wales. The poet The Hon W R Spencer immortalised this hound, Gelert in a poem. In his *Historie of Ireland* completed 1571, Blessed Edmund Campion gives a description of the hounds used for hunting the wolves on the Dublin and Wicklow mountains. He says: They (the Irish) are not without wolves and greyhounds to hunt them, bigger of bone and limb than a colt. Due to their popularity overseas many were exported to European royal houses leaving numbers in Ireland depleted. This led to a declaration by Cromwell himself being published in Kilkenny on 27 April 1652 to ensure that sufficient numbers remained to control the wolf population. References to the Irish wolfdog in the 1700s tell of its great size, strength and greyhound shape as well as its scarcity. Writing in 1790, Bewick described it as the largest and most beautiful of the dog kind; about 36 inches high, generally of a white or cinnamon colour, somewhat like the greyhound but more robust. He said that their aspect was mild, disposition peaceful, and strength so great that in combat the mastiff or bulldog was far from being an equal to them. The last wolf in Ireland is thought to have been killed at Myshall, Co Carlow in 1786 by a pack of wolfdogs kept by a Mr Watson of Ballydarton. The remaining hounds in the hands of a few families who were mainly descendants of the old Irish chieftains, were now symbols of status rather than hunters, they were said to be the last of their race.

Englishman Captain George Augustus Graham is responsilble with a few other breeders for reaffirming the dogs existence. In 1879 he wrote: "It has been ascertained beyond all question that there are few specimens of the breed still left in Ireland and England to be considered Irish wolfhounds, though falling short of the requisite dimensions. This blood is now in my possession." Captain Graham devoted his life to ensuring the survival of the Irish wolfdog. Owing to the small numbers of surviving specimens outcrossing was used in the breeding programme. It is believed that Great Dane, Deerhound and Mastiff dogs all played their part in Graham's creation of the dog we currently know. In 1885 Captain Graham with other breeders founded the Irish Wolfhound Club, and the Breed Standard of Points to establish and agree the ideal to which breeders should aspire.

The wolfhound is sometimes regarded as the national dog breed of Ireland but in fact no breed has ever been officially adopted as such. The wolfhound was historically a dog that only nobles could own and was taken up by the British during their rule in Ireland. This made it unpopular as a national symbol and the Kerry Blue Terrier was adopted by Irish Nationalists such as Michael Collins. However, in recent years, the wolfhound has been adopted as a symbol by both rugby codes, which are organised on an All-Ireland basis. The national rugby league team are nicknamed the wolfhounds, and the Irish Rugby Football Union, which governs rugby union, changed the name of the country's A (second-level) national team in that code to the Ireland Wolfhounds in 2010.

Further reading

- McBryde, M. (1998). *The Magnificent Irish Wolfhound*, Ringpress Books, Dorking. ISBN 1-86054-093-7, ISBN 978-1-86054-093-6.

External links

- http://www.iwsocietyofireland.com Irish Wolfhound Society of Ireland
- Irish Wolfhound Club of Ireland [8]

Norrbottenspets

Norrbottenspets

Other names	Nordic Spitz Norrbottenspitz Pohjanpystykorva
Country of origin	Sweden

Traits	

Classification and standards		
FCI	Group 5 Section 2 #276	standard [1]
AKC	Hound (FSS)	[? standard]
	The AKC Foundation Stock Service [3] (FSS) is an optional recording service for purebred dogs that are not yet eligible for AKC registration.	
CKC	Group 2 - Hounds	standard [2]
UKC	Northern Breeds	[? standard]

Notes
The UKC does not have an official breed standard.
Dog (Canis lupus familiaris)

The **Norbottenspets** is a breed of dog of the spitz type. It is an ancient breed whose original purpose was a farm and hunting dog but has recently became more popular as a companion dog. The Norrbottenspets is used to hunt black grouse, capercaillie and hazel grouse, but is also effective with small fur-bearing animals all the way up to moose and grizzly bear.

History

The breed originated in Norrbotten, Sweden and Lappland/Kainuuland, Finland, and have been documented as early as the 1600s. Sweden and Finland argue about the true home of the Norrbottenspets, but clearly the dog has spent much time in both countries. The dogs were mainly used as hunting companions. By the end of WW1, the Norbottenspets came close to extinction. Due to the very small number of norrbottens, Sweden closed its studbook in 1948. Although some dogs were preserved, they were in a non-Swedish speaking area and in the far north as a farm dog and companion. Enthusiasts sought out the few remaining dogs and started a successful breeding program between the 1950s and early 1960s. FCI confirmed a new breed standard in 1966 and the official name was confirmed as Norrbottenspets. In 1967 the Swedish Kennel Club accepted the breed for registration and a new standard was written. Finland accepted the standard and began registering dogs in 1973. In Finland these dogs are called Pohjanpystykorva. Immigrant farmers have given the dog an even longer name, Norbottens-skollandehund. There is a great effort in Finland to ensure the health of these fox-like hunting dogs and breeding is highly controlled. Healthy animals, that are only distantly related, are being bred with careful consideration of breeding consultants to create a strong background. Sweden has also had a dramatic impact on the preservation of this breed through strict breeding practices.

Characteristics

Appearance

The Norrbottenspets should be a light spitz dog, yet powerful in appearance. There should be lightness and power reflected in the dog. Males are noticeably more masculine than females, who are smaller and of lighter build. It should give the impression of being alert, spritely, and intelligent. In proportions the Norrbottenspets is slightly taller than long - fit for the original use as a hunter. The tail should curl over the back and rest on the hips.

The Norrbottenspets is a physical mixture of endurance, speed, and strength. The ribcage has elements of both speed and strength. Viewed from the front the ribcage is oval and relatively deep, half from height. The ribcage is also relatively long with well developed last ribs. The arched neck, distinguishable withers and slightly slanting croup makes the lines of the body very speedy. The underline has only a slight tuck up, which with the long ribcage reflects endurance.

Viewing the legs one can see both elements of speed and endurance. The relatively slanting shoulder blades, long upper arms and strong back angulations reflect endurance. The upper thigh forms a nearly 90 degree angle with the pelvis. Small, tight paws belong to an endurance trotter, but relatively long hocks add to the speed in gallop, especially in the start.

Although rare, bobtails do occur naturally, as in the Finnish Spitz and Karelian Bear Dog. This is an automatic disqualification for the showring for the Finnish Spitz and the Norrbottenspets, but not the Karelian. The hunting dog does not need a tail to be very efficient.

Coat and colour

The coat is hard, straight, dense, and lies close to the body. It must always have a double coat (although after a coat loss, the undercoat can be rather sparse), and the under-coat is softer than the outer-coat. The ground colour is white, with yellowish red or reddish brown markings. Also, markings of other colours are permitted. The ideal amount of white varies from 30% to nearly 100%, but in extreme cases it should have colour at least on the ears and a small spot near the base of the tail. The more coloured dogs must have a broken saddle(white crossing completely over the shoulders) with the white clearly dominant. Symmetry is not essential in facial colouring, nor is any pattern more correct than another. White on both ears, however, is highly correlated with deafness and is not desirable. Ticking(small spots of 0.25-1.0 cm) is allowed, as is a dark face. There is a gene that is dominant that leads to the dark coloured mask on the face. Often, the mask is accompanied by dark tipping of the guard hairs. For a show dog, symmetrical color can be preferred, but structure and the original purpose are always the most important.

Piebald colouring

Piebald colouring is normally a result of a single gene mutation. Usually a dog that has two copies of the mutated gene is piebald, and a single copy of the gene results in an Irish type spotting. Generally, two copies of the non-mutated gene produces dogs of a solid colour, although a small amount of white is seen. There are a few dogs that do not follow the normal inheritance patterns. The Norrbottenspets is one that does not(data collected by the University of Saskatchewan in Saskatoon Canada, fall 2008). Another one is the Icelandic Sheep Dog. There are a range of piebald colours - blond to red to darker brown. It is the form of the colouring that is important.

Size

The difference in size among the Scandinavian Hunting Breeds (Karelian Bear Dog, Finnish Spitz, and Norrbottenspets) promoted by the Finnish Spitz Club (SPJ) is distinct. The Norrbottenspets is clearly the smallest, without being toy breed-like. The standard calls for "a small and light spitz-dog". There is overlap in size between the Finnish Spitz and the Norrbottenspets.

The Canadian Kennel Club does not disqualify based on standard, but ideal height at the withers: Males- 45 cm (17.7"), Females- 42 cm (16.5"). Although the standard does not note this, variation of +/- 2 cm (0.8") is considered acceptable based on the home standards of Finland and Sweden. The Swedish and Finnish standards indicate that males over 47 cm and females over 44 cm should be disqualified.

The weight is approximately 11 to 15 kg (24 to 33 lb) for males, and 8 to 12 kg (18 to 27 lb) for females. Weight is not mentioned in the standard.

Movement and gait

Gait must show smooth, even movements with great drive, covering the ground well. The top-line must stay firm. Legs must be parallel in action. The ears may be back during gaiting. Good strength, balance, co-ordination and agility is needed when working on rough terrain or crossing waterways. A heavy dog would not live long in the woods. Working fitness is of high value – a large, lethargic dog is to be penalized. It is noteworthy that dogs may gain fat in the winter for warmth along with their heavier coat, but this should not impair their agility or endurance.

Hunting

When hunting the dogs use sight, scent, and sound unlike most hounds which tend to specialize as sight or scent hunters. The Norrbottenspets is released into a wooded area where it uses all its senses to find game. Once found the dog will flush the game and begin the chase. The dog will chase the game until it is cornered, treed, or stops. The dog then attempts to hold the game in that location by barking and continuous movement. This barking can be up to 120 barks per minute. In hunting trials the dog is required to bark at 100 barks per minute or faster. The purpose of this rapid barking is to confuse the game and cover any sounds made by the approaching hunter. This allows the hunter to find the game and get close to the game without it knowing the hunter is there.

Dog numbers

The Norrbottenspets fanciers have been very interested in registering dogs. In Finland, there are about 1200 Norrbottenspets currently living, as of 2008. Canada and the United States have approximately 300 living dogs, as of 2008. Sweden has approximately 1000 dogs, as of 2008. Finland's breeding program has used breeding consultants and computer programs to determine inbreeding coefficients to keep the risk of genetic diseases low given the small population.(Numbers collected by the Finnish Spitz Club, Finland.)

Related Breeds

- Finnish Spitz
- Karelian Bear Dog

Gallery

References

- *Dogs* by David Alderton
- *NORBOTTENSPETS* by the FCI
- *Soumen Pystykorvajarjesto - Finska Spetskulubben r.y. 70 vutta* by Finnish Spitz Club, Finland

External links

- http://www.nordicspitz.com
- http://www.manjusha-spitz.ca
- http://www.rnbkennels.com
- http://www.kennelliitto.fi/EN/etusivu.htm

Norwegian Elkhound

Norwegian Elkhound

A Norwegian Elkhound, showing the standard tightly curled tail – photographed on 29 August 2003.	

Other names	Norsk Elghund
	Grå Norsk Elghund
	Gray Norwegian Elkhound
	Small Grey Elk Dog
	Norwegian Moose Dog
Country of origin	Norway

Traits

Classification and standards

FCI	Group 5 Section 2 #242	standard [1]
AKC	Hound	standard [2]
ANKC	Group 4 (Hounds)	standard [3]
CKC	Group 2 - Hounds	standard [4]
KC (UK)	Hound	standard [5]
NZKC	Hounds	standard [6]
UKC	Northern Breeds	standard [7]

Notes

The FCI divides this into two breeds,
Grey (242) and Black (268).

Dog (*Canis lupus familiaris*)

The **Norwegian Elkhound** is one of the ancient Northern Spitz-type breed of dog and is the National Dog of Norway. The Elkhound has served as a hunter, guardian, herder, and defender. In a land of subzero temperatures, deep snow, thick forests, and rugged mountains, only the hardiest of the breeds could evolve to perform the variety of jobs at which the Elkhound excels. Its Spitz courage is probably a by-product or residue of the fact that a significant number of them were used to track and hunt moose and other large game, like bear or wolf. The Norwegian Elkhound was first presented at a dog exhibition in Norway in 1877.

The AKC breed name "Norwegian Elkhound" is a direct translation from its original Norwegian name "Norsk Elghund," meaning "Norwegian moose dog." (European settlers mistakenly called the North American cousin of the red deer an elk, when in fact in the Norwegian language the term elk or *elg* means moose.) Despite its name in America, it is not a hound dog; the Elkhound does not hunt like a hound dog nor is it directly related to hounds, however in Britain it is classed as a hound and in shows is grouped in the Hound group. The breed's goal in the hunt is to independently track down and hold the moose at bay — jumping in and out toward the moose, while signaling to the hunters by barking very loudly — until the hunter who follows the sound can arrive to shoot it. Another way of hunting with the dog is to let one of the hunters follow the dog, then chase the moose towards a row of hunters, so they can shoot it.

Description

Appearance

Norwegian Elkhound appearance	
Build:	medium, sturdy and squarely built
Weight:	40-70 pounds (18–27 kg.)
Height:	18-21 inches (46–53 cm.)
Coat:	Coarse, straight, with soft undercoat
Color:	Black and white coloring, often noted as grey or silver
Head:	Broad and wedge-shaped with a defined stop
Teeth:	Scissors bite
Eyes:	Dark brown with a keen, friendly expression
Ears:	Pointed, erect
Tail:	Rolled tightly over back
Limbs:	Straight and parallel
Life span:	12–16 years

The dog stands about 45–52 cm (20.5") high and weighs up to 24 kg (52 lbs). Its grey, white, and black coat is made up of two layers: an underlying dense smooth coat ranging from black at the muzzle, ears, and tip of its tail; to silvery grey on its legs, tail, and underbody; and an overlying black-tipped protective guard coat. An ideal Elkhound has a tightly curled tail, as the dog shown in the photograph on this page. The Elkhound is a medium-sized dog and extremely hardy.

Temperament

Norwegian Elkhounds are bred for hunting large game, such as wolf, bear and moose. Although the breed is strong and hardy, the dogs typically have an inseparable bond with their masters and are quite loyal. All Elkhounds have a sharp loud bark which makes them suitable as watchdog.

Norwegian Elkhounds are loyal to their "pack" and make excellent family dogs if given proper attention. It is bold, playful, independent, alert, extremely intelligent, and, at times, a bit boisterous. They rank 36th in Stanley Coren's The Intelligence of Dogs, being of above average working/obedience intelligence. This is a dog ready for adventure and is happiest if that adventure takes place outdoors in cold weather. It needs daily exercise, lest it become frustrated or even destructive. It is an exceptionally friendly breed. If untrained, it tends to pull when on leash. This dog needs attention for it to understand its place within the family (or the pack), else it may develop social problems and feel neglected. This is a very proud and noble breed that can easily have its feelings hurt if its owner deserts his or her allegiance or duty. An inevitable bond will develop between the dog's family, master, or pack, and if there is disloyalty, the dog will definitely feel it and be hurt. Although each dog is an individual, they generally are very gentle and get along great with children. They are happiest when they feel that they are part of the family. This, combined with their very loud bark, makes them a good watchdog.

Norwegian Elkhounds can be challenging to train because of their intelligence and deep independent streak, but they are acceptable obedience dogs, good-natured, and very understandable in their learning and training. For example, if they fail to "come" because there is something of greater interest in the other direction, they can be quick to learn the importance of the command if taught correctly but they are a willful breed and may never "come" on command. They can be wonderful in agility and are particularly good tracking dogs.

Care

Grooming

Norwegian Elkhound's thick coats are well suited to Norwegian weather, and provide protection from the elements in two main ways. Their outer coats shed rain, snow, and sleet easily, while their under coats keep them warm in low temperatures. Because their coat is so thick, they moult twice a year, producing copious amounts of fur indoors.

Elkhounds tend to remain clean because their coat sheds most dirt and because they seem to keep themselves clean instinctively. However, Elkhounds require regular everyday brushing; especially when they moult to avoid their oil glands becoming plugged and to help them stay cool in summer.

However, this can prove problematic for owners in warmer climates, for Elkhounds shed profusely in the summer, leaving soft white down-like hair everywhere.

Some owners save the hair from brushes and combs, spin the cleaned hair into yarn, and crochet or knit with it. The resulting fabric is soft and warm.

Walking

Elkhounds are very powerful animals, bred to hunt all day in cold climates, so they require plenty of exercise to feel satisfied and stay healthy. A minimum of 20–30 minute walk twice a day is absolutely necessary and recommended by many breeders. But for an Elkhound to feel really satisfied and healthy, daily walks up to two or three hours would be ideal.

Elkhounds are truly an outside dog at heart and need to have an owner with confidence who has the ability to establish clear dominance in the owner–pet relationship. An owner who does not establish this dominance will find that an Elkhound may be prone to running off when walking or when the door is open and ignoring any calls or commands.

Health

Norwegian Elkhounds sometimes carry a genetic predisposition to suffer from progressive retinal atrophy, or, like many medium and large breeds, hip dysplasia, renal problems and cysts, particularly in later life; they are also prone to thyroid problems. Overall, however, they are a hardy breed with few health problems.

Elkhounds are prone to rapid weight gain and must not be overfed .

They have a lifespan of 12–16 years.

History and Evolution

The Norwegian Elkhound is an ancient breed, having been developed over 6,000 years ago to help early Scandinavians hunt big game such as moose and bear. Remains of dogs remarkably similar to the modern Elkhound have been found in grave sites such as the Viste Cave in Jæren, Norway, where they were dated as far back as 4000–5000 BC. Archaeological excavations in Scandinavia suggest this breed existed and was domesticated in the Stone age. At the end of the 19th century the breed came to England, and in 1901 the The Kennel Club officially recognized it.

For many years, the Norwegian Elkhound was considered the oldest of all dog breeds, going back further than 6,000 years. Recent DNA analysis suggests, however, that several "ancient" breeds have been "recreated in more recent times from combinations of other breeds" (Ostrander et al., 2004). The researchers found "genetic evidence for a recent origin of the Norwegian Elkhound, believed to be of ancient Scandinavian origin" ([8]). But this study only includes 85 of the world's more than 400 dog breeds, omits many primitive lineages, and clusters the breeds together into just four major groups called clades. Nevertheless, some researchers say that the Norwegian Elkhound is a descendant of the ancient "primitive" Pariah Dog that existed 4,000–7,000 years ago.

Of the four major clades that Ostrander et al. clusters together, Clade II includes dogs with the genetic haplotype D8 from two Scandinavian dog breeds: the Norwegian Elkhound and the Jämthund. This genetic sequence haplotype is closely related to two wolf haplotypes found in Italy, France, Romania, and Greece, and is also related to a wolf haplotype found in western Russia (Vila et al., 1997). Clade II appears to be only seen in Norwegian breeds and exhibits a vast amount of divergences. It is suggested that this clade illustrates an ancient and independent origin from wolves that are now extinct (Raisor, 2004). The Norwegian Elkhound evolved, at least partially, from ancestral grey wolf subspecies now found in south central Europe and western Russia and may very well be one of the most ancient of all dog breeds.

In Medieval times it was known as a dyrehund, meaning "animal-dog" in Norwegian, and was highly prized as a hunting dog but rarely seen or bred outside of Norway.

Famous Norwegian Elkhounds

- President Herbert Hoover's "Weejie"

Cultural references

Literature

- "Canute" and others, in Virginia Woolf's novel, *Orlando: A Biography*

Television

- Mulder blocks Eugene Victor Tooms when stalking a potential victim by asking him about his Norwegian Elkhound, Heinrich in the episode Tooms

See also

- Tahltan Bear Dog (extinct)

References

- Lynch, Deborah and Jenny Madeoy. 2004 "Man's best research guide: Breeds hold key to shared ailments." presented at the annual meeting of the American Association for the Advancement of Science by Deborah Lynch of the Canine Studies Institute in Aurora, Ohio and Jenny Madeoy of the Fred Hutchinson Cancer Centre in Seattle. [9]

- Lynch, Deborah and Jenny Madeoy. 2004a "How top dogs took lead 7,000 years ago." presented at the annual meeting of the American Association for the Advancement of Science conference in Seattle by Deborah Lynch of the Canine Studies Institute in Aurora, Ohio and Jenny Madeoy of the Fred Hutchinson Cancer Centre in Seattle. [10]

- Ostrander et al. 2004. "Genetic Structure of the Purebred Domestic Dog." Science, vol. 304, pp. 1160–1164.

- Raisor, Michelle Jeanette. 2004. "Determining the Antiquity of Dog Origins: Canine Domestication as a Model for the Consilience Between Molecular Genetics and Archaeology." Dissertation, Department of Anthropology, Texas A&M University. [11]

- Vila, Caries, et al. 1997. "Multiple and Ancient Origins of the Domestic Dog." Science, vol. 276. [12]

Further reading

- **Books**
  - Norwegian Elkhound (Comprehensive Owner's Guide), 2005. ISBN 978-1593783068
  - Norwegian Elkhounds by Anna Katherine Nicholas. TFH, 1997. ISBN 978-0793823192
  - The Norwegian Elkhound (Pure Bred) by Nina P. Ross, PhD. Doral, 1995. ISBN 978-0944875391
  - The Elkhound in the British Isles by Anne Roslin-Williams. Witherby & Co., 1993. ISBN 1 85609 050 7
  - My 60 Years with Norwegian Elkhounds by Olav P. Campbell, 1988.
  - The New Complete Norwegian Elkhound, revised edition, by Olav Wallo. Howell, 1987.
  - Norwegian Elkhounds by Anna Katherine Nicholas. TFH, 1983.
  - Great Gray Dogs: The Norwegian Elkhound Factbook, 2nd edition. Great Gray Dogs, 1980.
  - Your Norwegian Elkhound by Helen E. Franciose and Nancy C. Swanson. Denlinger, 1974.
  - How to Raise and Train a Norwegian Elkhound by Glenna Clark Crafts. TFH, 1973. Reprint of the 1964 book with a different cover.

- **Magazine Articles**
  - Dearth, Kim D.R. "The Norwegian Elkhound" *Dog World* September 1999, Vol. 84 Issue 9, p12-17.
  - "Dog of the Vikings" *Dog Fancy*. April 1998.
  - "Norwegian Elkhound". *Dog World*. July 1997, Vol. 82 Issue 7. p86.

External links

- Norwegian Elkhound Association of America [13]
- Norwegian Elkhound Club of Great Britain [14]

Norwegian Lundehund

Norwegian Lundehund

Norwegian Lundehund	
Other names	Norsk Lundehund Norwegian Puffin Dog Lundehund
Country of origin	Norway
Traits	
Classification and standards	
FCI Group 5 Section 2 #269	standard [1]
AKC Miscellaneous Class	standard [2]
CKC Group 2 - Hounds	standard [3]
UKC Northern Breeds	standard [4]
Dog (*Canis lupus familiaris*)	

The **Norwegian Lundehund** (*Norsk Lundehund*) is a small breed of dog of the Spitz type that originates from Norway. Its name is composed of the prefix *Lunde*, from the Norwegian *lundefugl* (puffin), and the suffix *hund*, meaning dog. The breed was originally developed for the hunting of puffins and their eggs.

Appearance

The Norwegian Lundehund is a small, rectangular Spitz type dog. The Lundehund has a great range of motion in its joints, allowing it to fit into and extricate itself from narrow passages. Dogs of this breed are able to bend their head backwards along their own spine and turn their forelegs to the side at a 90-degree horizontal angle to their body, much like human arms. Their pricked, upright ears can be folded shut to form a near-tight seal by folding forward or backward. The Norwegian Lundehund is a polydactyl: instead of the normal four toes per foot, the Lundehund normally has six toes, all fully formed, jointed and muscled. Some specimens may have more, or less, than six toes per foot; although having less than six toes is frowned upon and will lose the dog points in a show ring. The outercoat is dense and rough with a soft undercoat. The Lundehund is adapted to climb narrow cliff paths in Røst where it originally would have hunted puffins.

History

The breed has a long history. As far back as 1600 it was used for hunting puffins along the Norwegian coast. Its flexibility and extra toes were ideal for hunting the birds in their inaccessible nesting locations on cliffs and in caves. Interest for the breed declined when new methods for hunting puffins were invented and a dog tax was created. Around 1900, they were only found in the isolated village of Mostad (spelled Måstad in Norwegian), Lofoten. The breed was nearly extinct around World War II when canine distemper struck Værøy and the surrounding islands. In 1963, the population was further decimated by distemper again. This time, only 6 dogs survived (1 on Værøy & 5 in southern Norway Hamar (these 5 were from the same mother)), creating a population bottleneck. Due to careful breeding with strict guidelines, there are now an estimated 1500-2000 dogs in the world, with around 1100 of the population in Norway and ~350 in the United States. Height:13-15 inches Weight: 12-15 pounds

Lundehund Gastroenteropathy

Lundehund gastroenteropathy is a set of digestive disorders that can lead to an overgrowth of digestive bacteria, and a loss of ability to absorb nutrients from food. In extreme cases the dog can starve due to its inability to derive nutrients and protein from food, regardless of food intake. All Lundehunds have the genetics to have this illness, though not every Lundehund is severely afflicted and some are symptom free. There is no cure, though the disease can be managed.

American Kennel Club

The Norwegian Lundehund, currently listed in the Foundation Stock Service was approved to move to the Miscellaneous Class of the American Kennel Club on November 13, 2007, by a unanimous vote of the AKC Board of Directors, effective date to be July 1, 2008. After an evaluation period in the Miscellaneous Class (reviewed in 6-month increments, effective in January & July), the breed is slated to progress into the Non-sporting Group. The Lundehund made its AKC conformation debut at the Roaring Fork Kennel Club show in Eagle, Colorado on July 12, 2008.

The Lundehund made its introductory premier at a major event at the 2008 AKC/Eukanuba National Championship show in Long Beach, California on December 13 and 14, 2008. Four Lundehunds were present for introductions and inspections by judges and the public at a meet-the-breed booth, constituting one of 153 breeds represented. From this event, the Norwegian Lundehund Association of America has been asked to instruct at several upcoming judges' education events - a major aspect of the AKC plan for full recognition of the breed.

Other aspects in the plan for full recognition include active participation in AKC events (conformation, agility, etc.) and expanding the general dog fancier's knowledge of the breed.

On February 12, 2010, the Board of Directors of the American Kennel Club voted to accept the Norwegian Lundehund "into the Stud Book of the AKC on December 1, 2010. The breed will be eligible to compete in the Non-Sporting Group beginning January 1, 2011."

References

General

- ISBN 0-7513-0856-0

Specific

External links

- Norwegian Lundehund Association of America, Inc. [1] - Recognized by the AKC as the Breed Parent Club for the USA
- The Norwegian Lundehund Club of America [2]
- The International Web Page of the Norwegian Lundehund [3]
- Norsk lundehund klubb [4] (Norwegian-language site)
- lundehund.hallwass.net - The international Community [5] (German-language site)
- LuvLundies [6] - a new message forum dedicated to all things Lundehund
- American Norwegian Lundehund Club [7] - UKC parent club

Otterhound

Otterhound

Otterhound	
Country of origin	Great Britain - England
Traits	

Classification and standards		
FCI	Group 6 Section 2 #294	standard [1]
AKC	Hound	standard [2]
ANKC	Group 4 (Hounds)	standard [3]
CKC	Group 2 - Hounds	standard [4]
KC (UK)	Hound	standard [5]
NZKC	Hounds	standard [6]
UKC	Scenthound	standard [7]
Dog (*Canis lupus familiaris*)		

The **Otterhound** is an old British dog breed, with Bloodhound ancestors, and one of the ancestors of the Airedale Terrier.

Appearance

The Otterhound is a large, rough-coated hound with an imposing head. Originally bred for hunting, it has great strength and a strong body with long striding steps. This makes it able to perform prolonged hard work. Otterhounds generally weigh between 80 and 120 pounds (36 to 54 kg). They have extremely sensitive noses which make them inquisitive and perseverant in investigating scents. Consequently, they need particular supervision. They are friendly dogs with a unique bass voice which they use frequently.

Hunting

The Otterhound hunts its quarry both on land and in water and it has a combination of characteristics unique among hounds; most notably an oily, rough, double coat and substantial webbed feet.

The use of otterhounds to hunt otters by scent ceased in Britain in 1978 when it became illegal to kill otters, at this point otter hunts switched to hunting mink or coypu.

Health

The breed lives to between 10 and 13 years old, although at least one hound is known to have lived to be 16 years old.

The Otterhound enjoys considerable exercise, but can also be a couch potato. They can be good family dogs but need to be kept in a secure property since they can jump fences up to 5 feet high.

common problems that can occur are elbow and hip dysplasia which is a malformation of the hip and elbow joints. They are not always painfull but can cause lameness and impair mobility with arthritis a possible result. Badly affected hounds should not be bred but most otterhounds have a fairly poor hip and elbow score. This problem can be reduced by making sure that developing otterhounds do not jump down from high places, go up and down the stairs or walk too much on very hard surfaces while bones are still growing.

Otterhounds can also be subject to ear infections, due to the shape of their ears, and bloat (or gastric torsion), due to their deep chest. Bloat is the biggest killer of large dogs and is very painful. There are ways to reduce the risk of getting bloat: 1. raising the feeding bowl so that the dog does not take in too much air while feeding 2 wait an hour either side of feeding before or after the dog is exercised. 3 do not feed them high cereal cheap food 4 calm the dog before feeding 5 if the dog eats quickly then put something large in the bowl to reduce the speed of consumption as this will reduce the amount of air in the stomach.

If your dog shows signs of bloat then immediate vetinary attention is required.

An endangered breed

There are only an estimated 1,000 or so Otterhounds in the world and somewhere between 350 and 400 in the US. Even in the early 20th century, when otter hunting was most popular as a sport, Otterhounds were not numerous. They are now considered the most endangered dog breed in Britain since only 51 were born there in 2006. They are on the list of Vulnerable Native Breeds as identified by the UK Kennel Club, and as much as possible is being done to save the breed. NB: It is important to remember that all dog breeds are essentially the same species (*Canis familiaris*) and varying characteristics of any one breed are the result of selective breeding by humans in order produce certain looks and traits. "Endangered" breeds such as the Otterhound are therefore closely related leaving them prone to inhereted diseases due to a lack of genetic diversity.

Famous Otterhounds

- Sandy in *Annie (film)*

External links

- Otterhound Club of America [8]
- www.otterhounds.de [9]

Petit Basset Griffon Vendéen

Petit Basset Griffon Vendéen

Two Petit Bassets Griffon Vendéen.	
Nicknames	PBGV
Country of origin	France
Traits	

Classification and standards		
FCI	Group 6 Section 1 #67	standard [1]
AKC	Hound	standard [2]
ANKC	Group 4 (hound)	standard [3]
CKC	Group 2 - Hound	standard [4]
KC (UK)	Hound	standard [5]
NZKC	Hounds	standard [6]
UKC	Scenthounds	standard [7]
Dog (*Canis lupus familiaris*)		

The **Petit Basset Griffon Vendéen** ("peh-TEE bas-SAY grih-FON vahn-day-AHN"), or "PBGV," is a breed of dog of the scent hound type, bred to trail hares in bramble filled terrain of the Vendée district of France.

Description

Appearance

Both sexes should be of similar size, range between 12.5 and 15.5 inches (32 to 40 cm) at the withers and between 25 and 40 pounds (15 to 20 kilograms).

Like the other 3 Griffon Vendéen breeds: the Grand Griffon Vendéen, Briquet Griffon Vendéen, and the Grand Basset Griffon Vendéen; they are solid dogs that appear rough and unrefined yet casual. They have short legs, a sturdy bone structure, and a body that is only slightly longer than it is tall at the withers. The body length is not as extreme as that of a basset hound or dachshund.

The dogs have a tousled appearance, with a harsh double coat that is both long and rough.The hair on the face and legs may be softer than body hair. The fur on the face resembles a beard and moustache. They usually have very long eyelashes.

The skull is domed, with drop, oval ears like many hounds share, though dogs tend to have higher domes than bitches. The ears are set low and hanging, and if stretched out should reach the tip of the nose. The tail is usually held upright, and is long and tapered to the end, similar in shape to a saber.

The coloring is primarily white with spots of orange, lemon, black, grizzle (gray-and-white hairs), or sable, sometimes with tan accents. They may be bicolor, tricolor, or have grizzling.

Temperament and Breeding

PBGVs are extroverted, friendly, and independent hounds. Sometimes called the "happy breed," PBGVs have tirelessly wagging tails and expressive, intelligent eyes. PBGVs are typically active and lively. While good with children, other dogs and pets, they may be unsuitable for very young children because of their energy and tendency to play bite. The PBGV standard states that the dog should "give voice freely" -- as is typical of hounds, petits are outspoken dogs. If their 'pack' begins howling or singing, the dog will join in, with amusing results. PBGVs may howl alone or with a companion; they may howl to music, for fun, or in protest at being left alone. PBGV companions report that sleeping dogs have been known to awaken and howl along with favorite songs.

The PBGV is not a quiet dog. While no PBGV would ever be called "yippy," their assertive, hound-bray is uncharacteristically loud for their petite stature. The outspoken nature of a PBGV varies from dog to dog, but even the shyest Petit will greet other dogs with a bark or call.

Like other hounds, Petits are stubborn, and sometimes may not respond well to training.

Because they are so extroverted, friendly, and happy, PBGVs make excellent therapy dogs.

PBGVs are excellent hunting and tracking dogs. A "Hunting Instinct Test" with associated AKC certification is currently in development as a part of optional breed credentialing. Petits who work in this manner do not hunt to kill. In the Vendee region of France, the dogs are used to flush and track rabbit in the bramble, sending rabbit out into the open where the hunter takes the rabbit with a shot.

Skilled hunting dogs work well with other dogs in the pack, alerting the pack to the presence of a rabbit, or to a rabbit in motion down a trail. "Saber tails," another PBGV nickname, are typically white at the tip of the tail, so the tail is easily identified by a hunter above the bramble and brush.

As a companion animal, this occasionally pronounced hunting instinct may manifest in the home as a dog that gives chase to birds, squirrel, and cats. For some PBGVs, this instinct may be difficult to overcome with training. Most PBGVs make fine companion animals, and have suitable manners to live among cats and other animals without assuming a hunting role. Potential PBGV owners are cautioned to be aware of this instinct and, if cats are present in the home, work to acclimate the puppy or dog to recognize that the cat is part of the home "pack."

As scent hounds, most PBGVs should be kept on-leash when in open outdoor areas. Even the most obedient dog may give chase when a scent is found. Petits are natural athletes, and they can run fast and long where scent is involved. Scent will typically trump obedience in the mind of a PBGV.

The outspoken nature and erect tail of a PBGV can be misinterpreted by other dogs, as these manners typically express dominance to other dogs. PBGVs can inspire a misguided need to express dominance on the part of passing dogs. PBGV owners need to be alert to this potential misinterpretation, as Petits are easily outclassed in both size and aggressiveness.

Health

The UK Kennel Club conducted a health survey of Basset Griffon Vendeens (both Petit and Grand varieties combined) in 2004. The Petit Basset Griffon Vendeen (PBGV) Club of America has conducted two health surveys, one in 1994 and one in 2000. The club is currently conducting another survey. These are apparently the only completed or on-going health surveys for Basset Griffon Vendeens (as of July 2007).

Mortality

Average longevity of PBGVs in the 2000 Club of America survey was 12.7 years (standard deviation 3.9). Sample size was not clear, but it appeared to be 45 dogs. No longevity data were collected in the 1994 survey. There was no information on causes of death.

Average longevity of 76 deceased Basset Griffon Vendeens (both varieties) in the 2004 UK Kennel Club survey was 12.1 years (maximum 17.3 years). Leading causes of death were cancer (33%), old age (24%), and cardiac (7%).

Compared to surveyed longevities of other breeds of similar size, Basset Griffon Vendeens have a typical or somewhat higher than average life expectancy.

Morbidity

In the PBGV Club of America 2000 survey, the most common diseases reported by owners of 640 dogs were persistent pupillary membranes, recurrent ear infections, hypothyroidism, neck pain, and epilepsy.

Among 289 live Basset Griffon Vendeens (both varieties) in the 2004 UKC survey, the most common health issues noted by owners were reproductive, dermatologic (dermatitis and mites), and aural (otitis externa, excessive ear wax, and ear mites).

Care

They should have daily walks to burn off excess energy. They need to be brushed regularly, but not daily, to avoid matting and tangles. To keep the coat well groomed it must be stripped. Hairs must be pulled out of the coat using either a special stripping tool or the finger and thumb. The coat is shallow rooted and is made to come out if trapped, so this grooming method causes no pain. They need regular ear cleanings to prevent yeast infections and clipping of the claws is normally needed once or twice a month.

Part of the charm of a PBGV is its tousled, unkempt appearance.

See also

- Basset Hound
- Basset Bleu de Gascogne
- Basset Fauve de Bretagne
- Grand Basset Griffon Vendéen
- Coat (dog)

External links

- Petit Basset Griffon Vendeen Club of America [8]
- Basset Griffon Vendeen Club of Great Britain [9] - Breed club for the Petit and Grand Basset Griffon Vendeens

Pharaoh Hound

Pharaoh Hound

A juvenile male Pharaoh Hound	
Other names	Kelb tal-Fenek (in country of origin)
Nicknames	Pharaoh
Country of origin	Malta
Patronage	Great Britain

Traits

Classification and standards

FCI	Group 5 Section 6 #248	standard [1]
AKC	Hound	standard [2]
ANKC	Group 4 (Hounds)	standard [3]
CKC	Group 2 - Hounds	standard [4]
KC (UK)	Hound	standard [5]
NZKC	Hounds	standard [6]
UKC	Sighthound and Pariah	standard [7]

Dog (*Canis lupus familiaris*)

The **Pharaoh Hound** is a breed of dog and the national hound of the Mediterranean nation of Malta. Its native name is ***Kelb tal-Fenek*** (plural: *Klieb tal-Fenek*) in Maltese, which means "rabbit hound". The dog is the traditional hunting companion of Maltese outdoorsmen. The breed has no conclusive links with Ancient Egypt and its name in English is a 20th century fabrication. It has variously been classified as a member of the sighthound group, yet its fieldwork description clearly determines it as a hound. It is indigenous to the islands and remains rare outside of Malta.

Description

Appearance

At first glance, the Pharaoh Hound should appear both graceful and elegant as well as powerful and athletic. Its build should be one of strength without bulkiness or excessive musculature. Its head is elegant without being fine or extreme. The skull should resemble a blunt wedge, and is long and chiseled with only a slight stop and a muzzle of good length. Its eyes are oval with a keen, noble, alert, and intelligent expression. It has a long, lean, and muscular neck that is slightly arched. Its body is slightly longer than its height at the withers. It has a deep chest that extends down to the elbows and a moderate tuck up. Its shoulders are long and well laid back. Its front legs are long and straight. The back legs are moderately angulated, parallel to each other, and must be in balance with the forelegs. It has a long, fine, straight tail that should reach down to a bit below the point of the hocks. The tail is carried down when relaxed but must not tuck between the legs. When the dog is in motion or is excited, the tail is carried up; either level with, or loosely curled above, the back. Its dewclaws may be removed.

Size

It stands between 21 to 25 inches at the withers and weighs between 40 to 60 lbs. Males are typically larger than females.

Coat and colour

The coat is fine and short with no feathering. The texture varies from silky to somewhat hard and it must never be so profuse as to stand away from the dog's skin. The only color accepted by most kennel clubs is red; though the shades of red color varies, and accepted shades range from a tan to a deep chestnut and all shades in between. White markings on the chest, toes, tail-tip, center of forehead, and the bridge of the muzzle are accepted, but not required. A white tail-tip is desired by some kennel clubs. In contrast, any white markings on the back of the neck, the sides, or the back of the dog are unacceptable by most standards. Pharaoh's eyes are always amber, and should compliment the coat colour. They are born with blue eyes, which change to a light gold or yellow color during early puppyhood and then begin to darken well into adulthood. The nose, whiskers, nails, paw-pads, and eye-rims should also be the same colour as the coat. Pharaohs also have a unique trait of "blushing" when excited or happy, with their ears and nose becoming bright pink.

Temperament

The Pharaoh Hound is an intelligent, trainable, playful, and active breed. It is sociable with other dogs and with people; however, it can be aloof or reserved with strangers. It is typically very open and affectionate with its family and those it knows. It is an independent-minded, occasionally stubborn breed, yet can be very trainable when appropriate positive training methods are used. It has a strong hunting instinct, and caution should be observed when it is around small pets such as cats, birds, and rodents. It is not a demonstrative breed but rather is quietly affectionate. It is a vocal breed without being yappy or barking just for the sake of barking. It makes a good watch dog; however, it is not well suited as guard dog as it is rarely aggressive with people. This is not a breed suited for kennel situations due to its intelligence and activity level. The breed tends to bond deeply with its people and thrives best when it feels included as a member of the family.

History

The first recorded mention of a Maltese hunting dog, which could have been identical with the modern Kelb tal-Fenek, was issued by Commendatore Fra. G. Fran. Abela (Maltese historian and Vice Chancellor of the Order of St. John) in 1647 who wrote 'There are dogs called 'Cernechi' esteemed for the hunting of rabbits , and as far as France are in demand primarily for stony, mountainous and steep locations'. The use of the word 'Cernechi' to name the breed should be no surprise as Italian was the language of scholars and the courts in Malta from at least 1091 up to WWII.

The first two specimens of the breed were brought to Britain from Malta in the 1920s, but at that time, no litter was bred. Again, some dogs were imported to the UK in the early 1960s, and the first litter was born in 1963. The breed standard was recognised by the The Kennel Club in 1974. The breed was called the *Pharaoh Hound* although this name was already used by the FCI as an alternative name for the Ibizan Hound at that time. When the FCI abolished this name in 1977 and decided to call the Ibizan Hound exclusively by its original Spanish name *Podenco Ibicenco*, the term Pharaoh Hound was transferred to the Kelb tal-Fenek, whose breed standard had been recognised by the FCI at the same time .

A number of other breeds that are similar to the Pharaoh Hound exist in different regions of the Mediterranean. One is the Cirneco dell'Etna from neighbouring Sicily, which is very similar in structure and appearance, but somewhat smaller (43–51 cm/17-20in). Other similar breeds include the Ibizan Hound, Podenco Canario, Podengo Português and other local breeds from the Mediterranean—each breed is slightly different with physical characteristics that match the terrain the dogs hunt on. It is not clear whether those breeds have descended from the same ancestral lines, or whether their similarities have developed due to similar environmental conditions.

Care

The Pharaoh Hound is independent-minded, highly intelligent, and occasionally stubborn, yet very trainable when positive methods are used. It is a very sensitive breed and responds poorly to compulsionary training methods and to being physically punished. Pharaohs can succeed in competition obedience, but they do not take to it naturally as many breeds that were bred to work alongside people. Pharaohs were bred to hunt and think for themselves, and they have retained this trait for thousands of years. They tire/bore easily with repetitive commands, therefore it is the trainer's job to ensure that their training remains interesting and positive in nature.

They have sensitive skin, and shampoo (canine or human) may cause allergic reactions; therefore, it is best to wash them with either a human baby shampoo or gentle dog shampoo. Grooming Pharaohs is as easy as a quick rub with a hound glove or a damp cloth. They are clean dogs, shed very little, and have no noticeable odor, even when wet.

They are a very active breed and need more than just a daily walk; a run every day is required. Though they are active, they should not be hyperactive. Because of their strong prey drive and independent nature, this breed should never be allowed off leash unless in a securely fenced area away from road traffic or other dangers. Their prey drive is so strong that if they see something they think is prey, they will chase after it, and no amount of training can stop them.

They are very adept jumpers, and fences meant to contain them must be more than five feet (1.52 metres) high, six feet (1.82 metres) or higher being preferable. Because they are such good jumpers, they are well suited to the sport of dog agility. They are often classified as sighthounds, and thus compete in lure coursing. Because they maintain very little body fat and have short coats, they are sensitive to cold and cannot be left outside for long in cold climates. Dog coats/jackets are a must for this breed in cold climates. Many Pharaoh Hounds enjoy snow, however, and will keep themselves warm through running, playing, and digging.

Health

Pharaoh hounds, being somewhat uncommon outside of the Maltese Islands of Malta and Gozo, and because they are not profitable for commercial breeding, have not been subjected to as much irresponsible breeding as some more popular breeds. Breeders try hard to prevent hereditary diseases from entering the gene pool. Pharaohs are basically free from genetic diseases. Reputable breeders continue to test their breeding stock for genetic conditions such as hip dysplasia, luxating patellas, and myriad eye conditions just to ensure that these disorders do not become a problem. Reputable breeders should be able to show documentation of health screening performed on their breeding dogs. Note that Pharaohs, like most sighthounds, are sensitive to barbiturate anaesthetics. Their ears are thin and prone to frostbite when in cold climates. Life expectancy is about 12–15 years or more

Hunting

The Kelb tal-Fenek is usually taken out to hunt at night when there are fewer distractions. Generally, the hunters will take their dogs into the countryside and release pairs of a male and a female dog in each compass direction. The dogs will then search out their prey using scent. When a rabbit is found the hounds will give chase, the small and more agile female in the lead with the male keeping the rabbit from darting too far to the sides. At this point the dogs giving chase will emit a high pitched bark, attracting the other dogs and the hunters, all of whom will come running. By the time the hunters and other dogs arrive the rabbit will almost always have taken to the ground. The hunters will then gather and leash all but one dog, then place nets over all of the likely escape holes of the rabbit. Finally the hunter will take a ferret (with a small bell attatched) from a round wicker basket, and places it into the last entrance to the rabbit's burrow. The Kelb tal-Fenek can hear the little bell up to 3 meters down under the rocky terrain. When the ferret flushes the rabbit out a hole, one free dog swoops down upon it. This style of hunting is mentioned by Strabo about hunting in the Balearic Islands under Roman rule , and the Maltese word for ferret--"nemes"--may have its roots in the Greek word 'nemesis'.

Competitions and Shows

Pharaoh Hound, International Champion XO EZ owned by Lori Evans, Joseph Buchanan and Ronald and Desiree Frank, placed 4th in the Hound Group at Crufts 2007.

A Pharaoh Hound, owned by Ms. J. Hall from Sweden, was Hound Group Winner at Crufts, 2009. However the Pharaoh Hound has yet to place at the group level in the Westminster Kennel Club Dog Show, due to a lack of hounds outside Malta.

Miscellaneous

It should be noted that the Kelb tal-Fenek is not the only breed of dog specific to the tiny islands of Malta. There is also the Kelb tal-But ("pocket dog", a toy breed), Kelb tal-Kaċċa ("gun dog", a breed used for bird hunting), and lastly a type of Mastiff which is now extinct (Kelb tal-Ġlied, sometimes called the Maltese Bulldog or Maltese Mastiff). It is number 141 out of 154 breeds by dogs registered in 2005 by the AKC.

Kelb Tal-Fenek were also used in the reconstruction and reconstitution of the Cirneco dell'Etna breed in Sicily.

External links

- Information
  - Website about the Maltese Kelb Tal-Fenek [8]
  - Field work description [9]
  - Breeder website containing detailed Pharaoh Hound Information from Europe and the USA [10]
  - Breeder website containing detailed Pharaoh Hound information [11]
  - The Pharaoh Hound Breed Forum [12]
- Clubs
  - Pharaoh Hound Club of America [13]
  - The Swedish Pharaoh Hound Club [14]
  - The Pharaoh Hound Club [15] breed club in the UK
- Sites

- The Pharaoh Hound in the UK [16]

Plott Hound

Plott Hound

Other names	Plott Plotthund
Country of origin	brought from Germany, started officially in United States
Traits	
Classification and standards	
AKC Hound Group	standard [1]
UKC Scenthound Breeds	standard [2]
Dog (*Canis lupus familiaris*)	

The **Plott Hound** is a large scent hound, specifically a coonhound, originally bred for hunting boar.

Description

The Plott Hound is one of the least known breeds of dog in the United States, even though they are the state dog of North Carolina. They make wonderful pets and hunting dogs.

Appearance

The Plott Hound should be athletic, muscular, and agile in appearance. It should be neither low-set and heavy, nor leggy and light: it has medium build. Its expression should be one of intelligence, confidence, and determination. Its skin should not be baggy like that of a Bloodhound.

The Plott is a beautiful, strongly built yet moderate hound, with a distinct brindle-colored coat. His appearance suggests the capacity for speed, stamina and endurance.

The Plott may have an identification mark on the hound used to identify the dog when out hunting. Such a mark is not penalized in conformation shows.

Coat and color

Fine to medium coarse in texture. Short or medium in length, with a smooth and glossy appearance.

The National Plott Hound Association's definition of the word "brindle": "A fine streaked or striped effect or pattern of black or tan hairs with hairs of a lighter or darker background color. Shades of colors accepted: yellow brindle, red brindle, tan brindle, brown brindle, black brindle, grey brindle, and maltese (slate grey, blue brindle.)" Grey muzzle accepted.

Acceptable colors are any of the above mentioned brindles, or black with brindle trim. Some white on chest and/or feet is permissible. White anywhere except on chest and/or feet is a fault.

Size

Plott Hounds are approximately 22 to 27 in (50 to 71 cm) at the withers for males, (50 to 58 cm) 21 to 25 in for females. Males should weigh 23 to 27 kg (50 to 75 lb). Females should weigh 18 to 25 kg (40 to 65lb).

Temperament

This breed is active, fast, bright, kind, confident, alert, cute and courageous. They are vicious fighters on game, have a super treeing instinct and take readily to water. They are quick to learn. They are often indifferent to other dogs but seek the attention of humans. Voice is open trailing, bawl and chop. Plott Hounds are also good family pets, but young children will not do well with this breed because of its hunting instinct.

History

Of the seven breeds of UKC registered Coonhounds, the Plott Hound and the American Leopard Hound do not trace their ancestry to the foxhound. And, of those seven breeds, we can be most certain of the Plott's heritage and the men most responsible for its development.

The ancestors of today's Plott Hounds were used for boar hunting in Germany many years ago. Johannes Plott left his native Germany and came to this country in 1750. He brought a few wild boar hounds with him. These dogs had been bred for generations for their stamina and gameness. Plott and his family settled in the mountains of western North Carolina. Though there is no evidence that Johannes ever came to western North Carolina, his son Henry settled there around 1800 and was responsible for the Plott hound legend of an incredible big game dog. The Plott Balsams are a mountain range that carries the family name to this day.

Plott supposedly kept his strain entirely pure, making no outcrosses. In 1780, the Plott pack passed into the hands of Henry Plott.

Shortly after, a hunter living in Rabun Gap, Georgia who had been breeding his own outstanding strain of "leopard spotted dogs" heard of the fame of the Plott Hounds and came to North Carolina to see for himself. He was so impressed that he borrowed one of Montraville Plott's top stud dogs for a year to breed to his own bitches. This single cross is the only known instance of new blood being introduced into the Plott Hound since they first came to this country. Eventually Mont decided not to continue this breeding practice and gave all the leopard dogs away, returning to his original breeding practices.

Other crosses possibly took place around the year 1900. G.P. Ferguson, a neighbor of the Plott family in North Carolina in those days, was a major influence on the Plott breed. He made a careful study of the Blevins hounds and the Cable hounds of that era. To what extent he used these bloodlines in his Plott breeding program is not known.

The Plott Hound was first registered with the United Kennel Club in the 1900's. Today's Plotts are known for their great courage and stamina. They have a clear voice that carries well.

References

- http://www.secretary.state.nc.us/pubsweb/symbols/sy-plott.htm
- http://www.akc.org/breeds/plott/
- http://www.slate.com/id/2184281/pagenum/all/#page_start
- http://www.ukcdogs.com/WebSite.nsf/Breeds/PlottHoundRevisedJanuary12009

Strike and Stay: The Story of the Plott Hound, Bob Plott, The History Press, 2007 pp. 25- 30

Portuguese Podengo

Portuguese Podengo

Wirehaired Portuguese Podengo Medio	
Other names	Podengo Portugues Portuguese Warren Hound
Country of origin	Portugal
Traits	
Classification and standards	
FCI Group 5 Section 7 #94	standard [1]
AKC Hound (FSS)	standard [2]
The AKC Foundation Stock Service [3] (FSS) is an optional recording service for purebred dogs that are not yet eligible for AKC registration.	
KC (UK) Hound	standard [3]
UKC Sighthound and Pariah	standard [4]
Dog (*Canis lupus familiaris*)	

The **Portuguese Podengo** is an ancient multi-sensory hound (sight and scent) breed of dog from Portugal. The Podengo comes in three sizes that are not interbred - small (Pequeno), medium (Médio) and large (Grande), each size with two hair coats (smooth and wire coat) and its own unique temperament. All three sizes love to hunt, its tradition in their native country. Typically, the dogs hunt in a pack with their human companion following them on large tracts of land with lots of game. Their hunting style is of an independent nature, with the dog(s) forging ahead with the hunter within their site range (which can be many acres). When game is found, they will kill it and bring it back to the hunter or wait for the hunter to catch up and shoot it. Each is capable of hunting game that is appropriate to their size and temperament. (Pequeno-rabbits, Medio-rabbits and wild boar, Grande-deer and wild boar).

The Portuguese Podengo is featured as the Portuguese Kennel Club's logo. It is a healthy breed and the Pequenos have been known to live twenty years, with the average lifespan of the breed approximately

15–17 years. The Médios can live to be approximately 12–15 years.

- The Portuguese Podengo in the UK is represented by The Portuguese Podengo Club of Great Britain [5], and the Podengo Pequeno was fully recognized by the Kennel Club in 2003. The Breed Standard was approved on January 1, 2006. The Podengo Poqueno was transferred from the Import Register into the Breed Register on January 1, 2008 at the Kennel Club. The Podengo Pequeno now has its own breed classes at Championship Shows and Open Shows (the other sizes are in the process of being included). The Podengo Pequeno was shown at Crufts for the first time in 2009. There are approximately 400 Podengos (primarily Pequeno) now resident in the UK.

- The Portuguese Podengo Pequeno is represented in the United States by Portuguese Podengo Pequenos of America [6], The American Portuguese Podengo Pequeno Club (APPPC) [7] and The Portuguese Podengo Pequeno Club of America [8]. The Portuguese Podengo Medio and Grande are represented in the United States by The American Portuguese Podengo Medio/Grande Club (APPMGC or 'MGC') [9] and The Portuguese Podengo Club of America [10]. The Podengo(s) is currently recognized in the US by the United Kennel Club [11], American Rare Breed Association [12] and Rarities (North American Kennel Club) [13]. It is also recognized by The American Sighthound Field Association [14] and is recorded in the American Kennel Club's [15] Foundation Stock Service, the first step towards full recognition by the AKC. The Portuguese Podengo participates in AKC's Companion Events - obedience, rally and agility and lure coursing. There are approximately 400 Podengos in the United States, most of them of the Pequeno size.

- In Europe, the Podengo is classified by the Fédération Cynologique Internationale (FCI) as Group 5: Spitz and primitive type, Section 7: Primitive type hunting dogs. The FCI breed standard, which originates in Portugal, governs all types and varieties of the Portuguese Podengo.

- Portugal registers the most Podengos, followed by the United Kingdom, Finland, and the United States.

- In both the United States and the UK the Portuguese Podengo is classified in the Hound Group.

- All Podengo types are hardy, intelligent and lively dogs, excelling at agility and making fine companions. Loyal and fearless, Podengos are also good house guards and are amenable to training by dog experienced people and those that enjoy primitive (unrefined, "less domesticated") dog behavior. The Médio, particularly the Wirehaired, presents behavioral and intellectual challenges that inexperienced or unprepared dog owners will find unacceptable such as inattentiveness, independence, dog-dog aggression, resource hoarding and guarding, very loud and persistent barking, serious recreational digging, fence jumping, destructiveness and running away.

Types and varieties

There are three sizes of Podengos: Podengo Grande, Podengo Medio and Podengo Pequeno.

Within each size type are two varieties: smooth (also referred to as smooth coat) and wire (also referred to as wire coat, wirehaired, longhaired or rough coat). All of these types are called 'Portuguese Podengo' as a 'breed,' although none of these six types are interbred.

1. Portuguese Podengo Pequeno (Smooth Coat)
2. Portuguese Podengo Pequeno (Wire Coat)
3. Portuguese Podengo Medio (Smooth Coat)
4. Portuguese Podengo Medio (Wire Coat)
5. Portuguese Podengo Grande (Smooth Coat)
6. Portuguese Podengo Grande (Wire Coat)

In its home country, the Podengo is referred to as Small, Medium or Large Podengo. It is acceptable for the hair description to come before or after the 'type' name.

In the United States, the American Kennel Club split the Podengo Pequeno from the other two sizes as a separate breed. This was done primarily to prevent the (registerable) interbreeding of the Pequeno with the Medio.

Portuguese Podengo History

The Portuguese Podengo's probable origin, like all other Mediterranean prick-eared breeds, is from unspecialized, primitive dogs used for various game (all once called 'kelb tal-fenek' or 'rabbit dogs') obtained and distributed by Phoenician traders during their navigations of Africa in 600 BC. They reached the Iberian Peninsula and the land that later became Portugal in the 8th Century BC (evidence of 8th Century BC Phoenician presence in Portugal has been found under Lisbon Cathedral, which was built in 1147). They traded and traveled extensively in this land, which was between their famous city of Gadir (Cádiz) in Iberia and Cornwall, England (where they obtained the valuable tin needed to make bronze). They also moved goods via river transport from their Iberian trading cities as well as storing goods safely on the island of Ibiza. It is entirely possible that the Phoenicians brought dogs with them to these areas at that time as it is very likely that hunting dogs were a valuable commodity for them. When the Moorish (North African) invaded and occupied the Iberian Peninsula (from the early 8th Century to the late 15th Century*) they probably brought their own version of these primitive dogs with them, which would have further influenced and refined Iberian breeds such as the Podengo in Portugal, Podengo Galego in Spain and the Charnigue Hound (or Charnègre Hound) in France.

Diverse recent genetics studies have concluded podenco is a type of dog very related to the rest of european hunting dogs and they are not more primitive than most of them.

The Portuguese Podengo was developed with 6 varieties, each suited to different climates, terrain, type of prey and hunting style. Each is a very versatile hunter and companion that uses all of its senses combined with agility, speed and endurance, running singly or in packs. The Wire Coat variety is better suited for hotter climates with its more open coat texture which provides better cooling and the Smooth variety is better suited for cooler climates with its tighter, denser coat which provides better insulation.

The Grande (large) was developed for deer and wild boar hunting. It will exhaust and hold down the prey and await the hunter's gun. The Grande is now very rare in its home country.

The Medio (medium) was developed for rabbit chasing, flushing, hunting and retrieval. Its hunting style includes catlike stalking and, similar to the Ibizan Hound, it often jumps above the prey before landing on or near it to flush it out of dense brush, rock crevices or burrows. It will dig if necessary to flush prey.

The Pequeno (small) was also developed for flushing rabbits from cover. It is also a good vermin exterminator and was probably kept on board explorer ships when the Portuguese initiated the European worldwide explorations in the 15th and 16th centuries.

In the United States the American Kennel Club (AKC) has divided the breed into the Portuguese Podengo Pequeno and the Portuguese Podengo (that includes the medio and grande size). Both breeds are hunting hounds. The Pequeno will be entering the AKC Misc class in January 2011. The Podengo currently at 124 needs to be at 150 to move to Misc.

Sources: 1) Phoenicians: Lebanon's Epic Heritage by Sanford Holst, leading expert on the Phoenician people 2) Golden Age of the Moor by Ivan Van Sertima 3) Nature Knows No Color-Line by J. A. Rogers 4) Encyclopedia Phoeniciana by Salim George Khalaf

Portuguese Podengo Pequeno

Appearance

- WIRE COAT

The WPP is a small-sized type with a rough coat. The single coat (without undercoat) does shed but not very much.

- SMOOTH COAT

The SPP is a small-sized type with a dense smooth single layer coat that is extremely low maintenance. It naturally sheds dust and dirt and dries very quickly. The single coat (without undercoat) does shed but not very much.

Temperament

Both kinds of Podengo Pequeno are small, friendly, hardy, lively and intelligent companions. They are very active and usually good with children and other animals when socialized from an early age. They enjoy time with their human family.

Like their Medio relatives, they are very watchful and observant and will bark when something gets their attention. They enjoy digging and sunshine and must have a secure enclosed fence. The Podengo Pequeno is trained well with positive techniques and should be kept on leash all of the time during training as they can be quite autonomous and have their own ideas about what constitutes proper behavior. They can be remarkably silly in the home, running around and jumping off furniture with abandon, therefore care must be taken to not allow them free roam of the house or hurting themselves by jumping from too high a perch. A walk with many Pequenos can be a delight and they will continually come back to the owner to make sure they are coming along.

History

The Portuguese Podengo Pequeno accompanied Portuguese explorers on their ships for ratting purposes after the Portuguese completed the reconquest of their country from the Moors in the 13th century.

Wire Coat Pequenos were first shown in the United States in 2001. Smooth Pequenos were first shown in the United States in 2003.

Wire Coat Pequenos were first imported to the UK in 2002. The smooth coated Pequeno followed in 2004.

Most (80%)of the purebred Portuguese Podengos in the United States consist of the Pequeno size, and most of these (75%) are of the wire coat variety.

Portuguese Podengo Medio

Appearance

- WIRE COAT

The WPM is a medium-sized type with a rough coat that functions as an air conditioner in the hot weather. This coat was preferred in the South of their native Portugal, which is very warm. The single coat (without undercoat) does shed but not very much.

- SMOOTH COAT

The SPM is a medium-sized type with a dense smooth single layer coat that is extremely low maintenance. It naturally sheds dust and dirt and dries very quickly. For that reason the Smooth Coat variety is preferred in the North of their native Portugal, which has rainy winters. The single coat (without undercoat) does shed but not very much.

Temperament

Both kinds of Podengo Medio are friendly, hardy and intelligent companions. They are very active and usually good with children and other animals, including livestock, especially when socialized from an early age.

They are watchful and observant and will bark when something gets their attention. Most enjoy digging and need a secure fence, optimally enclosing their own yard. As they are very agile, regular fencing might not be enough, as they are excellent jumpers and climbers. The best way to address this is with a high enough fence to prevent jumping and a "fence" below the ground, preferably of hardware cloth.

When trained, Podengo Medios can have good recall when not on leash. While hiking with them, they generally stay in visual distance and "check" on their owners frequently, always being aware of their position (although that can mean a few acres away). Of course, they must be trained with a reliable recall first.

They are an enthusiastic, trainable dog. This trainability led them to star in a number of movies in the 1990s, including Three Wishes, Homeward Bound II: Lost in San Francisco, Zeus and Roxanne and Soccer Dog: The Movie.

History

The Portuguese Podengo Medio, both smooth coat and wirehaired, has existed, unregistered, in the United States for decades in small numbers with Portuguese-Americans in private home settings, where they have been used for traditional rabbit hunting. They were never really popularized outside of their immigrant homesteads. They are attractive, nice family dogs, with a touch of mischief. The first group of Podengo Medio fanciers met in the US in the early 90's via the early internet Gopher (protocol) system and rec.pets.dogs.breeds.

Smooth Podengo Medios began being shown in America in 2004 and Wirehaired Podengo Medios began being shown in America in 2005.

They are still rare. Breeders in Portugal primarily breed for rabbit hunting, not pets. They are hunting dogs, often kept in kennels, not in homes. The idea of Wirehaired Podengo Medios being kept more as house pets began with breeders in Europe. Similarly, American-born Medios are socialized and tempered to household life.

Portuguese Podengo Grande

Appearance

- WIRE COAT

The WPG is a large-sized type with a tough but even temperament and a rough coat that primarily functions as a briar-protectant when hunting wild boar. The single coat (without undercoat) does shed but not very much. Registered WPGs are very rare, even in its home country and is not yet available to export.

- SMOOTH COAT

The SPG is a large-sized type with a dense smooth single layer coat that also functions as a briar-protectant when hunting wild boar. The registered SPG is still rare in its home country, with very few individuals available for export.

Temperament

Both kinds of Podengo Grande are known to be tough, hardy and intelligently observant animals. They must be socialized very well and carefully by a primitive breed-experienced handler. They are used primarily for hunting wild boar in large packs, where they are released from kennel trucks and sent to chase the boar to its den. They then continue to harass it until it emerges in its attack mode. The dogs then jump in and attach to the boar from all angles and dispatch it swiftly. The waiting hunter can then retrieve the prey.

They will be good guardians and require a securely fenced yard (at least 6 ft tall). They enjoy digging dens, also, like their other Podengo relations. It is most closely related to the Podengo Medio, in fact, Podengo Medios which grow too tall for the Medio standard may be classified as Podengo Grandes. This arrangement does not exist in any other way within the Podengo group.

Training will be firm but fair with the Podengo Grande as it must have respect for its handler and be amenable to training.

History

The Portuguese Podengo Grande may have existed, unregistered, in North America with Portuguese-Americans in private home settings, where they have been used for deer and wild pig hunting.

The first Podengo Grande was imported to the US in 2008 and the first litter born in 2009 as well as the import of 4 Grande of the wire coat. 2010 brought the second litter of Grande

Breeders in Portugal continue to breed primarily for hunting and the PG is kept and raised in kennels.

There is a unique system currently in place in Portugal where unregistered dogs (denoted by the kennel club of Portugal as R.I. or 'Registration Incomplete') may be evaluated by breed experts and used in a breeding program. Succeeding generations, also evaluated by said experts, may eventually result in a 3 generation pedigree of known, evaluated, 'R.I.' dogs which would thus create a full pedigree for certain formerly "RI" Podengos. This process is carried forth under rules established by the CPC and is not exportable to other countries as it relies on the presence of indigenous wild specimens of the breed.

In the United States the American Kennel Club (AKC) has determined that the Medio and Grande size together are to be called 'Podengo' as one breed.

Redbone Coonhound

Redbone Coonhound

Redbone Coonhound	
Nicknames	Reds
Country of origin	Southern United States
Traits	
Classification and standards	
AKC Hound	standard [1]
UKC Scenthounds	standard [2]
Dog (*Canis lupus familiaris*)	

The **Redbone Coonhound** is a breed of dog. They are widely used for hunting bear, raccoon, and cougar. Their agility allows them to be used for hunting from swamplands to mountains, and some can be used as water dogs. The Redbone Coonhound is the only solid colored coonhound. The AKC standard says, *"The Redbone mingles handsome looks and an even temperament with a confident air and fine hunting talents."* [3] This breed has been registered with the UKC since 1904. This is the type of hound that was used in the novel, *Where the Red Fern Grows*.

Description

Appearance

The Coonhound has the lean, muscular, well proportioned build typical to the coonhounds, with long straight legs, a deep chest, and a head and tail held high and proud when hunting or showing. The face has a pleading expression, with sorrowful dark brown or hazel eyes and long, drooping ears.These dogs are great at getting what they want because of their expressions. Their coat is short and smooth against the body, but coarse enough to provide protection to the skin while hunting through brush.Their paws should have thick pads; dewclaws are common. The nose should be black and prominent. The ears are floppy and should extend to nearly the end of the nose if stretched out. The nose is always black and the coat color is always a rich red, though a small amount of white on the chest, between the legs, or on the feet is permissible, though not preferred. Variations of black fur on the face and muzzle are also common. The toes are usually webbed.

Males should be 22-27 inches (56-68.5 cm) at the shoulder, with females slightly shorter at 21-26 inches (53–66 cm). Weight should be proportional to the size and bone structure of the individual dogs, with a preference towards leaner working dogs rather than heavier dogs. Generally, weights will range from 45 to 70 lbs (20.5 to 31.75 kg). Males are typically larger and heavier boned than females and carry a deeper bay.

Temperament

The Redbone Coonhound is an excellent companion and family pet, with some special considerations. They love to be with their owners and family, and are happy just doing things with their humans, or sitting nearby, watching them: a Redbone Coonhound who has been left out of the family fun or penned up during the party is often a heartbroken one. Overall, they are very affectionate and loving: they will often leap to their feet barking loudly to greet their master upon his return home and a typical Redbone will shower everyone with love, licking the face off of family and friends if left to his own devices. A dog of this breed usually won't come and ask for attention as a lab might. They are very happy if you pet them, and love it. They are also a very boisterous breed: as explained above, adult Redbones grow to a large size. They may not know how big and strong they are when young and thus may accidentally knock over elderly adults and young children if left untrained or never taught the command "heel," so basic obedience MUST be on the agenda with this breed. The Redbone is an extremely vocal dog, as would be expected of a hound: for generations (and even to the present day) their masters would follow the sound of their loud howls into the forest as they tracked quarry. It takes training to first control their excited, emotional, booming barks, but also to help provide the hounds an outlet for their 'tracking' desires that sometimes drive their vocalizations.

If not hunting with the dog, an excellent outlet is to train as a watchdog, seeing that it's a perfect alarm call as well as a highly alert and focused breed. As watchdogs, Redbones are unusually aware of the dress, ethnicity, and territory of their owners, and have been known to "protect" the yard against service providers such as postal workers and garbage collectors. Their deep bark and long canine teeth can be most intimidating to the unwary intruder.

Redbones do not reach full physical and mental maturity until the age of two years, comparatively slower than many other breeds. Puppies and adolescents are more energetic than adults and need lots of activity or they will become destructive, with chewing furniture, chewing shoes, and snooping around the garbage as particular forms of mischief. When going through obedience training, it is imperative for a master to know that harsher methods will not work with this breed: coonhounds are stubborn but also very sensitive and being overbearing will only result in a broken spirit, a dog terrified of everything. Once trained (and aware of its size) it is typically very gentle with even small children, easily tolerating a small child playing tag or a crawling baby tugging on its long ears. With older children they will happily jump into the family swimming pool to play when the weather is warm and can give more popular breeds like the Labrador Retriever a run for its money in swimming abiliy.

Coonhounds are in the same group as better known breeds like the Beagle, Basset Hound, and Bloodhound: they are bred to track game both with their noses and eyes over long distances, to jump over obstacles, and to "sing" as they catch up with their quarry. Therefore, this breed likes to chase small animals that may wander into a back garden, like rabbits, squirrels, badgers, or even cats: a Redbone Coonhound owner should have a fence at least 7 feet high to keep the dog in so as to make sure his dog does not follow his nose into trouble and wander from home.

Like many hunting dogs, they require a good deal of exercise to be happy and are best suited to the countryside or suburbs; urban environs are less than ideal but workable so long as they get roughly an hour and a half or more of walking per day. Redbones, especially those kept as family pets have an independent intelligence especially well suited for problem solving. This can be an issue if the problem they want to solve is their backyard fence or the dog-proof garbage. They are able to jump quite high so any fence is preferably one exceeding seven feet. Redbones have a very high tolerance for pain. Consequently, electric fences are not a useful means of keeping one's Redbone on one's property. Most Redbones require leashes to avoid wandering off. Because of their curiosity of smells, they are eager to follow their noses, ignoring their owners' commands-they should never be allowed off leash in a field unless that field has a large fence surrounding it.

History

In the late 1700s, many European type hunting dogs were imported to America, most of them of Scottish, French, English, and Irish ancestry: the English Foxhound, the Grand Bleu de Gascogne, the Welsh Hound, the beagle, and the Bloodhound were among these. Most often, these dogs were imported so that wealthy planters of the Tidewater could mimic the European gentry and engage in foxhunting, with smaller amounts of dogs winding up on small farms. However, after the American Revolution, as settlement pushed farther West and deeper South, hunters found they needed dogs that were much more suited to the environment and wildlife found there: the hounds of Europe at that time were bred to hunt in terrain that did not include bayous, wide open spaces, rugged mountains, cypress swamps, or animals that would fight back viciously like alligators, bears, porcupines, cougars, or raccoons. In addition, such dogs were found to be nearly useless unless their prey burrowed into the ground: when confronted with an animal that climbed a tree or (in some cases) tried to throw off their pursuers in deep, swampy water, they would mill about confused (when confronted with porcupines they would sometimes even flee.) Over time, Southern hunters would selectively breed dogs that wouldn't back down, had great stamina, and would tree their quarry: coonhounds.

In the late 1700s Scottish immigrants brought with them red colored foxhounds to Georgia, dogs which would be the foundation stock of the Redbone. Later, c. 1840 Irish Foxhounds and Bloodhound lines were added to the mix. The name would come from an early breeder, Peter Redbone of Tennessee, though other breeders of note are Georgia F.L. Birdsong of Georgia (contemporary) and the 19th Century's Dr. Thomas Henry. Over time, breeders followed a selective program that led to a coonhound that is more specialized for prey which climbs trees than European hunting dogs, was unafraid of taking on large (and ornery) animals, was agile enough to carry on over mountain or in meadow, and liked to swim if necessary. They were ideal for pack hunting of both small and larger prey. Originally, the Redbone had a black saddleback, but by the beginning of the 1900s, they were a pure red tone.

Like many American hunting dogs, especially those from the South, they were widely known and loved by hunters and farmers, but totally unknown in the show ring. Recently, this has changed, and the Redbone has found recognition by the two major American kennel clubs (Many young American students of school age today are familiar with this breed through a novel called Where the Red Fern Grows: the two dogs owned by the main character, Old Dan and Little Ann, are both Redbone Coonhounds.) Unfortunately, for reasons of its main use as a hunting dog rather than a show dog Redbones are extremely rare dogs outside of the United States. There are very few breeders outside of North America of this hound and it is virtually unknown in Europe or Australia.

External links

- Redbone Hounds in the Ozarks [4]
- UKC breeds [5]
- Hunting with coonhounds [6]

Rhodesian Ridgeback

Rhodesian Ridgeback

Other names	African Lion Dog African Lion Hound
Country of origin	Rhodesia
Traits	
Classification and standards	
FCI	Group 6 Section 3 #146 standard [1]
AKC	Hound Group standard [2]
ANKC	Group 4 (Hounds) standard [3]
CKC	Group 2 - Hounds standard [4]
KC (UK)	Hound standard [5]
NZKC	Hounds standard [6]
UKC	Sighthounds & Pariahs standard [7]
Dog (*Canis lupus familiaris*)	

The **Rhodesian Ridgeback** is a dog breed developed in Southern Africa where it was used (amongst other things) to hunt lions. This is most likely why this dog is known for its bravery. Its European forebears can be traced to the early pioneers of the Cape Colony of southern Africa, who crossed their dogs with the semi-domesticated, ridged hunting dogs of the Khoikhoi.

In the earlier parts of its history, the Rhodesian Ridgeback has also been known as **Van Rooyen's Lion Dogs**, the **African Lion Hound** or **African Lion Dog**—Simba Inja in Ndebele, Shumba Imbwa in Shona—because of their ability to distract a lion while awaiting their master to make the kill.

The original breed standard was drafted by F.R. Barnes, in Bulawayo, Rhodesia (today known as Zimbabwe), in 1922. Based on that of the Dalmatian, the standard was approved by the South African Kennel Union in 1926. This dog is now used to help athletes train.

History

The breed's history dates back to early in the 18th century, when the first European settlers found dogs domesticated by Khoi-khoi tribes with the hair on the spine turned forward. In the late 19th century, big game hunters needed a hunting dog that was tough, resistant to disease, and intelligent enough to avoid crocodiles and snakes, but brave and fast enough to face a lion. Also important was a tick-repellent smooth coat and tight paw pads to protect against thorns and rough terrain. Cornelius Van Rooyen of Plumtree, Rhodesia, was the main person behind the development of the breed. The history of the breed is disputed. It is commonly accepted that Van Rooyen used two ridged, rough-coated bitches from the Swellendam district brought to him by the Rev. Charles Helm in 1879. Van Rooyen crossed these bitches with members of his pack, noting that their ridged progeny excelled at lion hunting.

The breed took a further step in its formalization in 1922 just prior to the formation of the independent crown colony of Southern Rhodesia, when a group gathered at a farm in Bulawayo to set out the basic standard for ridged dogs that included the selection of the red wheaten to become the 'son of Africa'

The Breed Standard is loosely based on that of a slightly enlarged Dalmatian and was first registered by the South African Kennel Club, SAKU (now KUSA) in 1924. At that time KUSA was the only Kennel Club in the territory. Ridgebacks were first brought to the United States by Col. Morris DePass and his wife Maj. Ruth DePass who raised the breed in Kiln, Mississippi. The breed was admitted into the American Kennel Club in 1955 as a member of the Hound Group. The first ridgebacks in Britain were shown by Mrs Edward Foljambe in 1928.

As hunters, Ridgebacks were sent out in packs of two or more (usually twenty) to track down, then corner and wear down a lion by taunting and goading it into confusion, a tactic known as keeping the lion "at bay". The dogs, working in revolving groups, kept the lion at bay until the hunter arrived to dispatch the occupied lion with a well placed rifle shot from relatively close range.

Description

Appearance

The Rhodesian Ridgeback's distinguishing feature is the ridge of hair along its back, running in the opposite direction to the rest of its coat. It consists of a fan-like area formed by two whorls of hair (called "crowns") and tapers from immediately behind the shoulders down to the level of the hips. The ridge is usually about 2 inches (5 cm) in width at its widest point. It is believed to originate from the dog used by the original African dog population, which had a similar ridge. The first depiction of a Ridgeback is a wall painting describing the life of the Boers, housed in South Africa in the Voortrekker Monument.

Male Ridgebacks should stand (63–69 cm) at the withers and weigh about FCI Standard); females should be (61–66 cm) tall and about in weight many are much larger. Ridgebacks are typically muscular and have a light wheaten to red wheaten coat, which should be short, dense, sleek and glossy in appearance, and neither woolly nor silky. White is acceptable on the chest and toes. The presence of black guard hairs or ticking is not addressed in the AKC standard, although the elaboration of the AKC standard notes the amount of black or dark brown in the coat should not be excessive. The FCI Standard states that excessive black hairs throughout the coat are highly undesirable. Ridgebacks sometimes have a dark mask.

Ridgebacks have a strong, smooth tail, which is usually carried in a gentle curve backwards. The eyes should be round and should reflect the dog's color: dark eyes with a black nose, amber eyes with a brown (liver) nose. The brown (liver) nose is a recessive gene. It is not as common as a black nose; some breeders believe the inclusion of brown(liver)noses in a breeding program is necessary for maintaining the vibrancy of the coat.

The original standard allowed for a variety of coat colors, including brindle and sable. The modern FCI standard calls for light wheaten to red wheaten.

Other breeds with a ridge of fur along the spine include:

• Phu quoc ridgeback dog, Vietnam
• Thai Ridgeback
• Combai of Tamilnadu, India

Temperament

Rhodesian Ridgebacks are loyal and intelligent. They are, however, aloof to strangers. This is not to be confused with aggression; a Ridgeback of proper temperament will be more inclined to ignore, rather than challenge, a stranger. This breed requires positive, reward-based training, good socialization and consistency; it is often not the best choice for inexperienced dog owners. Ridgebacks are strong-willed, intelligent, and many seem to have a penchant for mischief, though loving. They are protective of their owners and families. If trained well, they can be excellent guard dogs.

Despite their athletic, sometimes imposing, exterior, the Ridgeback has a sensitive side. Excessively harsh training methods, that might be tolerated by a sporting or working dog, will likely backfire on a Ridgeback. The Ridgeback accepts correction as long as it is fair and justified, and as long as it comes from someone he knows and trusts. Francis R. Barnes, who wrote the first standard in 1922, acknowledged that "rough treatment ... should never be administered to these dogs, especially when they are young. They go to pieces with handling of that kind."

Health

Health conditions known to affect this breed are hip dysplasia and dermoid sinus. The Ridgeback ranks number six in terms of most affected breeds for thyroid problems recorded by the Orthopedic Foundation for Animals. Average lifespan is from 11 to 13 years, though they have been known on rare occasion to live to nearly 16 years.

Dermoid sinus

Dermoid sinus is a congenital neural-tube defect that is known to affect this breed. The dermoid is often likened to a thin "spaghetti noodle" beneath the skin. Puppies should always be screened at birth by the breeder and veterinarian, and the examination repeated as the puppies grow before they go to their new homes. This is done by palpation of the subcutaneous dorsal midline from the base of the skull to the insertion of the tail. Surgical removal is an option for affected neonates, puppies and adult dogs. All affected dogs, even those surgically corrected, should be spayed or neutered and never be bred. Since surgical dermoid sinus removal can be extremely cost prohibitive, and because all unremoved dermoid sinuses will eventually abscess, abscessed dermoid sinuses will cause the dog a painful death. However, it has been shown that supplementation of folic acid to the diet of the brood bitch before mating and during pregnancy reduces the incidence of dermoid sinus.

Deafness

While deafness is not a common problem in the breed, Rhodesian Ridgebacks do suffer from a breed specific form of the disease. Dr. Mark Neff and his team of researchers at the University of California at Davis have located the mutation that causes this relatively rare, but breed-specific, form of deafness.

Degenerative myelopathy

Degenerative myelopathy (DM) is a disease of the spinal cord causing progressive paraparesis, most commonly in the German shepherd dog breed. It affects Rhodesian Ridgebacks at a rate of only 0.75%.

Hypothyroid

Hypothyroidism is a growing problem in the Rhodesian Ridgeback, and this condition causes a multitude of symptoms, including weight gain and hair loss. Treatment for hypothyroidism in dogs consists of an inexpensive once-daily oral medication. Dr. Lorna Kennedy at the University of Manchester's Centre for Integrated Genomic Medical Research in England has found the haplotype (group of genes), which, when present, double the chances of a Ridgeback becoming hypothyroid due to lymphocytic thyroiditis. This is important to the breed because lymphocytic thyroiditis is the overwhelming cause of hypothyroidism in Ridgebacks.

Bloat

Like many other large, deep-chested breeds, Ridgebacks are prone to bloat. This is a potentially fatal condition that requires immediate treatment.

Resources

RRCUS H&G - The Rhodesian Ridgeback Club of the United States maintains a web site devoted to the breed's health issues that also gathers ongoing research for their Health & Genetics Committee. This group recommends that breeders perform at least four health screenings: hips, elbows, thyroid and eyes, with cardiac and hearing tests optional.

CRRHS - It is also recommend that all Ridgeback owners enter their dogs' information in the Comprehensive Rhodesian Ridgeback Health Survey.

Ridge genetics

The genotype responsible for the ridge was recently found by a consortium of researchers at the Swedish University of Agricultural Sciences (Nicolette Salmon Hillbertz, Göran Andersson, et al.), Uppsala University (Leif Andersson, Mats Nilsson, et al.) and the Broad Institute (Kerstin Lindblad-Toh, et al.).

The only disqualification in the AKC standard for this breed is "ridgelessness". This term refers to the purebred offspring of heterozygous parental animals that do not inherit a copy of the ridge mutation from either parent and are, in effect, normal dogs without a ridged back. The most current research suggests that the ridge mutation is autosomal dominant with complete penetrance. However, while the few studies that have analyzed the issue do not agree on the incidence of ridgelessness within the breed, they all show a ridgeless rate significantly lower than 25%, which cannot be explained using the Punnett square model for single gene/two allele inheritance.

One possible reason for these studies to deviate from the expected 25% incidence of ridgelessness is inclusion of parents who were not heterozygous (possessing a copy of both the ridgeless and ridged allele) in the study. The inclusion of homozygotes (possessing two copies of the ridged alleles) would make the observed incidence be less than 25% when averaged across the population in the study. Since a molecular genetic test for the ridge gene does not exist, heterozygotes are detected by mating the animal in question to either known heterozygotes or known homozygous recessives (other methods exist such as mating to offspring, but result in inbred offspring) and a heterozygote is detected when a ridgeless pup is born. Note that 1) many matings are required to have a high probability of detecting a homozygous dominant (once a ridgeless pup is produced, the animal in question is assumed to be homozygous without question), and 2) more than one sire can produce the pups in one litter. The latter fact can cast doubt on the calling of male heterozygotes by this method and could possibly lead to the results shown in studies testing the mode of inheritance of ridgelessness.

Traditionally, many ridgeback puppies were culled at birth for numerous reasons, including ridgelessness. Contemporary breeders are increasingly opting for surgical sterilization of these offspring to ensure they will not be bred but can live into maturity as non-showing, non-breeding pets. Some breed parent clubs and canine registries have even made the culling of ridgeless whelps a requirement.

Classification conundrum

The historic and modern hunting uses of Rhodesian Ridgebacks have included everything from upland game birds to larger 'dangerous game'. While the hunting versatility of the breed has served it well in the field, it has caused much confusion and contention among Ridgeback fanciers about what these dogs are, and are not, as hunting companions. Throughout its history, the Rhodesian Ridgeback has been a breed of dog that has somewhat defied the strict interpretation of most conventional group classification paradigms.

Classification history

In 1922 Bulawayo, Rhodesia, Francis Barnes standardized the breed using the existing Dalmatian standard as a model - there was no mention of a preferred group placement. Although no parent club was 'officially' recognized at the time, in September 1924 the South African Kennel Union or SAKU (now the Kennel Union of South Africa or KUSA http://www.kusa.co.za/) began taking "Lion Dog" registrations. In February 1926, SAKU (KUSA) officially recognized the Rhodesian Parent Club. At the behest of Barnes, SAKU also made two changes at this time:

- The Union's official name for the breed was changed from 'Rhodesian Lion Dog' to 'Rhodesian Ridgeback'.
- The breed was placed in the Union's 'Gundog' group.

On this second point Barnes was emphatic, stating "I am breeding a gundog." The Rhodesian Ridgeback remained classified as a Gundog for over 20 years thence.

Although the Rhodesian Ridgeback's bird hunting prowess has been well known throughout the breed's history (the original description from the South African parent club belabors this point in fact), it is important to note that the "Gundog" classification made in 1920's Rhodesia and South Africa was not specifically about bird hunting. To understand this it is necessary to understand the Union's classification system at that time. The two likely categories Barnes could have chosen from within the SAKU classification system at that time were, "Sporting" and "Gundog". In the "Sporting" group were the Sighthounds and Scenthounds. In the "Gundog" group were the Birddogs. This raises the question why Barnes rejected the group containing the Sighthounds and Scenthounds, and successfully lobbied in favor of the group containing the Birddogs. Barnes' reasoning becomes clear with an understanding of the distinction between the two groups. The Union's "Sporting" dogs were those that would find game above ground, and were then expected to dispatch the game without assistance. The Union's

"Gundogs" were those that find game above ground, and the human hunter was then expected to dispatch the game by means of a firearm. Within this context, the Rhodesian Ridgeback—which was clearly expected to hold the lion at bay for the hunter—not to attempt to dispatch the lion unassisted by the gun, placement in the Union's Gundog group becomes the logical choice within that system as it existed at that time.

Over time the culturally perceived meanings of the group labels had changed to those closer to their modern meanings, and the Union eventually became a federated member of the FCI, and therefore adopted its group categorization system. By 1940, Barnes had resigned from the Rhodesian Parent Club and prompted by the lobbying of a newer generation of leadership within the Rhodesian Parent Club, in the 1950s, the breed's group classification was changed from "Gundog" to "Hound".

Classification theories

Today, there are at least five competing theories concerning proper group placement for the Rhodesian Ridgeback.

1) Scenthound - This theory arises from the fact that the southern African landscape in general, and the Zimbabwean landscape specifically, is an extremely varied and diverse terrain, where a true sighthound would be severely handicapped in its finding ability in the game producing cover of the bushveldt, thornveldt, and kopjes. Proponents of the scenthound classification also observe that the Ridgeback bears very little resemblance to the decidedly northern African desert breed sighthounds, in either form or function. And while proponents of this theory freely admit that Ridgebacks are undoubtedly athletic 'running' dogs, they draw the distinction that Ridgebacks do not pursue game by sheer speed, which is typical of the true sighthounds associated with the northern half of the continent.

2) Sighthound - This theory is based on the fact that some of the foundation stock used by Cornelius Van Rooyen during the creation of the breed was Sighthound stock. Support for this theory has grown in areas (most notably in the United States) where Ridgebacks have been allowed to compete with sighthounds in lure-coursing field trials. The theory's detractors contend that success in lure coursing trials does not in and of itself make a dog a true sighthound, and further bolster their contention by pointing out that Ridgebacks are very poor performers when allowed to run in unofficial open field courses where they typically cannot keep up with the true sighthounds. Even so, no one can argue that Ridgebacks have not been successful at lure coursing events. In fact Ridgebacks have been very competitive in almost every lure coursing venue in which they have been allowed to compete. Proponents of this theory will often further defend it with a (hotly debated) claim that while Ridgebacks are versatile and use all their senses, their first and strongest inclination is to find game by sight—which itself is considered normal for dogs of any type, when the game is actually in sight.

3) U.K.C. Cur Dog - This theory is based on the United Kennel Club's (the leading 'working dog' registry in the U.S.) classification system which, within the scenthounds, includes a sub-group known as "Cur Dogs". Contrary to the traditional/historical meaning of the term "Cur", these dogs are neither mongrels, nor dogs of dubious breeding or value. Quite the contrary, the UKC Cur-Dogs are pure-bred, versatile hunting and livestock dogs. These pure breeds were typically developed by pioneering peoples who needed a dog that was highly protective of the family and farm, as well as a capable stock driver. Most importantly the dog was required to pursue various species of game both small and large game alike, in a manner inconsistent with the rest of the Hounds (sight or scent). The UKC Cur Dog does so using all of its senses - hearing, sight, and scent as the situation demands. This classification theory is consistent with old breed descriptions, which are somewhat contrary to the more classical sighthound/scenthound types, like the one offered in an advertisement run by the Rhodesian Parent Club in a show catalogue in 1926, "... Rhodesian Ridgeback (Lion Dogs) are unsurpassed for hunting and veld (sic) work. Ever faithful and loyal to their owners, highly intelligent and reliable guards."

4) Wagon Dog/Wagon Hound - This theory was forwarded at the 2008 Rhodesian Ridgeback World Congress, and contends that an honest evaluation of the breed's functional history indicates that during its formative development and early use as a breed, the Ridgeback was much more a "Hunter's/Farmer's Ox-Wagon Dog" than it was a "Lion Dog". This theory aligns itself with the current FCI classification of the breed, Group 6.3 (a special type of scenthound). However, the important distinction in this theory is not that the FCI classification of "scenthound" is accurate, but rather, that placing the Dalmatian and the Rhodesian Ridgeback (the only breeds currently in FCI group 6.3), breeds that historically have served as versatile hunting/wagon dogs, should indeed be classified as two examples of the same type of dog, but further asserts that such dogs' classification makes more sense as a discreet group. This classification theory is generally supported by historical accounts that mirror the one offered by Phyllis Archdale who went to Rhodesia in 1919 and bred Ridgebacks there in the 1920s, "Old timers told me that in early days most Dutch transport riders had a Ridgehound as guard to their wagons. They were used to bail up lion and wild pig. Mine did both..."

5) Ridged Primitive - There is also a group of Ridgeback fanciers who believe Rhodesian Ridgebacks should be thought of in terms of the FCI's group 5.8. FCI group 5 is the Spitz's and 'related primitives'. FCI group 5.8 specifically is "Primitive type Hunting Dogs with a ridge on the back". The theory's detractors note that the Rhodesian Ridgeback was not only developed in the late 1800s and standardized in the early 1900s, but developed specifically to "hunt to the gun" and as such is in fact a very modern creation, and anything but "primitive". But supporters of the theory contend that enough of the foundational stock is ancient, including the Greyhound and the Khoisan Dog (from which the ridged back derives), that even though it was developed relatively recently and for use with modern firearms, the breed can still be considered to be of a "primitive type".

Current registry classifications

Presently, the breed is categorized as a "hound" by every major registry throughout the world. For example, the British Kennel Club and the Canadian Kennel club both categorize the Rhodesian Ridgeback as a Hound, without any further specification. Both of the major registries in the United States, the AKC and the UKC, currently further distinguish the breed as a Sighthound. The FCI, the largest international canine governing body, which looks to the parent club in the country of origin (the Parent Club in Zimbabwe) for the breed standard and group classification, currently further distinguishes the Rhodesian Ridgeback as a Scenthound.

See also

- Lion hunting
- Hound Group

External links

National Parent Clubs

- National Rhodesian Ridgeback Council (Australia) [8]
- Rhodesian Ridgeback Club Österreich (Austria) [9]
- Rhodesian Ridgeback Club of Canada (Canada) [10]
- Rhodesian Ridgeback Klub Zagreb (Croatia) [11]
- Rhodesian Ridgeback Club Czech republic (Czech republic) [12]
- Belgian Rhodesian Ridgeback Club (Belgium) [13]
- Dansk Rhodesian Ridgeback Klub (Denmark) [14]
- The Rhodesian Ridgeback Club of Finland (Finland) [15]
- Rhodesian Ridgeback Club of Germany (Germany) [16]
- Rhodesian Ridgeback of Italy (Italy) [17]
- Dutch Rhodesian Ridgeback Club (Netherlands) [18]
- Norsk Rhodesian Ridgeback Klubb (Norway) [19]
- Rhodesian Ridgeback Club of Poland (Poland) [20]
- Rhodesian Ridgeback Club of Slovakia (Slovakia) [21]
- Rhodesian Ridgeback Club of Sweden (Sweden) [22]
- Rhodesian Ridgeback Club of Scotland (United Kingdom) [23]
- Rhodesian Ridgeback Club of the United States (United States) [24]
- South African Rhodesian Ridgeback Club (South Africa) [25]

General Information Websites

- Belgian Rhodesian Ridgeback [26]
- Rhodesian Ridgeback in Italy [27]

Preservation Groups

- Rhodesian Ridgeback International Foundation [28]
- The African Ridgeback Group (North America) [29]

Working Ridgeback Clubs

- Club for the Conservation of the Lion Hound of Southern Africa (Club ELSA (Germany)) [30]
- The Hunting Ridgeback Association (United States) [31]
- The Lion Dog Group (South Africa) [32]

Ridgeback Health Information

- Ridgeback Health and Genetics [33]
- Rhodesian Ridgeback of Italy (Italy) [17]

Ridgeback Pedigree Information Databases

- Rhodesian Ridgeback Pedigree Search (European) [34]
- POST - Pedigree Online Search Tool (American) [35]

Ridgeback Rescue Groups

- Rhodesian Ridgeback Rescue, Inc. [36]
- Texas Independent Rhodesian Ridgeback Rescue [37]
- Ridgeback Rescue of the United States [38]
- Etosha Rescue and Adoption Center [39]
- Ridgeback Rescue of Northern California [40]

Saluki

Saluki

Salukis come in a variety of coat colours.	
Other names	Gazelle Hound Royal Dog of Egypt Persian Greyhound
Country of origin	Middle Eastern Region

Traits

Classification and standards

FCI	Group 10 Section 1 #269	standard [1]
AKC	Hound	standard [2]
ANKC	Group 4 (Hounds)	standard [3]
CKC	Group 2 - Hounds	standard [4]
KC (UK)	Hound	standard [5]
NZKC	Hounds	standard [6]
UKC	Sighthounds & Pariahs	standard [7]

Dog (*Canis lupus familiaris*)

The **Saluki** (Arabic: سلوقي) is perhaps the oldest known breed of domesticated dog. A study published in the May 21, 2004, issue of *Science* confirms the Saluki's antiquity through DNA analysis identifying it as one of the earliest breeds to diverge from wolves. Like elsewhere in the Fertile Crescent region, Saluki-like animals appear on the ancient ceramics from Susa and Sialk of 3500 B.C.E. in Iran, as well as on Egyptian tombs of 2100 B.C.E. The breed had been occasionally imported to England before 1840, however there was no serious interest until the Hon. Florence Amherst imported a breeding pair of Salukis from Lower Egypt in 1895 and began working to popularize the breed. The Kennel Club recognized Salukis in 1923.

Widely admired for its beauty, speed and endurance, the Saluki is a sighthound and historically traveled throughout the Middle East with nomadic desert tribes over an area stretching from the Sahara to the Caspian Sea. As a result, different Saluki subtypes, varying mostly in colour and coat, can be found across this widely scattered area.

Although the greyhound is the fastest dog breed with a top speed of around 45 mph (72 km/h), the Saluki's strength lies in its great endurance and stamina. They are not the fastest sighthounds, but they can run for much longer than the sprinting breeds.

Description

Appearance

They are 58–71 cm and 13–30 kg in weight. The overall appearance of the Saluki is one of grace and symmetry. Salukis are "sight" hounds which means they sight the quarry, run it down, catch and retrieve/dispatch it. There are two coat types evident in the Saluki gene pool: smooth and feathered. In both varieties males may range from 23 to 28 inches at the top of the shoulder with females measuring somewhat smaller.

Temperament

A true Saluki retains the qualities of hunting hounds and may seem reserved and aloof. They learn quickly but can get bored with repetition, so training sessions should be short and varied. Sensitive and intelligent, the Saluki should never be trained using force or hard-handed methods.

They will "sing" (a high pitched howl, with oscillating volume) when they feel that something is wrong or when a member of the family is away for a long period of time. This "singing" can also be for bonding in the family (pack) group. Salukis have a fairly long life span, living an average of 13–16 years.

History

The Saluki has historically served as a courser, a speedy hunting dog that operated in packs. They often hunted in tandem with falcons which locate the prey for the dogs to run down.

Salukis appear on Egyptian tombs from 2100 B.C.E. The dogs were so esteemed that they were often mummified like the bodies of the Pharaohs themselves. Numerous Saluki remains have been found in the ancient tombs of the Upper Nile region.

In Muslim cultures, dogs are often seen as unclean. A saluki, however, is given a different status by the Arab culture. The Bedouin value them, breeding them for both beauty and hunting qualities. A saluki, instead of being viewed as unclean, often sleeps in tents with their owners, to be protected from the heat of the day and the cold of the night.

The Breed Established in the West

In England, a few specimens of the breed had been sporadically imported as curiosities since the mid-1700s. The first successful breeding line of Salukis begins in 1895 with the Honourable Florence Amherst (daughter of the 1st Baron Amherst of Hackney). Having seen Salukis on a Nile tour in that year, she imported a breeding pair from the Al Salihah area of Lower Egypt. A champion of breed purity, she struggled alone for nearly three decades and real Saluki popularity did not take hold until the early 1920s when officers returning from the war in the Middle East and the Arab Revolt brought their pet Salukis home with them.

One of these was Brigadier General Frederick Lance of the 19th Lancers, who, with his adventurous wife, Gladys, returned home with two Syrian Salukis from Sarona where he was stationed during the post-war occupation. The Lances were avid hunters and rode out with their Saluki pack and terrier to course jackal and Dorcas gazelle in the desert. Their imported male, Sarona Kelb, became a significant influence on the breed in the West.

Together, the Lances and Florence Amherst mounted a campaign for recognition of the Middle Eastern breed that luckily coincided with the phenomenon of "Tutmania" caused by Howard Carter's spectacular discovery of Tutankhamun's tomb in late 1922. In 1923, the Saluki or Gazelle Hound Club [8] was formed and the Kennel Club granted official recognition to the breed. Popularity of Salukis dramatically increased and The American Kennel Club would recognize the breed and the Saluki Club of America [9] was founded in 1927.

Imports to England during the inter-war years were chiefly from areas of British military influence and commerce: Bahrain, Egypt, Transjordan, and Iraq. Both Florence Amherst and the Lances imported breeding stock from the latter two countries. Despite substantial populations of Salukis in Germany, the Netherlands, and Sweden, none of these were imported to England.

English Salukis (chiefly descendents of Sarona Kelb) were exported to many countries, but by the mid-1930s, interest slackened, and with the outbreak of World War II, breeding and show activities almost entirely stopped. The number of litters was minimal – just enough to keep the breed alive. Food rationing reserved all edible meat for humans and rather than see their beloved Salukis starve or perhaps killed by bombs, some owners euthanized entire kennels. A small number of Saluki kennels survived the war, and along with fresh imports belonging to a second wave of soldiers returning from the Middle East, the slow process of re-establishing the breed began again.

Genetics

As is the case with some other pedigree breeds in the United States, including the Basenji and Portuguese Podengo, the current domestic population of Salukis is descended from a small number of founders introduced into the country within the last 100 years, and must be carefully mated to avoid inbreeding. However, the original dogs imported into the US came from throughout the Middle East, a vast geographical area, unlike most other breeds that come from very small areas, so, worldwide, Salukis have the largest genetic base among purebreds. Recently, the AKC (American Kennel Club) has allowed the third generation of COO (Country of Origin) salukis to be registered after inspections by recognised judges so the DNA base will broaden.

In popular culture

- Ivy from *Cats & Dogs*
- Cross from *Ginga: Nagareboshi Gin*
- Ken and George from *Ginga Densetsu Weed* (a sequel to *Nagareboshi Gin*) are the puppies of Cross and Ben (a Great Dane), so they are half-Saluki, half-Great Dane.
- Rita from *Oliver and Company*
- Southern Illinois Salukis

External links

- AKC Breed history [10]
- Salukis Breed-FAQ [11]
- The Arabian Saluki Center [12]
- The Wind Drinker [13]
- A day in the life of a Saluki - Guided Tour of Arabian Saluki Centre by Cultural Consultant Ali Al Saloom [14]

Reference Books

- Allan, Diana and Ken, *The Complete Saluki*, (New York: Howell Book House, 1st edition, 1991), ISBN 978-1860541957 [15]
- Duggan, Brian Patrick, *Saluki: The Desert Hound and the English Travelers Who Brought It to the West*, (Jefferson, NC: McFarland, 1st edition, 2009) ISBN 978-0-7864-3407-7 [16]
- Goodman, Gail, editor, *The Saluqi: Coursing Hound of the East*, (Apache Junction, AZ: Midbar Press Inc., 1st edition, 1995) ISBN 978-0963922403 [17]
- Waters, Hope and David, *The Saluki in History, Art, and Sport*, (Wheat Ridge, CO: Hoflin Pub. Ltd., 2nd edition; 1980) ISBN 978-0614045468 [18]
- Watkins, Vera H., *Saluki - Companion of Kings* (Hagerstown, MD: Copper Beech Press, 3rd edition, 1995) ISBN 0903879107

Scottish Deerhound

Scottish Deerhound

Other names	Deerhound		
Country of origin	Scotland		
Traits			
Classification and standards			
FCI	Group 10 Section 2 #164	standard [1]	
AKC	Hound	standard [2]	
ANKC	Group 4 (Hounds)	standard [3]	
CKC	Group 2 - Hounds	standard [4]	
KC (UK)	Hound	standard [5]	
NZKC	Hounds	standard [6]	
UKC	Sighthounds & Pariahs	standard [7]	
Dog (*Canis lupus familiaris*)			

The **Scottish Deerhound**, or simply the **Deerhound**, is a breed of hound (a sighthound), bred to hunt the Red Deer by coursing.

Description

Appearance

The Scottish Deerhound resembles a rough-coated Greyhound. It is however, larger in size and bone. It is one of the tallest sighthounds, with a harsh 3-4 inch long coat and mane, with somewhat softer beard and mustache, and softer hair on breast and belly. It has small, dark "rose" ears which are soft and folded back against the head unless held semi-erect in excitement. The harsh, wiry coat in modern dogs is only seen in self-coloured various shades of gray (blue-gray is preferred). Historically Deerhounds also could be seen with true brindle, yellow, and red fawn coats, or combinations. 19th century Scottish paintings tend to indicate these colours were associated with a wire haired coat, but, with show breeders preferring a longer coat, these genes now appear to be lost. A white chest and toes are allowed, and a slight white tip to the tail; a white blaze on the head or a white collar are not accepted. The head is long, skull flat, with little stop and a tapering muzzle. The eyes are dark, dark brown or hazel in colour. The teeth should form a level, complete scissor bite. The long straight or curved tail, well covered with hair, should almost reach the ground.

Temperament

The Scottish Deerhound is gentle and extremely friendly. The breed is famed for being docile and eager to please, with a bearing of gentle dignity. It is however a true sighthound which has been selected for generations to pursue game; consequently, most Deerhounds will be eager to chase. The Deerhound needs considerable exercise when young to develop properly and to maintain its health and condition. That does not mean it needs a large house to live in, however it should have regular access to free exercise in a fenced or otherwise "safe" area. Deerhounds should not be raised with access only to leash walking or a small yard, this would be detrimental to their health and development."Deerhound character" [8]

Young Deerhounds can sometimes, depending on the individual, be quite destructive especially when they are not given sufficient exercise; however, the average adult Deerhound may want to spend most of the day stretched out on the floor or a couch sleeping. They do require a stimulus, preferably another Deerhound, and a large area to exercise properly and frequently. They are gentle and docile indoors and are generally good around company and children (however they require supervision with young children due to their size).

Health

Barring major medical emergencies, Deerhounds can be expected to live to approximately 9–11 years of age. The serious health issues in the breed include cardiomyopathy, osteosarcoma (bone cancer), bloat and torsion (GDV).

History

The Scottish Deerhound is believed by some to have existed back to a time before recorded history. Its antecedents may have been kept by the Scots and Picts, and would have been used to help in providing part of their dietary requirements, namely from hoofed game (archaeological evidence supports this in the form of Roman pottery from around 1st Century AD found in Argyll which depicts the deerhunt using large rough hounds (these can be viewed at the National Museum of Scotland in Edinburgh). Other evidence can be found on standing stones from around the 7th century AD reflecting a hunt using hounds, such as the Hilton of Cadboll Stone). In outward appearance, the Scottish Deerhound is similar to the Greyhound, but larger and more heavily boned. However Deerhounds have a number of characteristics that set them apart. While not as fast as a Greyhound on a smooth, firm surface, once the going gets rough or heavy they can out run a Greyhound. The environment in which they worked, the cool, often wet, and hilly Scottish Highland Glens, contributed to the larger, rough-coated appearance of the breed. The Deerhound is closely related to the Irish Wolfhound and was the main contributor to the recovery of that breed when it was re-created at the end of the 19th century.

The Deerhound was bred to hunt red deer by "coursing", and also "deer-stalking" until the end of the 19th century. With modern rifles and smaller deer-forests, slower tracking dogs were preferred to fast and far-running Deerhounds.

In coursing deer, a single Deerhound or a pair of were brought as close as possible to red deer, then released to run one of them down by speed, which if successful would happen within a few minutes - rarely were there sustained chases.

With the eventual demise of the clan systems in Scotland, these hunting dogs became sporting animals for landowners and the nobility, but were also bred and hunted by common folk when feasible. As fast and silent hunters they made quick work of any game the size of a hare or larger and were highly regarded by nobility and poachers alike. One of the most precarious times in the breed's history seems to have been towards the end of the nineteenth century, when many of the large Scottish estates were split into small estates for sporting purposes, and few then kept Deerhounds. The new fashion was for stalking and shooting, which required only a tracking dog to follow the wounded animal, using a collie or similar breed. Although a few estates still employed Deerhounds for their original work, the breed was left in the hands of a few enthusiasts who made them a show breed.

In Australia Deerhounds have been used to hunt the kangaroo and wild boar; while according to Teddy Roosevelt, in "Hunting the Grisley and Other Tales", some American wolf hunters used them, see also [9]

Miscellaneous

Scottish Deerhounds compete in conformation, lure coursing, and where it is still legal, in some states of the USA, in hare coursing and coyote hunting. A few are trained to succeed in obedience competition but few excel in it, and fewer still excel in dog agility or flyball because the courses and activities are generally designed for smaller dogs with lower body weight and a much shorter stride.

See also

- List of domesticated Scottish breeds

Further reading

- Almirall, Leon V. *Canines and Coyotes*. Caldwell, Id.: The Caxton Printers, Ltd., 1941.
- Barrett, Kay. *Living with Deerhounds* [10]
- Bell, Weston. *The Scottish Deerhound*. 1892. (Reprinted by Hoflin Publishing Inc., 4401 Sephyr St., Wheat Ridge, Colorado, U.S.A. 80003.)
- Benbow, Audrey. *How To Raise and Train A Scottish Deerhound*. Neptune City, N.J.: T.F.H.Publications, 1965, 1993.
- Blaze, Elzear and Byng Hall, Herbert *The Sportsman and His Dog* London: Darling 1850 [11]
- Cassels, Kenneth. *A Most Perfect Creature of Heaven: The Scottish Deerhound*. K.A.H.Cassels, 1997.
- Crealock, Lt.-General Henry Hope. *Deerstalking in the Highlands of Scotland*. London: Longmans & Green, 1892.
- Cunliffe, Juliette. *Deerhound*. Dorking, Surrey, U.K.: Interpret Publishing, 2002.
- Cupples, George. *Scotch Deerhounds and their Masters*. Edinburgh: William Blackwood, 1892. (Reprinted in 1978 by Hoflin Publishing Inc.)
- Dalziel, Hugh. *British Dogs - Their Varieties, History, Characteristics, Breeding, Management And Exhibition* London: The Bazaar Office circa 1879 [12]
- Grimble, Augustus. *Deer-stalking* London: Chapman & Hall 1886 [13]
- Hartley, A.N. *The Deerhound*. 1986. (Available from the Scottish Deerhound Club of America and the Deerhound Club (U.K.))
- Heidenreich, Barbara. *Your Scottish Deerhound Primer*, Fern Hill, Ontario, 1989,1999,2005.[14]
- Macrae, Alexander. *A Handbook of Deer-stalking* Edinburgh: William Blackwood 1880 [15]
- Scrope, William. *The Art of Deer-stalking*. London: John Murray 1839.[16]
- Shaw, Vero. *The Illustrated Book of the Dog*. London: Cassell 1881 [17]
- St. John, Charles. *Sketches of the Wild Sports & Natural History of the Highlands* London: John Murray 1878 [18]
- Van Hummell: "The Deerhound", in *The American Book of the Dog* Editor George O. Shields. Chicago: Rand Mcnally 1891 [9]

External links

- A global community for the Scottish Deerhound enthusiast [19]
- Scottish Deerhound Club of America [20]
- Scottish Deerhound Club of the UK [21]
- Scottish Deerhound diary from Scotland [22]
- Cusidh Scottish Deerhounds, bred in Scotland [23]
- Deerhounds Racing at the Sussex Longdogs [24]

Segugio Italiano

Segugio Italiano

Other names	Italian Hound
Nicknames	Segugio
Country of origin	Italy

Traits	

Classification and standards		
FCI	Group 6 Section 1.2 #337 (Short-haired), 198 (Coarse-haired)	short-haired [1] coarse-haired standard [2]
KC (UK)	Hound	standard [3]

Dog (*Canis lupus familiaris*)

The **Segugio Italiano** is an Italian breed of dog of the scenthound family. It comes in both short-haired and wire-haired varieties. It is thought to be an ancient breed, descended in pre-Roman eras from progenitor scenthounds in ancient Egypt.

The Segugio is a square dog, whose length should be equal to its height at the withers. It is fawn-coloured or black and tan. The dogs are 45–52 cm tall at the withers and roughly 20–23 kg in weight. Its determination to track a scent is similar to that of a Bloodhound, but unlike the Bloodhound the Segugio is also interested in the capture and kill of its victim. In 2009 ENCI (the Italian Kennel Club) registered 4,500 specimens of the short-haired variety and 1,740 wire-haired specimens , making this one of the top ten breeds in Italy. Its popularity in Italy is due to its outstanding performance as a hunter of game. Although Italians also use other hound breeds, such as Ariegeois, Petit Gascon Santongeois, Porcelaine, Posavatz and Istrian Hounds, the Segugio Italiano has remained the choice of most Italian hunters due to its exceptional abilities. Hunters who hunt hare alone or in small groups find this dog to be ideal. The Segugio Italiano can also hunt larger game, such as wild boar (although it not considered a specialist for this quarry), wild sheep or goats or ungulates of the deer family. The Segugio Italiano works alone or in packs, depending on the quarry. This dog is first and foremost a working dog, and it is rarely kept as only a pet.

External links

- Short-haired [4], Wire-haired [5] at the Italian federation (ENCI).
- Segugio Italiano Video [6]
- Segugio Italiano video 2 [7]
- Segugio Italiano video 3 [8]
- Segugio Italiano Hunts Wild Boar in Piedmont [9]

Sloughi

Sloughi

Other names	Arabian Greyhound Sloughi Moghrebi
Country of origin	Morocco

Traits	

Classification and standards		
FCI	Group 10 Section 3 #188	standard [1]
AKC	Hound (FSS)	standard [2]
	The AKC Foundation Stock Service [3] (FSS) is an optional recording service for purebred dogs that are not yet eligible for AKC registration.	
ANKC	Group 4 (Hounds)	standard [3]
KC (UK)	Hounds	standard [4]
NZKC	Hounds	standard [5]
UKC	Sighthounds & Pariahs	standard [6]

Dog (*Canis lupus familiaris*)	

The **Sloughi** () is a Moroccan breed of dog, specifically a member of the sighthound family. Sloughis are likely closely related to the Azawakh, but not to the Saluki [7].

Description

Appearance

The Sloughi belongs to the Sighthound family. In appearance, it is a short-haired, middle-sized, strong sighthound with drooping ears. Its expression is often described to be melancholy. Its muscular system is "dry", that is, the Sloughi has flat and long muscles, which must not be as brawny as those of Greyhounds or Whippets, even when in excellent physical condition. Its back is nearly horizontal (the lumbar region must be slightly vaulted). It has a moderate angulation and a tucked up underline.

The Sloughi's eyes are ideally dark brown, though sometimes of amber colour. Its coat colour varies from light-sand, to red-sand, red- or mahogany with or without brindling, black mantle, black mask, black ears. According to the standard, a Sloughi may only have a small white patch on its chest. Extensive white markings and parti-colored coats are not allowed. The Sloughi's gait is feather-light, with a moderate and energy-efficient stride.

The Sloughi's general view is compact and strong; it may not be too dainty.

Temperament

It is of a sensitive nature yet is an alert and intelligent hound. It is said that Sloughis have a mighty longing for moving and that is not easy to keep them in flats with families; however, a Sloughi does not need more exercise than other dogs of similar size. It loves variety, walking on the leash, romping in the countryside, and racing. A Sloughi is faithful to his owner and it needs him close by. Sloughis are easy to bring up and to train, if you know how to do it. Because the Sloughi is somewhat sensitive, its training shouldn't be oppressive, and any punishment should be omitted. What it likes is a friendly confirmation of its behaviour.

Health

The Sloughi is largely unchanged from ancient times, and so retains a robust genetic health. Only a few genetic conditions have been noted in the breed, in particular Progressive retinal atrophy (PRA). Fortunately the Sloughi is one of the breeds in whom this condition can be tested for with a small blood sample, and breeders are working to eliminate PRA from the gene pool. Like all sighthounds, the Sloughi is very sensitive to anesthesia, and can be sensitive to vaccines, worming, and other medications - so these routine treatments should be spaced apart instead of given all at once. Otherwise the breed tends to enjoy excellent health into old age.

History

The Sloughi's origin is mostly a matter of speculation. It is thought that Sloughis originally came from the Orient or from what is today Ethiopia (the tributes to the Pharaohs included smooth Lop-eared Sighthounds from Nubia, south of Egypt). The Sloughi is one of the two African Sighthound breeds recognized by the FCI. On old fragments of earthenware (about 3000 B.C.), a short-haired sighthound with lop ears was discovered that looks like a Sloughi. Today, the Sloughi is found mainly in Morocco, Algeria, Tunisia, Libya, and Morocco is responsible for the breed's FCI Standard. It is not to be confused with the smooth Saluki of the Arabian peninsula and the Middle East, which is a variety of the Saluki breed. It is also not to be confused with the smooth Afghan Hound, which is a variety of the Afghan Hound. The Sloughi was and is still used for hunting in its native countries, and is also a reliable guarding dog.

References

- *Sloughi: The Arabian Sighthound,*1996, by Ermine Moreau-Sipiere, Alet Publishing.
- "Sloughi", 2004, by Dr. M.-D Crapon de Caprona, Kennel Club books
- "The Sloughi 1852-1952" 2008, by Dr. M.-D. Crapon de Caprona, Signature printing.

External links

Sloughi World (including 'Preserving the Sloughi site') [8]

American Sloughi Association [9]

Sloughi in Europe [10]

Sloughi Rescue [11]

The Sloughi Fanciers Association of America [12]

Sloughi Pedigree Database [13]

Whippet

Whippet

Whippet	
Country of origin	England

Traits		
Weight	(−14 kg).)	
Height	Male	18.5 to 22.5 inches (47 to 57 cm)
	Female	17.5 to 21.5 inches (44 to 55 cm)
Coat	Fine, dense	
Litter size	6-8 pups	
Life span	12-15 years	

Classification and standards		
FCI	Group 10 Section 3 #162	standard [1]
AKC	Hound	standard [2]
ANKC	Group 4 (Hounds)	standard [3]
CKC	Group 2 (Hounds)	standard [4]
KC (UK)	Hound	standard [5]
NZKC	Hounds	standard [6]
UKC	Sighthounds & Pariahs	standard [7]

Dog (*Canis lupus familiaris*)

The **Whippet** is a breed of dog in the sighthound family. They are active and playful and are physically similar to a small greyhound. Their popularity has led to the reuse of the Whippet name on a large number of things, from cars to cookies.

Description

Whippets are a medium-size dog averaging in weight from 15 to 30 lb (6.8–14 kg), with height (under the FCI standard) of 18.5 - 20 inches (47 - 51 cm) for males and (44–47 cm) for females. Whippets tend to be somewhat larger in the United States and Canada with their population in show, coursing and some race whippets required to be within the AKC standard of 18.5 to 22.5 inches (47 to 57 cm) for males, and 17.5 to 21.5 inches (44 to 55 cm) for females. Because colour is considered immaterial in judging Whippets, they come in a wide variety of colours and marking patterns, everything from solid black to solid white, with red, fawn, brindle, blue, or cream. All manner of spots and blazes and patches are seen, sometimes all in the same litter.

Temperament

Whippets are generally quiet and gentle dogs, and may be content to spend much of the day resting. Although especially attached to their owners, they are friendly to visitors. Because of their friendly nature, whippets are known to have been used in aged care facilities. They may bark when strangers arrive but are not suited to being guard dogs.

Unlike some other breeds, male whippets are as easy to housebreak as females. Females can be a little more complex, moody and strong-willed. Males tend to be one to two inches taller and three to six pounds heavier than females.

Whippets are not well-adapted for living in a kennel, or as outside dogs. Their short coats do not provide insulation to withstand prolonged periods in cold temperatures. Their natural attachment to people makes them happiest when kept indoors. They are most at home in the company of their owners—in their lap or lying next to them on the lounge. Whippets are quiet and thus well suited to apartment life, although like all dogs they need regular, healthy exercise. The chance to run free in open spaces should be made available to the whippet; however care should be taken with whippets on the street as it is difficult to instil any sort of traffic sense into them.

The whippet may look mild and gentle (and for the most part are), but make no mistake, when in pursuit of any game such as a rabbit the whippet will demonstrate the heart of a lion. Whippets are excellent hunting dogs for small game, which comes from their original role as providers of meat for the table. Often owning a whippet meant the difference between having meat for dinner or not.

Whippets have been called a "poor man's racehorse." As their heritage would suggest, whippets are outstanding running dogs and are top competitors in lure coursing, straight racing, and oval track racing. Typically in these events, a temporary track and lure system is set up. The lure is usually a white plastic trash bag, sometimes in conjunction with a "squawker" to simulate a sort of prey sound or with a small piece of animal pelt. With the advent of new methods in motivational obedience training being used, whippets are becoming successful obedience dogs. Many enjoy flyball and agility.

A May 7, 2007 article in *Science Daily* reported on a genetic mutation that may account for the abnormally high athletic ability of whippets.

The elegance and ease of grooming of the whippet have made it a somewhat popular in the sport of conformation showing.

Health

Given proper nutrition, exercise, and veterinary care, most whippets live for 12 to 15 years. They are generally healthy, and are not prone to the frequent ear infections, skin allergies, or digestive problems that can afflict other breeds. Genetic eye defects, though quite rare, have been noted in the breed. Because of this the American Whippet Club recommends that all breeders test for this defect in their breeding stock. Hip dysplasia is unknown in whippets. Undescended testicles are common in the breed. Like most sighthounds, they are intolerant of barbiturate anaesthetics.

The heart of a whippet is large and slow beating, often being arrhythmic or even intermittent when the animal is at rest This sometimes causes concern to the owner, or to the vet not experienced with the breed. Whippets will, however, demonstrate a regular heartbeat during exercise. In a health survey conducted by The Kennel Club (UK) cardiac problems were shown to be the second leading cause of mortality in Whippets. It is not clear, however, whether this is at all related to the breed's somewhat unusual heart function. See athletic heart syndrome.

A 2007 study identified a myostatin mutation particular to whippets that is significantly associated with their athletic performance. Whippets with a single copy of this mutation are generally very fast; those with two copies have disproportionately large musculature and are known as "bully whippets" although their temperament is not affected by this.

A Whippet owner should take notice that Whippets are, just like other sighthounds, sensitive to a number of anaesthetics. This may be due to their low concentration of body fat. Any Whippet should have a sighthound-knowledgeable veterinarian.

History

Whippets were bred to hunt by sight, coursing game in open areas at high speeds. One can find numerous representations of small greyhound-like hounds in art dating back to Roman times but the first written English use of the word "whippet" with regard to a type of dog was in 1610. There is a picture by Jean Baptiste Oudry (1686–1755) of "Misse", one of two English whippets presented to Louis XV, in the Washington National Gallery and another, with her companion, "Turlu", by the same artist in the Musée National de Fontainebleau. However, some French sources, notably the Ministry of Culture, use the word "levrette" to describe Misse and Turlu. Levrette translates as "female greyhound". In the nineteenth century, whippet racing was a national sport in England, more popular than football. It is only beginning with this period that the existence of the whippet as a distinct breed can be stated with certainty. The age of the modern whippet dawned in 1890 when the English Kennel Club granted the breed official recognition, thus making the whippet eligible for competition in dog shows, and commencing the recording of their pedigrees. In the United States, the whippet was recognized in 1888 by the American Kennel Club. Early specimens were taken from the race track by dog fanciers of the time and exported all over the world. The whippet's versatility as a hunting, racing, exhibition or companion dog soon made it one of the most popular of the sighthound breeds.

References

Whippet (dog information) [1] on petinfospot.com

External links

- Breed Clubs
  - The Whippet Club of Great Britain [2]
  - National Whippet Club of Canada [3]
  - Whippet Club of British Columbia [4]
  - American Whippet Club [5]
  - The Whippet Club inc New Zealand [6]
  - The Dutch Whippet Club [7]
  - German Whippet Club [8]
  - Finnish Whippet Club [9]
  - Lithuanian Sighthound Club [10]
- Racing and coursing sanctioning bodies
  - North American Whippet Racing Association [11]
  - National Oval Track Racing Association [12]
  - 2010 NAWRA and NOTRA National Racing Titles website [13]
  - Whippet Racing Association [14]
  - The Whippet Racing Club of Queensland [15]
  - American Sighthound Field Association [16]

Article Sources and Contributors

Breed Groups (dog) *Source*: http://en.wikipedia.org/?oldid=371298317 *Contributors*: 1 anonymous edits

American Kennel Club *Source*: http://en.wikipedia.org/?oldid=373448194 *Contributors*: 07bargem

Hound Group *Source*: http://en.wikipedia.org/?oldid=368267445 *Contributors*: Jafeluv

Afghan Hound *Source*: http://en.wikipedia.org/?oldid=375710800 *Contributors*:

American Foxhound *Source*: http://en.wikipedia.org/?oldid=375242201 *Contributors*: Ronk01

Australian Dingo *Source*: http://en.wikipedia.org/?oldid=376231396 *Contributors*: Chiefmanzzz

Azawakh *Source*: http://en.wikipedia.org/?oldid=371415712 *Contributors*: Hutcher

Basenji *Source*: http://en.wikipedia.org/?oldid=376053617 *Contributors*: Francish7

Basset Bleu de Gascogne *Source*: http://en.wikipedia.org/?oldid=347285726 *Contributors*: Hebrides

Basset Fauve de Bretagne *Source*: http://en.wikipedia.org/?oldid=375093162 *Contributors*: 1 anonymous edits

Basset Hound *Source*: http://en.wikipedia.org/?oldid=376347589 *Contributors*: Jtalledo

Bavarian Mountain Hound *Source*: http://en.wikipedia.org/?oldid=354703803 *Contributors*:

Beagle *Source*: http://en.wikipedia.org/?oldid=376356045 *Contributors*: Tide rolls

Black and Tan Coonhound *Source*: http://en.wikipedia.org/?oldid=339654010 *Contributors*:

Bloodhound *Source*: http://en.wikipedia.org/?oldid=368397355 *Contributors*: 1 anonymous edits

Bluetick Coonhound *Source*: http://en.wikipedia.org/?oldid=375946436 *Contributors*: 1 anonymous edits

Borzoi *Source*: http://en.wikipedia.org/?oldid=375143045 *Contributors*: The Blade of the Northern Lights

Cirneco dell'Etna *Source*: http://en.wikipedia.org/?oldid=370310570 *Contributors*: Mgiganteus1

Dachshund *Source*: http://en.wikipedia.org/?oldid=376655049 *Contributors*: 1 anonymous edits

Drever *Source*: http://en.wikipedia.org/?oldid=282159351 *Contributors*:

English Foxhound *Source*: http://en.wikipedia.org/?oldid=369526902 *Contributors*: SE7

Finnish Spitz *Source*: http://en.wikipedia.org/?oldid=373682840 *Contributors*: Pitke

Grand Basset Griffon Vendéen *Source*: http://en.wikipedia.org/?oldid=327933762 *Contributors*:

Grand Bleu de Gascogne *Source*: http://en.wikipedia.org/?oldid=347083915 *Contributors*:

Greyhound *Source*: http://en.wikipedia.org/?oldid=376698584 *Contributors*: 1 anonymous edits

Hamiltonstövare *Source*: http://en.wikipedia.org/?oldid=366238681 *Contributors*: 1 anonymous edits

Harrier (dog) *Source*: http://en.wikipedia.org/?oldid=369434848 *Contributors*: 1 anonymous edits

Ibizan Hound *Source*: http://en.wikipedia.org/?oldid=374793680 *Contributors*:

Irish Wolfhound *Source*: http://en.wikipedia.org/?oldid=376180242 *Contributors*:

Norrbottenspets *Source*: http://en.wikipedia.org/?oldid=369545215 *Contributors*: Bruinfan12

Norwegian Elkhound *Source*: http://en.wikipedia.org/?oldid=372591970 *Contributors*: 1 anonymous edits

Norwegian Lundehund *Source*: http://en.wikipedia.org/?oldid=372663180 *Contributors*: 1 anonymous edits

Otterhound *Source*: http://en.wikipedia.org/?oldid=368582747 *Contributors*: K9kmal

Petit Basset Griffon Vendéen *Source*: http://en.wikipedia.org/?oldid=370781562 *Contributors*: IronGargoyle

Pharaoh Hound *Source*: http://en.wikipedia.org/?oldid=375856287 *Contributors*:

Plott Hound *Source*: http://en.wikipedia.org/?oldid=375708218 *Contributors*: 1 anonymous edits

Portuguese Podengo *Source*: http://en.wikipedia.org/?oldid=375960958 *Contributors*: Agilepod

Redbone Coonhound *Source*: http://en.wikipedia.org/?oldid=373259810 *Contributors*: Bruinfan12

Rhodesian Ridgeback *Source*: http://en.wikipedia.org/?oldid=375695000 *Contributors*: Yerpo

Saluki *Source*: http://en.wikipedia.org/?oldid=376431916 *Contributors*: 1 anonymous edits

Scottish Deerhound *Source*: http://en.wikipedia.org/?oldid=374454496 *Contributors*: Rjwilmsi

Segugio Italiano *Source*: http://en.wikipedia.org/?oldid=367954822 *Contributors*:

Sloughi *Source*: http://en.wikipedia.org/?oldid=375829148 *Contributors*:

Whippet *Source*: http://en.wikipedia.org/?oldid=374298334 *Contributors*: Notacupcakebaker

8